Dave Armstron

A Biblical Defense of Catholicism

SOPHIA INSTITUTE PRESS®
Manchester, New Hampshire

A *Biblical Defense of Catholicism* was originally published in 2001 by 1stBooks Library, Bloomington, Indiana. This 2003 edition by Sophia Institute Press® does not include the indexes in the original edition and contains minor editorial revisions to the original text.

Printed in the United States of America

Cover illustration and design by Theodore Schluenderfritz

For further related reading, see the author's website: *Biblical Evidence for Catholicism* (http://ic.net/~erasmus/RAZHOME.HTM)

Sophia Institute Press®
Box 5284, Manchester, NH 03108
1-800-888-9344
www.sophiainstitute.com

Library of Congress Cataloging-in-Publication Data

Armstrong, Dave, 1958-
A biblical defense of Catholicism / Dave Armstrong.
p. cm.
Includes bibliographical references.
ISBN 1-928832-95-4 (pbk. : alk. paper)
1. Catholic Church — Apologetic works. 2. Bible
Criticism, interpretation, etc. I. Title.
BX1752.A76 2003
230′.2 — dc21 2003005245

06 07 08 09 10 9 8 7 6 5 4

Dedication

To Father John A. Hardon, S.J., of blessed memory, a tireless, extraordinarily dedicated, saintly servant of God, who encouraged and exhorted thousands of aspiring Catholic catechists, writers, apologists, teachers, converts, and others to pursue their pastoral and evangelistic callings as laymen, and especially to write.

I shall never forget, and will always be thankful for, the many nights spent at the University of Detroit in the early 1990s, benefitting from the wise teaching of this singularly gifted and knowledgeable man, and observing the example of his manifest humility and kindliness. By God's grace, I hope to live — as he did — by the maxim of the founder of the Jesuits, St. Ignatius Loyola:

Teach us, good Lord,
to serve thee as thou deservest;
to give and not to count the cost;
to fight and not to heed the wounds;
to toil and not to ask for rest;
to labor and not to ask for any reward
save knowing that we do thy will.

"Always be prepared to make a defense to anyone who calls you to account for the hope that is in you, yet do it with gentleness and reverence."

1 Peter 3:15

Contents

Appendixes

Foreword

By Father John A. Hardon, S.J.
(1914-2000)

Please allow me to introduce to you Dave Armstrong. I know Dave and his wife, Judy, personally. I received him into the Church on February 8, 1991, and baptized both their children, Paul and Michael. Dave has attended my classes on spirituality and catechetics. He was formerly a missionary as an Evangelical Protestant and has spent twelve years in intensive study of various theological topics. He carries this evangelistic zeal with him into the Catholic Church.

In particular, I highly recommend his work *A Biblical Defense of Catholicism*, which I find to be thoroughly orthodox, well written, and effective for the purpose of making Catholic truth more understandable and accessible to the public at large. Dave has edited and compiled much material from great Catholic writers past and present, interspersed with his own commentary and analysis. It is, I firmly believe, a fine book of popular Catholic apologetics.

Throughout his writing, Dave has emphasized the inability of Protestantism to explain coherently the biblical and historical data concerning Christian doctrine and practice. I feel this is very important in light of the inroads of Protestant thought into the hearts and minds of millions of insufficiently catechized Catholics.

In our Lord,
John A. Hardon, S.J.
September 17, 1993

Acknowledgments

I wish to express my heartfelt thanks and deepest gratitude to my friends, my colleagues in the Catholic apologetics community, my mentors, and my family, who have offered me much needed encouragement and helped to maintain my hopes and dreams through the years, as I endured the usual frustrations and disappointments that writers in all fields experience.

Particularly I wish to thank Fr. Peter M. J. Stravinskas, Patrick Madrid, Marcus Grodi, Dr. Kenneth Howell, Fr. Ray Ryland, Dr. Scott Hahn, Steve Ray, Lynn Nordhagen, David Palm, Gary Michuta, Art Kelly, Robert Sungenis, Gerard Serafin Bugge, Don Ross, Diane Kamer, Stephen Hand, Leno Poli, John McAlpine, Pete Vere, Kristine Franklin, Michael Forrest, Shawn McElhinney, Paul Thigpen, John Betts, Andrew Holt, Dick Kelley, Jared Olar, Tom Wilkes, Chris LaRose, and two esteemed Anglican friends, Bret Bellamy and Fr. George Burns. There are many others as well. I hope no one feels left out if I didn't mention their names. They know who they are! Without their support, this book would not have seen the light of day.

Most of all, I want to express my love and profound appreciation for my one-of-a-kind, beautiful wife, Judy, and my three precious sons, Paul, Michael, and Matthew, for their undying faith in me and unending patience in allowing Daddy or hubby to work countless hours on his computer. Their support is crucial for my motivation and zeal. They will never know how much I love all of them, at least not in words, for no words are adequate to express how I feel.

It is written — proverbially — in Holy Scripture, that "a man's enemies shall be in his own household" (cf. Matt. 10:36). That is most assuredly *not* the case in my house, and I will be eternally grateful to God and thankful to my wonderful family for this blessing (life provides more than enough frustrations as it is). They are (on an earthly, human plane) my joy, my hope, and my happiness.

Introduction

During the course of 1990, I was actively and sincerely engaged in a lengthy historical and biblical critique of Catholicism (primarily having to do with papal infallibility) as a result of the ongoing dialogue taking place in an ecumenical discussion group I had initiated. I thought I might entice my Catholic friends out from under the alleged "yoke" of Rome. Little did I know that before the year was over, *I* would be the one to change *my* mind!

With heartfelt joy and a keen sense of discovery, I now attempt to uphold what I formerly attacked and to critique many of the Evangelical Protestant interpretations of Scripture that I strongly affirmed not long ago. Formerly, as an Evangelical countercult and campus missionary, I was committed to the defense of *mere*, or *generic*, Christianity. Now I seek to defend that Faith which might be called ancient or historic.

The present work endeavors to show that Catholicism can more than hold its own with regard to the evidence of the Bible, as it relates to distinctive doctrines that are considered unbiblical or even antibiblical by many evangelical Protestants. Our separated brethren often contend that Catholics (to understate it) are very unfamiliar with the Bible. This is, sadly, probably true as a general observation (although biblical illiteracy is certainly not confined to Catholics).

Nevertheless, it has no bearing on the question of whether the Bible in fact upholds the teachings of Catholicism. Many Catholic biblical arguments and interesting exegetical conclusions are entirely unfamiliar to most Protestants (and for that matter, most Catholics as well).

I myself learned of the vast majority of these scriptural evidences in favor of Catholicism while engaged in the research for this book, which was itself originally intended as a defense of my newfound views, primarily for the sake of Protestant friends who were curious as to the rationale behind my conversion to Catholicism. The more I studied Catholic apologetic works (many of which were older books obtained at used bookstores), the more I realized what a wealth of biblical material existed in favor of Catholic positions on a number of "controversial" doctrines.

I was continually amazed at the depth and solidity of these arguments, and pleasantly surprised that the Bible, which I had loved and studied intensely for ten years, could so confidently be utilized as a bulwark in defense of the Catholic Faith. Catholicism, rightly understood, is — I believe strongly — an eminently and thoroughly *biblical* belief system. This was entirely contrary to what I had so cavalierly assumed as an Evangelical Protestant. Reputable Protestant commentaries often ignore, overlook, or present very unsatisfactory explanations for Catholic biblical evidences, sometimes offering no more than an unsubstantiated denial of the Catholic interpretation, with no alternative.

The weight of the evidence herein presented is all the more compelling, I think, by virtue of its cumulative effect, which is well-nigh overwhelming. Time and time again, I discovered that Catholicism is altogether consistent with biblical teaching. Many claim that distinctive Catholic beliefs are simply not found in Scripture. Often, however, those who present this charge have little or no understanding of the notion of the *development* of doctrine, *implicit* biblical evidence, or the complementary (and biblically based) roles of Tradition and the Church. All of these factors and other related ones will be examined in this work.

Catholics need only to show the harmony of a doctrine with holy Scripture. It is not our view that every tenet of the Christian Faith must appear whole, explicit, and often in the pages of the Bible. We also acknowledge sacred Tradition, the authority of the Church, and the development of understanding of essentially unchanging Christian truths, as is to be expected with a living organism (the Body of Christ) guided by the Holy Spirit. A belief implicitly biblical is not necessarily antibiblical or unbiblical. But we maintain that the Protestant principle of *sola Scriptura* ("Scripture alone"), on the other hand, is incoherent and — I dare say — quite unbiblical.

In fact, many doctrines accepted by Protestants are either not found in the Bible at all (for example, *sola Scriptura* and the Canon of Scripture), are based on only a very few direct passages (for example, the Virgin Birth), or are indirectly deduced from many implicit passages (for example, the Trinity, the two natures of Jesus, and many attributes of God, such as his omnipresence and omniscience).

I have no *formal* theological training, although I have done a great deal of independent study over the last twenty years. This work is intended primarily as a layman's observations for other laymen, without pretending to be anything beyond that. C. S. Lewis, the great Anglican Christian apologist (and my favorite author) often made a similar claim for his own writings. He was formally educated in English literature, not in theology. To my knowledge, neither G. K. Chesterton nor Malcolm Muggeridge had any formal theological education either. They were journalists by trade and self-definition. Yet they — along with Lewis — are among the most celebrated Christian apologists of the twentieth century.

Furthermore, my relative lack of credentials might actually be somewhat of an advantage on my part, from the vantage point of

Protestant assumptions about the perspicuity, or "clearness," of the Bible (in terms of its outlines of the means whereby a man can be saved). Martin Luther made a famous remark to the effect that even a "plowboy" could interpret Scripture in the main without the necessary help of the Church. This is, then, largely a Catholic "plowboy's" attempt to learn and to share from Scripture itself, although without in the least denying the authoritativeness of the Church and Tradition.

I am always wholeheartedly willing to interact with scholars and reflective and thoughtful nonscholars who hold opposing viewpoints. If, however, even superior theological education cannot suffice for an adequate, reasonable alternate explanation over against the Catholic interpretations of various portions of Scripture presented herein, then it seems to me that this would serve only to strengthen the case I have made as an ordinary layman.

The widespread existence of Evangelical Protestant commentaries and various lexicons, Bible dictionaries, concordances, and so forth, for the use of laypeople, is based on a presupposition that individuals without formal theological education can arrive at conclusions on their own. This is largely what I am attempting presently. The only difference is that I am willing to modify or relinquish any conclusions of mine that turn out to be contrary to the clear teachings and dogmas of the Catholic Church, whereas the quintessential Protestant *ultimately* can stand on his own (like Luther), "on the Bible," against, if need be, the whole Tradition of the Christian Church. I formulate my conclusions based on the work of Church councils, great Catholic scholars, Fathers, Doctors, and saints, just as the conscientious Protestant would consult the scholars and great pastors and theologians of his own persuasion.

Far from having to force Scripture to conform to Catholic teaching, or to equivocate, or to rationalize away glaring contradictions, I've found that, invariably and delightfully, the converse is true: Catholicism is indeed the round peg, so to speak, that naturally fits into the round hole of Scripture. I have not undergone any torments of conscience or "intellectual suicide" in this endeavor, and I am more confident than ever that the Catholic Church is the "Bible Church" par excellence.

This discovery will never cease to be wondrous and marvelous to me, as well as to many other fellow converts to the Catholic Church via Evangelical Protestantism. For it means that we can continue to be Evangelical in every proper and true sense of that word: to love and cherish the Scriptures, to follow Jesus with all our heart, soul, strength, and mind, and to proclaim the message found in the Bible in its fullness and apostolic integrity unmingled with the error of excessively individualistic interpretation and competing, contradicting denominational beliefs. Accordingly, this work cites hundreds of scriptural passages from 229 of the 259 chapters in the New Testament (eighty-eight percent), and more than 250 Old Testament references.

Catholicism is not a blind Faith, but rather, one that is altogether reasonable, as far as reason goes (without excluding at all the essential religious characteristics of mystery, miracle, supernatural revelation, and love). A Catholic need not forsake hermeneutical rigor or critical acumen in any way.

Catholics can, assuredly, learn much from many positive and godly attributes of Evangelicalism and Protestantism in general. Likewise, a Protestant can derive much benefit from Catholicism, whether he feels compelled to convert or not. The non-Catholic can — after grappling with facts and arguments such as those presented herein — eventually recognize that Catholics are able to put forth a very strong biblical case for their beliefs. Likewise, the average Catholic in the pew, who often suffers from a marked lack of spiritual confidence, can greatly benefit from an increased familiarity with the biblical arguments that bolster the Catholic position.

Each chapter contains an authoritative definition and a relatively brief exposition of the Catholic doctrine to be defended, followed by extensive scriptural commentary on individual passages. Footnotes will direct the reader who wishes to pursue issues in greater depth to other relevant works and reinforce the arguments from scholarly sources, but will not interrupt the flow of the writing — intended to be popular and relatively nontechnical in style.

It is not my intention to minimize the importance of Tradition, councils, papal pronouncements, and suchlike at all. Rather, I seek to exhibit as many of the biblical evidences as can be brought to bear on any particular distinctively Catholic doctrine (at least all that I have found; certainly more exist). Doctrines held in common with Protestants and Eastern Orthodox Christians, such as the Trinity, the bodily Resurrection of Christ, Heaven and Hell, and so forth are not here dealt with.

All Christians agree that it is worthwhile to study and meditate upon the Bible — God's own inspired revelation for all mankind. Non-Catholics and even non-Christians might receive here some biblical food for thought, even if they are unconvinced by my arguments. It is a worthwhile endeavor to build bridges of understanding between Christians of all stripes, as commanded in Scripture. If this work causes the reader to delve more deeply into holy Scripture or into various Catholic sources, or to think more critically and deeply about the biblical evidences for various Protestant and Catholic doctrines, then it will have fulfilled its purpose.

A Biblical Defense of Catholicism

Chapter One

Bible and Tradition

"Maintain the traditions . . ."

Catholicism and Protestantism differ fundamentally with regard to the relationship between sacred Scripture and sacred Tradition: the Bible on the one hand and the historical doctrines and dogmas of the Christian Church on the other. Protestantism tends to see a certain dichotomy between the pure Word of God in the Bible and the Tradition of the Catholic Church, which is considered to be too often corrupted by "arbitrary traditions of men" (in this vein Matthew 15:3-6, Mark 7:8-13, and Colossians 2:8 are cited).[1]

For Protestants, Scripture alone, or *sola Scriptura*, is the source and rule of the Christian Faith. As such, it is superior to and judges all Tradition. It is sufficient in and of itself for a full exposition of Christianity and for the attainment of salvation.[2]

[1] John Calvin, *Institutes of the Christian Religion*, Bk. 4, ch. 10; G. C. Berkouwer, *Studies in Dogmatics: Holy Scripture*, trans. Jack B. Rogers (Grand Rapids, Michigan: Eerdmans, 1975), 299-300, 306; Martin, Marty, *A Short History of Christianity* (New York: Meridian, 1959), 216.

[2] Calvin, *Institutes of the Christian Religion*, Bk. 1, chs. 6-9; Clark Pinnock, *Biblical Revelation* (Chicago: Moody Press, 1971), 113-17.

The concept of *sola Scriptura,* it must be noted, is not in principle opposed to the importance and validity of Church history, Tradition, ecumenical councils, or the authority of Church Fathers and prominent theologians. The difference lies in the relative position of authority held by Scripture and Church institutions and proclamations. In theory, the Bible judges all of these, since, for the Evangelical Protestant, it alone is infallible, and the Church, popes, and councils are not.[3]

In actuality, however, this belief has not led to doctrinal uniformity, as the history of Protestant sectarianism abundantly testifies. The prevalence of *sola Scriptura,* according to Catholic thinking, has facilitated a widespread ignorance and disregard of Church history among the Protestants in the pews.[4] Protestantism is clearly much less historically oriented than Catholicism, largely for the above reasons. Recently, several evangelical scholars have frankly critiqued the weakness of either *sola Scriptura* itself,[5] or else the extreme version of it, which might be called "Bible Only" (a virtually total exclusion of Church history and authority).[6]

Whereas Protestantism takes an either-or approach on this issue and many other theological ideas, Catholicism has a both-and

3 Martin Luther, *On the Councils and the Churches,* 1539; R. C. Sproul, "*Sola Scriptura:* Crucial to Evangelicalism," in James Montgomery Boice, ed., *The Foundation of Biblical Authority* (Grand Rapids, Michigan: Zondervan, 1978), 109; Robert McAfee Brown, *The Spirit of Protestantism* (Oxford: Oxford University Press, 1961), 67.

4 Pinnock, *Biblical Revelation,* 118-119; Brown, *The Spirit of Protestantism,* 215-216.

5 Berkouwer, *Studies in Dogmatics,* 268-271, 286, 305; Brown, *The Spirit of Protestantism,* 171; Marty, *A Short History of Christianity,* 206.

6 Bernard Ramm, "Is 'Scripture Alone' the Essence of Christianity?" in Jack B. Rogers, ed., *Biblical Authority* (Waco, Texas: Word Books, 1977), 116-117, 119, 121-122.

perspective. Thus, Scripture and Tradition are inextricably linked: twin fonts of the one spring of revelation.[7]

Tradition is defined as the handing on of beliefs and practices by written as well as oral means.[8] The Bible is part of a Tradition larger than itself, of which it is an encapsulation or crystallization, so to speak.[9]

The first Christians preached; they didn't hand out copies of the New Testament (most of which was not yet written, much less established in its final form). Catholicism claims that its Tradition is neither more nor less than the preserved teaching of Christ as revealed to, and proclaimed by, the Apostles. Development occurs, but only in increased *understanding*, not in the *essence* of this apostolic Tradition. Catholicism claims to be the guardian or custodian of the original deposit of Faith which was "once for all delivered to the saints."[10]

It must also be pointed out that the written word and mass literacy have been widespread only since the invention of the movable-type printing press, around 1440. Thus, it could not have been the primary carrier of the gospel for at least fourteen centuries. Christians before the time of the Protestant Reformation learned mostly from homilies, sacraments, the Liturgy and its year-long calendar, Christian holidays, devotional practices, family instruction, church architecture, and other sacred art that reflected biblical themes. For all these Christian believers, *sola Scriptura* would have appeared as an absurd abstraction and practical impossibility.

[7] *Catechism of the Catholic Church (CCC)*, par. 80; John A. Hardon, *The Catholic Catechism (CC)* (Garden City, New York: Doubleday, 1975), 47-48.

[8] CCC, pars. 81, 83; John A. Hardon, *Pocket Catholic Dictionary (PCD)* (New York: Doubleday Image, 1980), 437.

[9] CCC, par. 82.

[10] Jude 3; CCC, par. 84; Hardon, CC, 41-43.

New Testament evidence for Tradition

Tradition, even in the extensive Catholic sense, permeates Scripture. Only an antecedent prejudice against such a notion or an undue concentration on Jesus' rejection of *corrupt* human pharisaical traditions, could blind one to the considerable force of the scriptural data. Put another way, Scripture does not teach *sola Scriptura*, a concept that constitutes the use of a document (the Bible) contrary to the same document's explicit and implicit testimony. In other words, Scripture alone should lead the impartial seeker *to* Tradition and the Church, rather than to a disdain of Tradition. G. K. Chesterton called Tradition the "democracy of the dead." It is foolish for any Christian to disregard what God has taught millions of other Christians throughout the centuries.

We must all do our best to avoid approaching Scripture with a philosophy that is itself not at all biblical, and forcing Scripture (and Christianity) into our own mold. The Bible itself has plenty to say about its own authority vis-à-vis that of Tradition and the Church.

The Bible is not all-inclusive

In the New Testament, first of all, we find clear-cut testimony to the effect that Scripture does not contain the whole of Christ's teaching. Probably no one would deny this, but Protestants usually deny that any of Christ's teachings *not* recorded in Scripture could possibly be faithfully transmitted orally by primitive apostolic Tradition. Reflection upon the closeness of Jesus to his disciples and on the nature of human interaction and memory makes quite dubious any such fancy. Who could make the claim that the Apostles remembered (and communicated to others) absolutely nothing except what we have in the four Gospels?

We might compare the Bible to the U.S. Constitution, which is not coterminous with the constitutional law that derives from it (and ultimately from the natural law alluded to in the Declaration of Independence). Nor is the Constitution workable in practice apart from judges who interpret it. The analogy is not perfect, but close enough to make the point.

The commentary in this chapter, it should be emphasized, is intended, not to denigrate Scripture in the least, but rather, to set it in its proper context within the living Christian community (the Church), and to accept it *on its own terms*. It seems that whenever the Catholic argues that the Bible is not the be-all and end-all of the Christian Faith, he is accused of disrespecting God's Word, etc. This is one of many unfortunate Protestant false dichotomies that will be dispelled in the course of our examination of Scripture.

> **Mark 4:33:** "With many such parables he spoke the word to them. . . ."

In other words, by implication, many parables are not recorded in Scripture.

> **Mark 6:34:** "He began to teach them many things."

None of these many things are recorded here.

> **John 16:12:** "I have yet many things to say to you, but you cannot bear them now."

Perhaps these "many things" were spoken during his post-Resurrection appearances alluded to in Acts 1:2-3 (see below). Very few of these teachings are recorded, and those that are contain only minimal detail.

> **John 20:30:** "Now, Jesus did many other signs in the presence of the disciples, which are not written in this book."

> **John 21:25:** "But there are also many other things which Jesus did; were every one of them to be written,

> I suppose that the world itself could not contain the books that would be written."
>
> **Acts 1:2-3:** "To [the Apostles] he presented himself alive after his passion by many proofs, appearing to them during forty days, and speaking of the kingdom of God" (see also Luke 24:15-16, 25-27).

Paradosis ("Tradition")

The most important Greek word in the New Testament for *tradition* is *paradosis*. It is used four times in reference to Christian tradition:

> **1 Corinthians 11:2:** "I commend you because you remember me in everything and maintain the traditions even as I have delivered them to you."
>
> **Colossians 2:8:** "See to it that no one makes a prey of you by philosophy and empty deceit, according to human tradition, according to the elemental spirits of the universe, and not according to Christ."

Paradosis simply means something handed on or passed down from one person to another. This "tradition" might be bad (Matt. 15:2 ff.; Col. 2:8), or opposed to the will of God (Mark 7:8 ff.), or entirely good (1 Cor. 11:2 and many other passages below). This distinction must be constantly kept in mind in the debate over the utility and propriety of Tradition.

> **2 Thessalonians 2:15:** "Stand firm and hold to the traditions which you were taught by us, either by word of mouth or by letter."
>
> **2 Thessalonians 3:6:** "Keep away from any brother who is living in idleness and not in accord with the tradition that you received from us."

Tradition in the Bible may be either written or oral. It implies that the writer (in the above instances, St. Paul) is not expressing his own peculiar viewpoints, but is delivering a message received from someone else (see, e.g., 1 Corinthians 11:23). The importance of the tradition does not rest in its *form*, but in its *content*.

Word of God/Word of the Lord

When the phrases "word of God" or "word of the Lord" appear in Acts and in the Epistles, they are almost always referring to oral preaching, not to Scripture. The Greek word usually used is *logos*, which is the title of Jesus himself in John 1:1: "The Word was God." Indeed, this holds true for the entire Bible, as a general rule. Protestants, unfortunately, tend to think "written word" whenever they see *word* in Scripture, but even common sense tells us that the English *word* refers also to spoken utterances. The latter is a more common and dominant motif in Scripture than the former. Much of Scripture is a recording of what was originally oral proclamation (for example, the Ten Commandments, Jesus' entire teaching — since he wrote nothing himself — or St. Peter's sermon at Pentecost). Thus, the oral component of Christianity is unavoidable, and a position that attempts to undermine this aspect is self-defeating from the outset.

Tradition according to Jesus Christ and St. Paul

Colossians 2:8 (see above) has often been used by evangelical Protestants (especially fundamentalists) to condemn both philosophy and Tradition, but offers no support for either position. For St. Paul is here contrasting the traditions and philosophies of men with that of Christ. He isn't condemning things in essence, but rather, in *corrupt* form. We've seen how St. Paul uses the same word for "tradition" positively in three instances.

Likewise, Jesus uses *paradosis* in condemning corrupt human traditions of the Pharisees (Matt. 15:3, 6; Mark 7:8-9, 13), not apostolic Tradition per se, since to do so would contradict St. Paul's use of the same word, as well as his own upholding of true Jewish teachings in the Sermon on the Mount and elsewhere. Notice, too, that in the instances above, Jesus qualifies the word *tradition* in every case by saying "your tradition" or "traditions of men," as does St. Paul in Colossians 2:8. When St. Paul speaks of apostolic Tradition, he doesn't qualify the word at all.

Paradidomi ("deliver")

A related word, *paradidomi*, is used with reference to Christian tradition, in the sense of "deliver," at least seven times:

> **Luke 1:1-2:** "Inasmuch as many have undertaken to compile a narrative of the things which have been accomplished among us, just as they were delivered to us by those who from the beginning were eyewitnesses . . ."

St. Luke is saying that these traditions handed down, or delivered, are not mere fables, legends, myths, or suchlike, but were dependable eyewitness accounts. Here also we have oral as well as written sources, with the former predominant at this point.

> **1 Corinthians 11:23:** "For I received from the Lord what I also delivered to you, that the Lord Jesus on the night when he was betrayed took bread . . ." (see also 1 Cor. 11:2 above; Rom. 6:17).

> **1 Corinthians 15:3:** "For I delivered to you as of first importance what I also received, that Christ died for our sins in accordance with the Scriptures."

It is striking here how Tradition and Scripture are one unified revelation, as in Catholic teaching. True Tradition can never contradict Scripture, but rather complements, explains, and expands upon it.

> **2 Peter 2:21:** "For it would have been better for them never to have known the way of righteousness than, after knowing it, to turn back from the holy commandment delivered to them."

> **Jude 3:** "Contend for the Faith which was once for all delivered to the saints."

Paralambano ("received")

The word *paralambano* ("received") appears also at least seven times with regard to Christian or apostolic Tradition. Thus, there are three related concepts: the tradition or doctrine that is given or, literally, "handed down," and the acts of delivering and receiving the tradition:

> **1 Corinthians 15:1-2:** "I preached to you the gospel, which you received, in which you stand, by which you are saved, if you hold it fast — unless you believed in vain" (see also 1 Cor. 11:23 and 15:3 above).

Note the reference to memory: the whole drift of the passage is an oral gospel and tradition transmitted by preaching and preserved by memory.

> **Galatians 1:9, 12:** "If anyone is preaching to you a gospel contrary to that which you received, let him be accursed. . . . For I did not receive it from man, nor was I taught it, but it came through a revelation of Jesus Christ."

This sounds rather like the anathema[11] statements of the Council of Trent, which are so objectionable to many. Here St. Paul

[11] See page 58, fn.

completely dissociates the gospel he received (which he elsewhere equates with Tradition) from traditions derived from men. The true Tradition originates wholly from above. *This* is the Tradition of which Catholicism claims to have been merely the custodian for nearly two thousand years. The next passage reiterates this:

> **1 Thessalonians 2:13:** "When you received the word of God which you heard from us, you accepted it not as the word of men, but as what it really is, the word of God" (see also 2 Thess. 3:6 above).

Tradition, Gospel, and
Word of God are synonymous

It is obvious from the above biblical data that the concepts of *Tradition*, *Gospel*, and *Word of God* (as well as other terms) are essentially synonymous. All are predominantly oral, and all are referred to as being delivered and received:

> **1 Corinthians 11:2:** "Maintain the traditions . . . even as I have delivered them to you."

> **2 Thessalonians 2:15:** "Hold to the traditions . . . taught . . . by word of mouth or by letter."

> **2 Thessalonians 3:6:** ". . . the tradition that you received from us."

> **1 Corinthians 15:1:** ". . . the gospel, which you received . . ."

> **1 Galatians 1:9:** ". . . the gospel . . . which you received."

> **1 Thessalonians 2:9:** "We preached to you the gospel of God."

> **Acts 8:14:** "Samaria had received the word of God."

> **1 Thessalonians 2:13:** "You received the word of God, which you heard from us. . . ."
>
> **2 Peter 2:21:** ". . . the holy commandment delivered to them."
>
> **Jude 3:** ". . . the Faith which was once for all delivered to the saints."

In St. Paul's two letters to the Thessalonians alone, we see that three of the above terms are used interchangeably. Clearly then, *tradition* is not a dirty word in the Bible, particularly for St. Paul. If, on the other hand, we want to maintain that it is, then *gospel* and *Word of God* are also bad words! Thus, the commonly asserted dichotomy between the gospel and Tradition, or between the Bible and Tradition, is unbiblical itself and must be discarded by the truly biblically-minded person as (quite ironically) a corrupt tradition of men.

Oral Tradition according to St. Paul

In his two letters to Timothy, St. Paul makes some fascinating remarks about the importance of oral tradition:

> **2 Timothy 1:13-14:** "Follow the pattern of the sound words which you have heard from me. . . . Guard the truth which has been entrusted to you by the Holy Spirit who dwells within us."
>
> **2 Timothy 2:2:** "And what you have heard from me before many witnesses entrust to faithful men who will be able to teach others also."

St. Paul says that Timothy is not only to receive and "follow the pattern" of his *oral* teaching, in addition to his *written* instruction, but also to teach others the same. The Catholic Church seeks to do this with regard to the entire "deposit of Faith," or the Apostles' teaching (Acts 2:42), in accordance with St. Paul.

Church, not Scripture, "pillar and ground of truth"

Almost any informed Evangelical Protestant, if asked to define the "pillar and ground of the truth" according to the Bible, would surely reply, "The Bible itself, of course." Yet Scripture does not so pronounce; it states, in perfect accord with Catholicism and in opposition to *sola Scriptura:* ". . . the church of the living God, the pillar and bulwark of the truth" (1 Tim. 3:15).

Other Bible translations render *bulwark* as "ground," "foundation," or "support."

Two sola Scriptura proof texts debunked

> **2 Timothy 3:16-17:** "All Scripture is inspired by God and profitable for teaching, for reproof, for correction, and for training in righteousness, that the man of God may be complete, equipped for every good work."

This is the most-often-used supposed proof text for *sola Scriptura*, yet a strong argument can be put forth that it teaches no such thing. John Henry Cardinal Newman (1801-1890), the brilliant English convert to Catholicism from Anglicanism, shows the fallacy of such reasoning:

> "It is quite evident that this passage furnishes no argument whatever that the sacred Scripture, without Tradition, is the *sole rule of faith;* for although sacred Scripture is *profitable* for these ends, still it is not said to be *sufficient*. The Apostle requires the aid of Tradition (2 Thess. 2:15). Moreover, the Apostle here refers to the Scriptures which Timothy was taught in his infancy. Now, a good part of the New Testament was not written in his boyhood: some of the Catholic Epistles were not written even when St. Paul wrote this, and none of the books of the New Testament were then placed on the canon of the Scripture books. He

> refers, then, to the Scriptures of the *Old* Testament, and if the argument from this passage proved anything, it would prove *too* much, viz., that the Scriptures of the *New* Testament were *not* necessary for a rule of faith. It is hardly necessary to remark that this passage furnishes no proof of the inspiration of the several books of sacred Scripture, even of those admitted to be such. . . . For we are not told . . . what the books or portions of *inspired Scripture* are.[12]

In addition to these logical and historical arguments, one can also differ with the Protestant interpretation of this passage on contextual, analogical, and exegetical grounds. In 2 Timothy alone (context), St. Paul makes reference to oral Tradition three times (1:13-14; 2:2; 3:14). In the last instance, St. Paul says of the tradition, "knowing from whom you learned it." The personal reference proves he is not talking about Scripture, but of himself as the tradition-bearer, so to speak. Elsewhere (exegesis), St. Paul frequently espouses oral tradition (Rom. 6:17; 1 Cor. 11:2, 23, 15:1-3; Gal. 1:9, 12; Col. 2:8; 1 Thess. 2:13; 2 Thess. 2:15, 3:6). The "exclusivist" or "dichotomous" form of reasoning employed by Protestant apologists here is fundamentally flawed. For example, to reason by analogy, let's examine a very similar passage, Ephesians 4:11-15:

> And his gifts were that some should be apostles, some prophets, some evangelists, some pastors and teachers, for the equipment of the saints, for the work of ministry, for building up the body of Christ, until we all attain to the unity of the faith and of the knowledge of the Son of God,

[12] John Henry Cardinal Newman, "Essay on Inspiration in Its Relation to Revelation," London, 1884, Essay 1, section 29, in Newman, *On the Inspiration of Scripture*, J. Derek Holmes and Robert Murray, ed. (Washington: Corpus Books, 1967), 131 (emphasis in original).

> to mature manhood, to the measure of the stature of the fullness of Christ; so that we may no longer be children, tossed to and fro and carried about with every wind of doctrine, by the cunning of men, by their craftiness in deceitful wiles. Rather, speaking the truth in love, we are able to grow up in every way into him who is the head, into Christ.

If the Greek *artios* (Revised Standard Version [RSV], *complete*; King James Version [KJV], *perfect*) proves the sole sufficiency of Scripture in 2 Timothy, then *teleios* (RSV, *mature manhood*; KJV, *perfect*) in Ephesians would likewise prove the sufficiency of pastors, teachers, and so forth for the attainment of Christian perfection. Note that in Ephesians 4:11-15, the Christian believer is "equipped," "built up," brought into "unity and mature manhood," "knowledge" of Jesus, "the fullness of Christ," and even preserved from doctrinal confusion by means of the teaching function of the Church. This is a far stronger statement of the "perfecting" of the saints than 2 Timothy 3:16-17, yet it doesn't even mention Scripture.

Therefore, the Protestant interpretation of 2 Timothy 3:16-17 proves too much, since if all nonscriptural elements are excluded in 2 Timothy, then, by analogy, Scripture would logically have to be excluded in Ephesians. It is far more reasonable to synthesize the two passages in an inclusive, complementary fashion, by recognizing that the mere absence of one or more elements in one passage does not mean that they are nonexistent. Thus, the Church and Scripture are both equally necessary and important for teaching. This is precisely the Catholic view. Neither passage is intended in an exclusive sense.

> **1 Corinthians 4:6:** ". . . that you may learn by us not to go beyond what is written, that none of you may be puffed up in favor of one against another."

The clause emphasized above, which is used as a proof for *sola Scriptura,* is thought to be difficult in the Greek, so much so that one Protestant translator, James Moffatt, considered it beyond recovery and refused to translate it! Yet the meaning seems fairly clear when the whole context is taken into consideration (at the very least, verses 3-6). This basic principle of biblical interpretation (context) is often neglected, even by good scholars, presumably due to presuppositional bias. For example, the great Evangelical theologian G. C. Berkouwer, who writes many insightful and edifying things about Scripture, falls prey to this tendency repeatedly, in using this portion of a verse to imply the notion of *sola Scriptura,* in his *magnum opus* on Scripture.[13]

One simply has to read the phrase following the "proof text" to see what it is to which St. Paul is referring. The whole passage is an ethical exhortation to avoid pride, arrogance, and favoritism and as such, has nothing to do with the idea of the Bible and the written word as some sort of all-encompassing standard of authority apart from the Church. St. Paul's teaching elsewhere (as just examined) precludes such an interpretation anyway. One of the foundational tenets of Protestant hermeneutics is to interpret obscure portions of Scripture by means of clearer, related passages.[14] St. Paul is telling the Corinthians to observe the broad ethical precepts of the Old Testament (some translators render the above clause as "keep within the rules"), as indicated by his habitual phrase "it is written," which is always used to precede Old Testament citations throughout his letters. Assuming that he is referring to the Old Testament (the most straightforward interpretation), this would again prove too much, for he would not be including the

[13] Berkouwer, *Studies in Dogmatics*, 17, 104-105, 148.

[14] See, e.g., Bernard Ramm, *Protestant Biblical Interpretations* (Grand Rapids, Michigan: Baker Book House, 1970), 104-106.

entire New Testament, whose Canon (that is, the list of books that belong to it) was not even finally determined until 397 A.D.

To summarize, then, 1 Corinthians 4:6 (that is, one part of the verse) fails as a proof text for *sola Scriptura* for at least three reasons:

- The context is clearly one of *ethics*. We cannot transgress (go beyond) the precepts of Scripture concerning relationships. This doesn't forbid the discussion of ethics outside of Scripture (which itself cannot possibly treat every conceivable ethical dispute and dilemma).

- The phrase does not even necessarily have to refer to Scripture, although this appears to be the majority opinion of scholars (with which I agree).

- If "what is written" refers to Scripture, it certainly points to the Old Testament alone (obviously not the Protestant "rule of faith"). Thus, this verse proves too much and too little simultaneously.

All "proof texts" for *sola Scriptura* are demonstrably inadequate and run up against biblical (and Catholic) teachings of Tradition and Church, as well as the insuperable difficulty of the Canon of the Bible, and how it was determined (by the Catholic Church).

Cardinal Newman, bristling with insight as always, gets right to the core of the issue in the following critique of Protestants' allegiance to *sola Scriptura:*

> That Scripture is the Rule of Faith is in fact an assumption so congenial to the state of mind and course of thought usual among Protestants, that it seems to them rather a truism than a truth. If they are in controversy with Catholics on any point of faith, they at once ask, *Where do you find it in Scripture?* and if Catholics reply, as they must do, that it is not necessarily in Scripture in order to be true, nothing can

persuade them that such an answer is not an evasion, and a triumph to themselves. Yet it is by no means self-evident that all religious truth is to be found in a number of works, however sacred, which were written at different times, and did not always form one book; and in fact it is a doctrine very hard to prove. . . . It [is] . . . an assumption so deeply sunk into the popular mind, that it is a work of great difficulty to obtain from its maintainers an acknowledgment that it is an assumption.[15]

The New Testament Canon

Although the question of the nature of the New Testament Canon is, strictly speaking, a historical one, we will examine it briefly, since it is obviously of crucial importance to biblical authority and to the notion of *sola Scriptura*.

For Protestants to exercise the principles of *sola Scriptura*, they first have to accept the antecedent premise of what books constitute Scripture — in particular, the New Testament books. This is not as simple as it may seem at first, accustomed as we are to accepting without question the New Testament as we have it today. Although indeed there was, roughly speaking, a broad consensus in the early Church as to which books were scriptural, nevertheless, enough divergence of opinion existed reasonably to cast doubt on the Protestant concepts of the Bible's *self-authenticating* nature, and the *self-interpreting* maxim of *perspicuity* (see Appendix One). The following overview of the history of acceptance of biblical books (and also nonbiblical ones as Scripture) will help the reader to avoid overgeneralizing or oversimplifying the complicated historical process by which we obtained our present Bible.

[15] John Henry Cardinal Newman, *An Essay in Aid of a Grammar of Assent* (Garden City, New York: Doubleday Image, 1955), 296.

The History of the New Testament Canon[16]

Explanation of Symbols:

* *Book accepted (or quoted)*

? *Book personally disputed or mentioned as disputed*

x *Book rejected, unknown, or not cited*

New Testament Period
and Apostolic Fathers (30-160)

Summary: The New Testament is not clearly distinguished from other Christian writings

Gospels: Generally accepted by 130

Justin Martyr's "Gospels" contain apocryphal material

Polycarp first uses all four Gospels now in Scripture

Acts: Scarcely known or quoted

Pauline Corpus: Generally accepted by 130, yet quotations are rarely introduced as scriptural

Philippians, 1 Timothy: x Justin Martyr

2 Timothy, Titus, Philemon: x Polycarp, Justin Martyr

Hebrews: Not considered canonical

? Clement of Rome

x Polycarp, Justin Martyr

James: Not considered canonical; not even quoted

x Polycarp, Justin Martyr

1 Peter: Not considered canonical

2 Peter: Not considered canonical, nor cited

[16] Sources for New Testament Canon chart (all Protestant): J. D. Douglas, ed., *New Bible Dictionary* (Grand Rapids, Michigan: Eerdmans, 196), 194-198; F. L. Cross and E. A. Livingstone, ed., *The Oxford Dictionary of the Christian Church* (Oxford: Oxford University Press, 1983), 232, 300, 309-310, 626, 641, 724, 1049, 1069; Norman L. Geisler and William E. Nix, *From God to Us: How We Got Our Bible* (Chicago: Moody Press, 1974), 109-112, 117-125.

1, 2, 3 John: Not considered canonical
x Justin Martyr
1 John ? Polycarp / **3 John** x Polycarp
Jude: Not considered canonical
x Polycarp, Justin Martyr
Revelation: Not canonical
x Polycarp

Irenaeus to Origen (160-250)

Summary: Awareness of a Canon begins toward the end of the second century

Tertullian and Clement of Alexandria first use the phrase "New Testament"

Gospels: Accepted
Acts: Gradually accepted
Pauline Corpus: Accepted with some exceptions:
2 Timothy: x Clement of Alexandria
Philemon: x Irenaeus, Origen, Tertullian, Clement of Alexandria
Hebrews: Not canonical before the fourth century in the West
? Origen
* First accepted by Clement of Alexandria
James: Not canonical
? First mentioned by Origen
x Irenaeus, Tertullian, Clement of Alexandria
1 Peter: Gradual acceptance
* First accepted by Irenaeus, Clement of Alexandria
2 Peter: Not canonical
? First mentioned by Origen
x Irenaeus, Tertullian, Clement of Alexandria
1 John: Gradual acceptance
* First accepted by Irenaeus
x Origen

2 John: Not canonical
? Origen
x Tertullian, Clement of Alexandria
3 John: Not canonical
? Origen
x Irenaeus, Tertullian, Clement of Alexandria
Jude: Gradual acceptance
* Clement of Alexandria
x Origen
Revelation: Gradual acceptance
* First accepted by Clement of Alexandria
x Barococcio Canon, c. 206
Epistle of Barnabas: * Clement of Alexandria, Origen
Shepherd of Hermas: * Irenaeus, Tertullian, Origen, Clement of Alexandria
The Didache: * Clement of Alexandria, Origen
The Apocalypse of Peter: * Clement of Alexandria
The Acts of Paul: * Origen
* Appears in Greek, Latin, Syriac, Armenian, and Arabic translations
Gospel of Hebrews: * Clement of Alexandria
Muratorian Canon (c. 190)
Excludes Hebrews, James, 1 Peter, 2 Peter
Includes The Apocalypse of Peter, Wisdom of Solomon

Origen to Nicaea (250-325)

Summary: The "Catholic epistles" and Revelation are still being disputed
Gospels, Acts, Pauline Corpus: Accepted
Hebrews: * Accepted in the East
x, ? Still disputed in the West
James: x, ? Still disputed in the East
x Not accepted in the West

1 Peter: Fairly well accepted
2 Peter: Still disputed
1 John: Fairly well accepted
2, 3 John, Jude: Still disputed
Revelation: Disputed, especially in the East
x Dionysius

Council of Nicaea (325)

Questions canonicity of James, 2 Peter, 2 John, 3 John, and Jude

From 325 to the Council of Carthage (397)

Summary: St. Athanasius first lists our present twenty-seven New Testament books as such in 367. Disputes still persist concerning several books, almost right up until 397, when the Canon is authoritatively closed.

Gospels, Acts, Pauline Corpus, 1 Peter, 1 John: Accepted
Hebrews: Eventually accepted in the West
James: Slow acceptance
Not even quoted in the West until around 350!
2 Peter: Eventually accepted
2, 3 John, Jude: Eventually accepted
Revelation: Eventually accepted
x Cyril of Jerusalem, John Chrysostom, Gregory Nazianzen
Epistle of Barnabas: * Codex Sinaiticus — late fourth century
Shepherd of Hermas: * Codex Sinaiticus — late fourth century
Used as a textbook for catechumens, according to Athanasius
1 Clement, 2 Clement: * Codex Alexandrinus — early fifth century (!)

Protestants do, of course, accept the traditional Canon of the New Testament. By doing so, they necessarily acknowledged the authority of the Catholic Church. If they did not, it is likely that Protestantism would have disappeared like almost all of the old heresies of the first millennium of the Church.

Chapter Two

Justification

"Faith apart from works is barren"

Justification, according to Catholicism, is a true eradication of sin, a supernatural infusion of grace, and a renewal of the inner man.[17] The Catholic Church holds that true faith in Jesus Christ is not saving faith unless it bears fruit in good works, without which spiritual growth is impossible.[18] In this way, good works are necessary for salvation, and sanctification is not separated from justification. Rather, the two are intrinsically intertwined, as with the Bible and Tradition.[19]

Sanctification is the process of being made actually holy, not merely legally declared so.[20] It begins at Baptism,[21] is facilitated by means of prayer, acts of charity, and the aid of sacraments, and is

17 CCC, pars. 1987-1992; Council of Trent, *Decree on Justification* (January 13, 1547), chs. 7-8. All Trent citations are from *Dogmatic Canons and Decrees (DJ)* (Rockford, Illinois: TAN Books and Publishers, 1977); John A. Hardon, *PCD*, 214-215.

18 CCC, pars. 144-147, 2008-2009; *DJ*, chs. 11, 16; Hardon, *PCD*, 259.

19 CCC, par. 1995; *DJ*, ch. 10, canons 24-26, 31.

20 CCC, pars. 1987, 1990, 2000.

21 CCC, pars. 1265-1266, 1987, 1992, 1997; Hardon, *PCD*, 39.

consummated upon entrance into Heaven and union with God.[22] Good habits help to make a man good, and bad habits make him bad. Once this premise is accepted, all sorts of pious devotional and penitential practices (often denigrated in some fashion by Protestants) become valuable helps in the Christian walk, rather than hindrances to "pure" worship.[23] *Grace* is defined in Catholicism as the gratuitous benevolence shown by God toward the human race, and it is an absolutely unmerited, free gift of God, made possible through our Redeemer, Jesus Christ, and his atoning death on the Cross for us.[24] When, therefore, Catholics speak of merit on the part of man, it must be understood in a secondary, derivative sense.[25]

St. Augustine wrote:

> The Lord made Himself a debtor, not by receiving something, but by promising something. One does not say to Him, "Pay for what You received," but, "Pay what You promised."[26]

Likewise, the Second Council of Orange in 529 declared:

> Whatever good works we do are deserving of reward, not through any merit anterior to grace; their performance, rather, is due to a prior gift of grace to which we have no claim.

The Bible teaches that God rewards good works, and that these are not antithetical at all to saving faith, as we shall see. Nor is

[22] CCC, pars. 826, 1127, 1133, 2003, 2030, 2098; Hardon, *PCD*, 393.

[23] CCC, par. 2015; Hardon, *PCD*, 380; Hardon, CC, 555-559.

[24] CCC, pars. 1996, 1998-1999, 2001; Hardon, *PCD*, 166.

[25] CCC, pars. 2007-2009; Hardon, *PCD*, 259.

[26] Commentary on Psalm 83:16. From William A. Jurgens, ed. and trans., *The Faith of the Early Fathers (FEF)* (Collegeville, Minnesota: Liturgical Press, 1970), Vol. 3, 19.

human motivation for doing good works at all denied in Catholicism. Mere external works done without purity of heart and charity are of little worth (1 Cor. 13:3).

Catholicism holds that a person cannot save himself by his own self-originated works. This is Catholic dogma and always has been, notwithstanding any distortions of it by nominal and undereducated Catholics or ill-informed anti-Catholic polemicists. Nor is anyone saved or redeemed by Mary or a pope or anyone else besides our Lord and Savior Jesus Christ.

On this particular matter, there is no difference whatsoever between Catholic and Protestant.[27] The doctrine of "works salvation," often wrongly attributed to Catholicism, is a heresy known as Pelagianism, which was in fact roundly condemned by St. Augustine (354-430), the above-mentioned council in 529, and the Council of Trent (canon 1 on Justification, January 13, 1547).

Catholicism also makes a distinction between mortal and venial sins. A mortal sin is a serious transgression of God's moral law, committed with full self-conscious knowledge and consent of the will. It causes a destruction of sanctifying grace and therefore the supernatural death of the soul. If not remedied by Confession and absolution or, in some extreme circumstances, perfect contrition alone, it will cause a person to be barred from Heaven.[28]

A venial sin (from the Latin, *venia*, "pardon") is a less serious transgression, not involving the elements of mortal sin as just outlined. It does not deprive the soul of sanctifying grace or destroy the soul's ability to effect a cure from within.[29] It does not follow,

[27] CCC, pars. 613-614, 970, 2010-2011; *DJ*, chs. 5-6, canon 33. Previous citation from the Second Council of Orange (canon 18) from Louis Bouyer, *The Spirit and Forms of Protestantism*, A. V. Littledale, trans. (London: Harvill Press, 1956), 68.

[28] CCC, pars. 1854-1859, 1861; Hardon, *PCD*, 167, 271.

[29] CCC, pars. 1854-1855, 1860, 1862-1863; Hardon, *PCD*, 449.

however, that Christians can therefore commit venial sins with impunity. That would be as foolish as a man cutting himself all over his body except at the jugular vein, on the grounds that, since such acts will not *kill* him, they are of little concern.

All of these important distinctions work in harmony to form a consistent system of salvation theology, or soteriology, which is, in this instance, explicitly grounded in Scripture. Different definitions, premises, and assumptions in many of these areas account for the variant system of soteriology found in Protestantism.

Most Protestants believe in external, or forensic, justification, where righteousness is merely declared, or imputed, by God to the sinner, who remains outwardly unchanged, at least in the beginning.[30] For Luther, Calvin, and most evangelical Protestants, sin is essentially defined as unbridled passion, over which the sinner, in a state of total depravity, has no control. Thus, the only hope for redemption is an act of God that operates absolutely independently of man's free choice or free will to do good, a capacity completely lost at the Fall in the Garden of Eden.

Luther thought his most important book was *The Bondage of the Will*, a work devoted to proving these very principles. Man lives and dies in iniquity: thus taught Luther.[31] Although classic

[30] See Augustus H. Strong, *Systematic Theology* (Westwood, New Jersey: Fleming H. Revell, 1967), 849 — a Baptist work; Charles Hodge, *Systematic Theology*, Edward N. Gross, ed. (Grand Rapids, Michigan: Baker Book House, 1988), 458, 461 — a Presbyterian work.

[31] Strong, *Systematic Theology*, 637-644; Hodge, *Systematic Theology*, 296-312. John Calvin sets forth essentially the same teaching in his *Institutes of the Christian Religion* (1559 ed.), Bk. 2, ch. 2, sect. 26-27; ch. 3, sect. 1-7; ch. 4, sect. 1-5. God's greatness and supremacy does not consign man to virtual worthlessness, as in classic Protestantism, but rather, man, created in God's image, is raised to even greater heights by virtue of Christ's Incarnation. For example, 2 Peter 1:4 speaks of human beings' becoming "partakers of the divine nature."

"Reformational" Protestantism most certainly doesn't deny the importance of good works in the Christian life, it regards them as manifestations or results of the necessary imputed justification, rather than as necessities in their own right.[32]

In Catholicism, on the other hand, man retains a small measure of free will to choose God and the good. This enables him — by the necessary assistance of God's enabling and preceding grace at every turn — to *cooperate* with God as he sanctifies and saves.[33] In Catholic theology, whoever rejects God and goes to Hell does so of his own volition and free choice,[34] whereas in Calvinist Protestant "Reformational" doctrine, God predestines people to Hell from eternity without (ultimately) their own choice being a factor at all (a doctrine known as double predestination).[35]

The Christian is being redeemed on the earth and (assuming perseverance) is destined for glorification in Heaven.

32 Strong, *Systematic Theology*, 869-871; Hodge, *Systematic Theology*, 464-465, 471-472; Calvin, *Institutes of the Christian Religion*, Bk. 3, ch. 16, sect. 1-4; *Augsburg Confession* (Lutheran, 1530), sect. 20.

33 CCC, pars. 1993, 2001-2002; Hardon, *PCD*, 339; Hardon, CC, 80; *DJ*, canons 4-6.

34 CCC, pars. 1033, 1036-1037; Hardon, *PCD*, 175; *DJ*, canon 17.

35 Strong, *Systematic Theology*, 353-370; Hodge, *Systematic Theology*, 387-394, 428-431; Calvin, *Institutes of the Christian Religion*, Bk. 3, ch. 21-24. For a scholarly Evangelical exposition of Calvin's predestinarianism, see Alister E. McGrath, *Reformation Thought* (Grand Rapids, Michigan: Baker Book House, 1993), 123-128. Most Protestants today, it must be noted, espouse free will; for example, Lutherans (starting with Philip Melanchthon, Luther's successor: see McGrath, *Reformation Thought*, 131), Anglicans, Methodists, many Baptists, and virtually all Pentecostal/Holiness Christians (who derive historically from Methodism), as well as a great many "nondenominational" Evangelical groups. When Protestant denominations reject Calvinism, they are taking a step back in the direction of Catholicism.

Even St. Augustine, contrary to the contentions of many Protestant apologists, never denied human free will as pertains to matters of salvation and damnation,[36] although he developed a strong view of predestination, as did the Catholic Church. The key difference relates to the nature and limits of man's free will, and whether God positively decrees souls to reprobation (damnation) or not. Calvinism affirms positive reprobation, while Catholicism vigorously denies it. Likewise, Catholics maintain that Jesus Christ died for all men (Universal Atonement) rather than only for the elect, those who will ultimately go to Heaven (Limited Atonement), as in the Calvinist schema.[37]

[36] In 427 St. Augustine wrote a book entitled *Grace and Free Will*, in which he sought to instruct those "who believe that free will is denied, if grace is defended. . . ." (citation from Ludwig Ott, *Fundamentals of Catholic Dogma*, Patrick Lynch, trans. [Rockford, Illinois: TAN Books and Publishers, 1974], 247). Thus, he espoused a view on human free agency that is diametrically opposed to the positions of Luther and Calvin, even though they constantly attempted to cite him as their forerunner. Even the prominent Evangelical apologist Norman Geisler admits that St. Augustine always upheld freedom of the will, denied double predestination, and rejected forensic, or imputed, justification (*Roman Catholics and Evangelicals: Agreements and Differences*, co-author Ralph E. MacKenzie [Grand Rapids, Michigan: Baker Books, 1995], 85, 89, 93, 99. In the same book, on page 502, it is conceded that virtually no one taught imputed justification in the whole 1,450-year period from St. Paul to Luther!) St. Augustine's perspective (and that of the Catholic Church) on human free will is that it mysteriously and paradoxically coexists with God's sovereign prevenient grace, which encompasses it within the sphere of his providence. It is one thing to acknowledge inscrutable mysteries, another altogether thereby to deny outright elements such as human free will, because we do not possess full understanding of God's ways.

[37] CCC, pars. 30, 74, 605; Hardon, *PCD*, 34. God's desire for and exercise of Universal Atonement is well-attested in Scripture: John 1:29, 3:15-18, 4:42, 11:51-52; Rom. 5:18; 2 Cor.

In Catholic theology, salvation is a lifelong process (Phil. 2:12-13; 3:10-14) begun at Baptism, rather than a one-time event (the Evangelical Protestant experience of "getting saved."[38] The Protestant "assurance" of instantaneous salvation and declaratory justification does not take into account the biblical data in its totality, as will be shown.

We can readily see how the issue of justification played a central role in the religious controversies and division of the sixteenth century and the rise of Protestantism. Yet — thankfully — there are also many similarities in the two broad theological positions that are helpful to recognize, in the spirit of openness, Christian unity, and ecumenism.

Simply put, both sides agree that faith is absolutely necessary for salvation and that we are clearly commanded by God to do good works. The Anglican C. S. Lewis once wryly remarked that an emphasis on either faith or works to the exclusion of the other was like thinking that one blade in a pair of scissors was more necessary than the other. The tendency in practice is for Catholics to minimize the first aspect and Protestants the second. Likewise, each side often thinks that the other denies one of these principles.

In fact, however, at the level of creeds, catechisms, confessions, and councils, both sides completely concur on these two maxims. The split comes over the precise nature of the relationship of faith and works to each other and to justification and salvation. We must not minimize theological divisions, nor should we exaggerate them. The first approach flows from the duty of honesty; the second from the demands of charity and understanding among Christians in the Body of Christ.

5:14-15; 1 Tim. 2:4-6; Heb. 2:9; 1 John 2:2. This was also the unanimous view of the Church Fathers.

[38] CCC, par. 2005; *DJ*, chs. 9, 11-14, canon 30.

*New Testament teaching
on justification and salvation*

> **Matthew 5:20:** "For I tell you, unless your righteousness exceeds that of the scribes and Pharisees, you will never enter the kingdom of Heaven."

Our Lord here shows us that it is necessary not only to believe in him, but also to keep all the Commandments (as the Pharisees were scrupulous in their observance of Mosaic Law). This standard indicates the very high level of perfection to which we are called. "Faith alone" is refuted.

> **Matthew 7:16-27:** "You will know them by their fruits. Are grapes gathered from thorns, or figs from thistles? So every sound tree bears good fruit; but the bad tree bears evil fruit. A sound tree cannot bear evil fruit, nor can a bad tree bear good fruit. Every tree that does not bear good fruit is cut down and thrown into the fire. Thus you will know them by their fruits. Not every one who says to me, 'Lord, Lord,' shall enter the kingdom of Heaven, but he who does the will of my Father who is in Heaven. On that day many will say to me, 'Lord, Lord, did we not prophesy in your name, and cast out demons in your name, and do many mighty works in your name?' And then will I declare to them, 'I never knew you; depart from me, you evildoers.' Everyone, then, who hears these words of mine and does them will be like a wise man who built his house upon the rock; and the rain fell, and the floods came, and the winds blew and beat upon that house, but it did not fall, because it had been founded on the rock. And everyone who hears these words of mine, and does not do them will be like a foolish man who built his house upon the

> sand; and the rain fell, and the floods came, and the winds blew and beat against that house, and it fell; and great was the fall of it."

Jesus puts salvation into very practical terms. He reiterates the teaching of Matthew 5:20 by emphasizing acts of obedience, as opposed to mere verbal proclamations or head knowledge. Even some miraculous works are not necessarily under his superintendence.

A similar dynamic is also present in Matthew 25:31-46, the great scene of the separation of sheep and goats, where Christ continually makes the works of faith the central criterion of judgment. And again in Luke 18:18-25, where the rich young ruler asked Jesus what he must do to inherit eternal life, Jesus asks if he has kept the Commandments. Upon finding out that he has, he commands him to sell all his possessions and give the money to the poor. Jesus was quite an incompetent missionary, according to the pragmatic evangelistic techniques and criteria for "success" which prevail among many of today's Evangelicals.

Nothing whatsoever is spoken about faith alone in any of these passages, as would be rightfully expected if Luther were correct about the nature of saving faith. All Christians agree that a person living unrighteously is in great danger. Catholics say that such a one has lost the state of grace through mortal sin, whereas most Evangelicals contend that they were likely never saved at all. In any event, the actual outcome is the same in both cases if the sinning persists: hellfire.

> **Matthew 16:27:** "For the Son of Man is to come with his angels in the glory of his Father, and then he will repay every man for what he has done."

Cardinal Newman comments:

Faith has a certain prerogative of dignity under the Gospel. At the same time, we must never forget that the more usual

> mode of doctrine both with Christ and His Apostles is to refer our acceptance to obedience to the commandments, not to faith. . . .
>
> There are multitudes who would avow with confidence and exultation that they put obedience only in the second place in their religious scheme, as if it were rather a necessary consequence of faith than requiring a direct attention for its own sake; a something subordinate to it, rather than connatural and contemporaneous with it. . . .
>
> These declarations,[39] so solemnly, so repeatedly made, must hold good in their plain and obvious sense, and may not be infringed or superseded.[40]

> **Luke 14:13-14:** "But when you give a feast, invite the poor, the maimed, the lame, the blind, and you will be blessed, because they cannot repay you. You will be repaid at the resurrection of the just."

The idea here appears to be the same one expressed by our Lord in Matthew 16:27: that of differential rewards in Heaven commensurate with deeds done in his grace and with heartfelt devotion.

> **John 1:29:** "Behold, the Lamb of God, who takes away the sin of the world!"

Here we see that sins are obliterated, not merely "covered over." There are many other passages in the same vein:

> **2 Samuel 12:13:** "The Lord also has put away your sin."

[39] He cites, in addition to Matthew 16:27, 2 Corinthians 5:10, Acts 10:42, James 2:24, and Revelation 22:14.

[40] Sermon: "Faith and Obedience," 1836. All cited Newman sermons can be found in his *Parochial and Plain Sermons* (San Francisco: Ignatius Press, 1987) and come from his Anglican period.

1 Chronicles 21:8: "Take away the iniquity of thy servant."

Psalm 51:2, 7, 9-10: "Wash me thoroughly from my iniquity, and cleanse me from my sin! . . . Purge me with hyssop, and I shall be clean; wash me, and I shall be whiter than snow. . . . Blot out all my iniquities. Create in me a clean heart, O God, and put a new and right spirit within me."

Psalm 103:12: "As far as the east is from the west, so far does he remove our transgressions from us."

Isaiah 43:25: "I am he who blots out your transgressions for my own sake."

Isaiah 44:22: "I have swept away your transgressions like a cloud, and your sins like mist, for I have redeemed you."

Ezekiel 37:23: "I . . . will cleanse them."

Acts 3:19: "Repent, therefore, and turn again, that your sins may be blotted out."

1 John 1:7: "The blood of Jesus, his son, cleanses us from all sin."

1 John 1:9: "He is faithful and just, and will forgive our sins and cleanse us from all unrighteousness."

The Greek word for "blotted out" in Acts 3:19, *exalipho*, is used in Revelation 3:5, where names from the book of life are blotted out — obviously an obliteration, with the most dire consequences. In Revelation 7:17 and 21:4, the word has reference to God's wiping away tears in Heaven: again, clearly an absolute act of removal. Therefore, the notion that the above passages are only metaphorical or symbolic would appear to be a strained and implausible interpretation. The language is so definite as to leave no doubt: sin is taken away, put away, swept away, washed, purged, cleansed, blotted out, or removed.

Likewise, the word for "cleanse" in 1 John 1:7, 9 is *katharizo*, which is used to describe the cleansing of lepers throughout the Gospels (e.g., Matt. 8:3, 11:5; Mark 1:42; Luke 7:22). This is indisputably an "infused" cleansing, rather than an "imputed" one. Why should God settle for anything less when it comes to our sin and justification?

To be fair, Protestants stress this actual sanctification, as we have already acknowledged, but in separating it in principle, and abstractly, from justification and the "working out" of one's salvation, they have constructed yet another unnecessary dichotomy, the net result of which has been a lessening of the vital role of works, which thereby tend to be regarded as far less compulsory, to the detriment of holiness.

> **John 3:36:** "He who believes in the Son has eternal life; he who does not obey the Son shall not see life, but the wrath of God rests upon him."

The Greek word for "believes" is *pistuo*, and the Greek for "does not obey" is *apitheo*. There is a parallelism in this verse, whereby *belief* and *obedience* are essentially identical. When all is said and done, believing in Christ *is* obeying him. This ought to be kept in mind by Protestant evangelists and pastors who urge penitents to "believe in Christ," "accept Christ," etc. To disobey Christ is to be subject to the wrath of God. Thus, again, we are faced with the inescapable necessity of good works — wrought by God's grace, and done in the spirit of charity — for the purpose and end of ultimate salvation, holiness, and communion with God.

St. Peter, in 1 Peter 2:7, uses the same parallelism, with the same two identical Greek words (*believe/disobedient* in KJV). St.

Paul uses *apitheo* with regard to disobedience to parents in Romans 1:30 and 2 Timothy 3:2, and in a more general sense (describing sinners) in Titus 1:16 and 3:3. Obviously, no one disbelieves in the existence of his parents. St. Paul is speaking of disobeying parents' commands. In the same sense, such disobedience (not mere lack of faith) is said to be the basis of the loss of eternal life in John 3:36.

To speculate further, if it be granted that *pistuo* ("believe") is roughly identical to "obeying," as it indisputably is in John 3:36, by simple deduction, then its use elsewhere is also much more commensurate with the Catholic view of infused justification rather than the more abstract, extrinsic, and forensic Protestant view; for example, the "classic" Protestant evangelistic verse John 3:16, Jesus' constant demand to believe in him in John 5 through 10, and St. Paul's oft-cited salvific exhortations in Romans 1:16, 4:24, 9:33, and 10:9, generally thought to be irrefutable proofs of the Protestant viewpoint on saving faith.

> **John 6:27-29:** "Do not labor for the food which perishes, but for the food which endures to eternal life, which the Son of man will give to you; for on him has God the Father set his seal. Then said they to him, 'What must we do, to be doing the works of God?' Jesus answered them, 'This is the work of God, that you believe in him whom he has sent.' "

In verses 28 and 29, *working* and *belief* in Christ are equated, much like *obedience* and *belief* in John 3:36. In the marvelous phrase "doing the works of God," we see that our works and God's are intertwined if indeed we are doing his will. This is the Catholic viewpoint: an organic connection of both faith with works, and God's unmerited grace coupled with our cooperation and obedience. Our Lord constantly alludes to the related ideas of *reward* and *merit*, which are complementary: Matthew 5:11-12, 6:3, 18,

10:42, 12:36-37, 25:14-30; Luke 6:35, 38; 12:33. St. Paul, using the same word for "works" (*ergon*), speaks in Acts 26:20 of the process of repenting, turning to God, and doing deeds worthy of their repentance. In other words, they will thus prove their repentance by their deeds.

> **Acts 10:31:** "Cornelius, your prayer has been heard, and your alms have been remembered before God."

> **Acts 10:35:** "But in every nation anyone who fears him and does what is right is acceptable to him."

The Gentile Cornelius is told by an angel that his alms (works done in faith) put him in good stead with God vis-à-vis becoming a Christian. Later, St. Peter reiterates this by stating that whoever "fears him and does what is right" is accepted by God; that is, both faith and allegiance must be present. The ongoing principle of the organic closeness of faith and works is again evident.

> **Acts 22:16:** " 'And now, why do you wait? Rise and be baptized, and wash away your sins, calling on his name.' "

Cardinal Newman comments on this verse:

> A man may . . . [think] that in St. Paul's Epistle to the Romans nothing is said about channels and instruments; that faith is represented as the sole medium of justification. . . . Yet from other parts of the history, we learn . . . that an especial revelation was made to Ananias, lest Saul should go without Baptism; and that, so far from his being justified immediately on his faith, he was bid not to tarry, but "to arise and be baptized, and *to wash away his sins*. . . ."
>
> Here, then, we have a clear instance in St. Paul's case, that there are priestly services between the soul and God, even under the Gospel; that though Christ has purchased

inestimable blessings for our race, yet that it is still necessary ever to apply them to individuals by visible means.[41]

The Protestant has difficulty explaining this passage, for it is St. Paul's own recounting of his odyssey as a newly "born-again" Christian. We have here the Catholic doctrine of (sacramental) sanctification/justification, in which sins are actually removed. The phraseology "wash away your sins" is reminiscent of Psalm 51:2, 7; 1 John 1:7, 9; and similar texts dealing with infused justification, dealt with earlier. We note also a similarity to St. Peter's first sermon in the Upper Room upon being filled with the Holy Spirit:

> **Acts 2:38:** "Repent, and be baptized, every one of you, in the name of Jesus Christ for the forgiveness of your sins; and you shall receive the gift of the Holy Spirit."

According to the standard Evangelical soteriology, the apostle Paul would have been instantly "justified" at the Damascus-road experience when he first converted (almost involuntarily!) to Christ (Acts 9:1-9). Thus, his sins would have been "covered over" and righteousness imputed to him at that point. If so, why would St. Paul use this terminology of washing away sins at Baptism in a merely symbolic sense (as they assert), since it would be superfluous? The reasonable alternative, especially given the evidence of other related scriptures, is that St. Paul was speaking literally, not symbolically.

There is even more remarkable proof of this: The Greek word for "wash away" in Acts 22:16 is *apolouo*. It only appears one other time in the Bible, also in St. Paul's writing:

> **1 Corinthians 6:11:** "And such were some of you. But you were washed, you were sanctified, you were

[41] Sermon: "The Christian Ministry," 1835.

> justified in the name of the Lord Jesus Christ and in the Spirit of our God."

There is much here that indicates the Catholic view of the doctrines under present consideration: washing (baptismal regeneration), sanctification, justification, and even the Holy Spirit (and the Trinity). Protestant "dogma" attempts to separate all four elements, to more or less degrees. Granted, it isn't logically certain that the three acts or processes are equivalent in this particular text, but at any rate, St. Paul is surely associating them together closely, as in Catholic teaching.

Baptism and regeneration are often correlated in Scripture: Jesus says we must be "born of water and the Spirit" to enter God's kingdom (John 3:5). Many Protestants rather desperately claim that the water refers to childbirth! St. Peter informs us that "Baptism . . . now saves you" (1 Pet. 3:21). St. Paul writes that "He saved us . . . by the washing of regeneration" (Titus 3:5) and equates Baptism with "put[ting] on Christ" (Gal. 3:27). Catholics do not hold that Baptism alone is sufficient for eternal salvation (assuming a person lives for a while after it) and interpret these verses in harmony with the rest of the biblical teaching of salvation as a lifelong process of perseverance. On the other hand, the Protestant must admit that there is definitely more to these verses than mere symbolism. We do indeed see here baptismal regeneration, by which the newly baptized initiate is sanctified and made holy — all of which is consistent with infused justification.

St. Paul and justification

Al Kresta, the host of a Catholic talk-radio show[42] and a former nondenominational pastor, a man thoroughly acquainted with

[42] "Kresta in the Afternoon," on WDEO, 990 AM, from Ann Arbor, Michigan, and WCAR, 1090 AM, from metropolitan Detroit, from 3-6 p.m. weekdays.

Protestant thinking on justification, makes some very cogent observations about St. Paul's theology of salvation:

> Unlike the modern Evangelical-Protestant revivalistic preaching tradition, the Apostle Paul was not preoccupied with his acceptance as a sinner before a holy and righteous God. That was Luther's crisis. Protestants have tended to read Paul through the lens of Luther's experience.
>
> 1. . . . Luther said he feared God but clung to the Apostle Paul. All the constitutive elements of the classic Luther-type experience, however, are missing in both the experience and the thought of the Apostle.
>
> Unlike Luther, Paul was not preoccupied with his guilt, seeking reassurance of a gracious God. He was rather robust of conscience, even given to boasting, untroubled about whether God was gracious or not [Phil. 3:4 ff.; 2 Cor. 10, 11]. He knew God was gracious. He never pleads either with Jews or Gentiles to *feel* an anguished conscience and then receive release from that anguish in a message of forgiveness. . . . Paul's burden is not to "bring people under conviction of sin," as in revival services. Forgiveness is simply a matter of fact.
>
> When Paul speaks of himself as a serious sinner, it is . . . very specifically because . . . he had persecuted the Church and missed God's new move — opening the covenant community to the Gentiles (1 Cor. 15:9-10; Eph. 3:8; Gal. 1:13-16; 1 Tim. 1:13-15).
>
> What is now set right in his life is not that he is no longer trying to work his way to Heaven, abandons self-exertion, and now trusts Christ; it is rather that he now sees that God has inexplicably chosen him to reveal this new and more inclusive covenant community made up of Jew and Gentile (Eph. 2:11-3:6). . . .

2. Paul's arguments against works of the law are not fundamentally arguments against human participation in or human cooperation with the saving purposes of God, but arguments against Judaistic pride that sought to define membership in the covenant community by reference to Jewish marks of identity, such as circumcision, Sabbath-keeping, etc. and not fundamentally faith in Jesus as Messiah. . . .[43]

[43] Al Kresta continues his somewhat technical exposition of St. Paul's viewpoint on the Jews and "works of righteousness" as follows:

"Contrary to the pronouncements of popular preachers, first-century Judaism did not believe in salvation by works. They believed that they were God's elect people by grace; lawkeeping was their response to God's grace. Salvation was understood to be granted by God's electing grace, not according to a righteousness based on merit-earning works. But most Protestant scholars since Luther have read Paul as saying that Judaism misunderstood the gracious nature of God's covenant with Moses and perverted it into a system of attaining righteousness by works.

"Wrong! Luther's experience was not Paul's. New Testament scholars, for the most part, now understand 'works of law' not as synonymous with human effort but as the activities by which the Jews maintained their distinct status from the Gentiles. . . .

"For Paul, these boundary-defining features distinguished Israel in the flesh (Rom. 2:28) and encouraged Jews to boast in their national identity (Rom. 3:27-29; Gal. 2:16; 6:13). They were obstructing the extension of God's grace to the nations through Christ. In so doing, they were undermining their very purpose of existence: all the nations were supposed to be blessed by the offspring of Abraham (Gen. 12:3; Deut. 4:6; Isa. 66:20). So when Paul says of the Jews that "they sought to establish their own righteousness" (Rom. 10:3), he doesn't mean that they were trying to earn their salvation through human exertion, but that they arrogated to themselves the authority to set the conditions by which believing Gentiles could be regarded as full members in the new covenant community. They rejected the authoritative apostolic

3. Even in Paul, justification cannot be isolated from the other images he employs to describe God's salvific activity toward us. While righteousness/justice/justification is the primary way the Apostle describes what God does for us in Christ, it is complemented by other images which express aspects of God's activity in nonlegal terminology that refers to personal and corporate transformation. Paul recognized that Christ had "once for all" (Rom. 6:10) died to sin and had justified human beings (Gal. 2:16; Rom. 3:26-28, 4:25, 5:18), but he freely described what this involves under such other images as:

- Salvation (2 Cor. 7:10; Rom. 1:16, 10:10, 13:11);
- Expiation of sins (Rom. 3:25);
- Redemption of sinners (1 Cor. 1:30; Rom. 3:24, 8:32);
- Reconciliation of sinners to God (2 Cor. 5:18-20; Rom. 5:10-11, 11:15);
- Adoption into the family of God (Gal. 4:5; Rom. 8:15, 23);
- Sanctification (1 Cor. 1:2, 30; 6:11);
- Freedom (Gal. 5:1,13; Rom. 8:1-2, 21);
- Transformation (2 Cor. 3:18; Rom. 12:20);
- Glorification (2 Cor. 3:10; Rom. 8:30);
- New Creation (Gal. 6:15; 2 Cor. 5:17; cf. 1 Cor. 15:45).

teaching that the Gentiles and Jews constituted one body (Acts 15:1, 24; Gal. 1:7, 2:12, 5:10; Eph. 2-3:13), and they sought to thwart God's inclusion of the Gentiles by insisting that Gentiles first become Jews through circumcision, etc., rather than through faith in Jesus, who is the 'aim' or 'end' of the law (Phil. 3:2; Gal. 5:6, 6:15; 1 Cor. 7:19; Rom. 10:4). They were retrogressive. . . ."

Protestants see justification, sanctification, and glorification as three successive phases of salvation — related, but essentially distinct. Catholics see them as three aspects of the same process begun at the same moment in time. . . .

A Catholic understanding of justification is that it is the glorious voice of the Lord declaring us to be righteous. The word of the Lord, however, is a creative word. It is powerful enough to effect what it says. God's word is not a mere statement; it will not return to him void, but will accomplish that which he pleases. When God declares a man just, he makes him just (cf. Isa. 44:22; Ps. 32:5, 51:3 ff.). . . . Our righteousness is, so to speak, the imprint upon us of the righteousness of Another.[44]

Romans 2:5-13: "But by your hard and impenitent heart you are storing up wrath for yourself on the day of wrath when God's righteous judgment will be revealed. For he will render to every man according to his works: To those who by patience in well-doing seek for glory and honor and immortality, he will give eternal life; but for those who are factious and do not obey the truth, but obey wickedness, there will be wrath and fury. There will be tribulation and distress for every human being who does evil, the Jew first and also the Greek, but glory and honor and peace for everyone who does good, the Jew first and also the Greek. For God shows no partiality. All who have sinned without the law will also perish without the law, and all who have sinned under the law will

[44] These observations are taken from unpublished lecture notes entitled "Some Further Thoughts on Justification by Faith Through Grace" (1993) and are used by express permission of the author.

> be judged by the law. For it is not the hearers of the law who are righteous before God, but the doers of the law who will be justified."

Judgment, according to St. Paul in his quintessential treatise on salvational theology, his letter to the Romans, is according to works, just as Christ also explicitly taught. This is a theme that runs through St. Paul's writings (for example, 1 Cor. 3:13, 4:5; 2 Cor. 5:10; Gal. 6:7-9; Col. 3:23-25). That this is the case is admitted even by staunchly Reformed evangelical theologians, such as G. C. Berkouwer.[45]

This passage easily synthesizes with Catholic soteriology, but is shockingly dissimilar to Protestant thought. To summarize: The concept of "demerits" is present (verse 5). Differential rewards for works (by implication, differential "merit") exist (verse 6). Eternal life is correlated with well-doing (verses 7, 10). Divine wrath is due to disobedience (verses 8, 9). Obedient doers of the law shall be justified (verse 13; a striking similarity to James 1:22-23; 2:24).

The theme of obeying the gospel, or the obedience of faith, is also common in St. Paul's writings (for example, Rom. 1:5, 6:17, 10:16, 15:18-19, 16:25-26; 2 Thess. 1:8; cf. Acts 6:7; Heb. 11:8).

> **Romans 3:28:** "For we hold that a man is justified by faith apart from works of law."

Hartmann Grisar, the great Jesuit scholar and biographer of Luther, asserts:

> Here he merely excludes the works "of the law," i.e., according to the context such works as do not rest on faith but

[45] G. C. Berkouwer, *Faith and Justification* (Studies in Dogmatics), Lewis B. Smedes, trans. (Grand Rapids, Michigan: Eerdmans, 1954), 103-105.

> precede faith, whether the purely outward works of the Mosaic ceremonial law, or other natural works done apart from, or before, Christ.[46]

This is the verse to which Luther, with no basis in the Greek text, arbitrarily added the word *alone* after the word *faith* in his German translation, in order to bolster his novel doctrine of *sola fide*. The notion of "faith alone" does, however, occur in the Bible twice, in James 2:17 and 2:24, where it is condemned. It comes as no surprise, then, to learn that Luther described the book of James as an "epistle of straw" and regarded it as an inferior, second-tier book of the New Testament (and in fact nearly threw it out altogether).

> **Romans 5:17-19:** "If, because of one man's trespass, death reigned through that one man, much more will those who receive the abundance of grace and the free gift of righteousness reign in life through the one man Jesus Christ. Then as one man's trespass led to condemnation for all men, so one man's act of righteousness leads to acquittal and life for all men. For as by one man's disobedience many were made sinners, so by one man's obedience many will be made righteous."

It seems unlikely, in light of the clear parallelism in verse 19 ("made sinners . . . made righteous") that the righteousness is merely imputed, since all agree that Original Sin is actual. Likewise, verse 17 gives us a clue as to St. Paul's meaning, since it refers to a received "abundance of grace" and "the gift of righteousness" — phrases that are more in line with infused justification.

46 Hartmann Grisar, *Luther*, E. M. Lamond, trans., Luigi Cappadelta, ed. (London: Kegan Paul, Trench, Trubner and Co., 1917), Vol. 1, 309.

> **1 Corinthians 3:8-9:** "Each shall receive his wages according to his labor. For we are God's fellow workers; you are God's field, God's building."

> **1 Corinthians 15:10:** "But by the grace of God I am what I am, and his grace toward me was not in vain. On the contrary, I worked harder than any of them, though it was not I, but the grace of God which is with me" (see also 1 Cor. 15:58; Gal. 5:6, 6:7-9).

St. Paul again regards faith and the human cooperation of works (labor) as two sides of the same coin, both proceeding from grace. Elsewhere, the apostle writes of the "works of faith" and related concepts (1 Thess. 1:3; 2 Thess. 1:11; Titus 1:15-16). Faith and works are not at all incompatible in all these Pauline passages. Salvation is described as a struggle, a process, a goal — not merely an abstract, past, instantaneous event.

As we labor faithfully as Jesus' disciples, we store up corresponding rewards (1 Cor. 3:8; cf. 1 Tim. 6:18-19): the idea of merit (which most Protestants deny). It is by virtue of our union with our Lord Jesus Christ that our actions — worthless in and of themselves — become meritorious.

> **2 Corinthians 5:17:** "If anyone is in Christ, he is a new creation; the old has passed away; behold, the new has come."

The curious thing here (for the Protestant) is the seemingly instantaneous change of sanctification, which would accompany justification. If "all things are new" (as in the KJV), how does this square with mere declaratory, forensic, extrinsic justification? The whole drift of the passage seems to be actual transformation in the person now in Christ, whereas in Protestant justification, only the individual's "legal" standing with God is changed. In fact, justification and sanctification are intimately related aspects of our ultimate salvation.

> **Ephesians 2:8-10:** "For by grace you have been saved through faith; and this is not your own doing; it is the gift of God — not because of works, lest any man should boast. For we are his workmanship, created in Christ Jesus for good works, which God prepared beforehand, that we should walk in them."

The first portion of this passage (2:8-9) is one of the most frequently used biblical citations in Protestant evangelistic circles. What is noteworthy upon reflection is how verse 10 clarifies the two preceding verses. When it is included in proper context, we see that works are not antithetical to faith, but rather, the necessary "outworking" of it. In verses 8 and 9, St. Paul is stressing the causational primacy of grace and faith, and the futility of mere human works not preceded by grace. But in verse 10 he teaches that good works ordained by God, and always proceeding from His grace, are equally part of salvation and justification. The whole passage is more in accord with Catholic both-and thinking than with the Protestant either-or dichotomous perspective.

> **Philippians 2:12-13:** "Work out your own salvation with fear and trembling; for God is at work in you, both to will and to work for his good pleasure."

Cardinal Newman elaborates:

> In truth, the two doctrines of the sovereign and overruling power of divine grace, and man's power of resistance, need not at all interfere with each other. They lie in different provinces, and are (as it were) incommensurables. Thus St. Paul evidently accounted them; else he could not have introduced the text in question with the exhortation, "Work

out or accomplish your own salvation with fear and trembling," for it is God which worketh or acts in you. So far was he from thinking man's distinct working inconsistent with God's continual aiding, that he assigns the knowledge of the latter as an encouragement to the former. . . .

It is quite certain that a modern Predestinarian never could have written such a sentence [as Phil. 2:12-13].[47]

> **Titus 3:5-8:** "He saved us, not because of deeds done by us in righteousness, but in virtue of his own mercy, by the washing of regeneration and renewal in the Holy Spirit, which he poured out upon us richly through Jesus Christ our Savior, so that we might be justified by his grace and become heirs in hope of eternal life. . . . Those who have believed in God may be careful to apply themselves to good deeds; these are excellent and profitable to men."

Here St. Paul refers to Baptism (verse 5: "washing of regeneration") and says we are saved in the sense of initial justification. That this is a conditional security, we have seen from several other passages already considered, and more to come. Assuming for the sake of argument that the salvation here spoken of is permanent and "eternally secure," the Evangelical would still have to extricate himself from the position of baptismal regeneration, which most Protestants deny vehemently. Once again, St. Paul utilizes a beautifully symmetrical argument, such as in Philippians 2:12-13 and Ephesians 2:8-10, balancing complementary aspects (which are often unnecessarily dichotomized by Protestantism).

Most interesting is the use of *deeds* in two different senses in the same passage. In verse 5, he teaches that we cannot be saved by purely human works, preceding the grace of God (that is, the

[47] Sermon: "Human Responsibility," 1835.

heresy of Pelagianism is denied). But in verse 8, he urges in very strong terms that good deeds are profitable, as indeed he often stresses elsewhere in several ways.

Catholics need not minimize the aspects of St. Paul's teaching that deal with human responsibility, nor set his teaching on works against his supposed teaching on extrinsic justification, nor his predestinarian texts against his numerous exhortations of vigilance and watchfulness concerning one's own state of friendship with God, nor oppose him to St. James or our Lord Jesus, etc. When the *whole* teaching of the Bible is taken into consideration (as objectively as humanly possible), the synthesis arrived at will be seen to be not unlike that which has been maintained in the Catholic Church, with increasing fullness as time goes on.

> **Hebrews 5:9:** "And being made perfect, he became the source of eternal salvation to all who obey him" (see also Heb. 6:9-10; 10:24).

Obviously, obedience is regarded here as essential for salvation. There is no sense whatsoever in this passage of a "faith alone" viewpoint, which somehow puts sanctification in a separate category, not necessary for salvation.

> **James 1:22:** "But be doers of the word, and not hearers only, deceiving yourselves."

> **James 2:14-26:** "What does it profit, my brethren, if a man says he has faith, but has not works? Can his faith save him? If a brother or sister is ill-clad and in lack of daily food, and one of you says to them, "Go in peace, be warmed and filled," without giving them the things needed for the body, what does it profit? So faith by itself, if it has no works, is dead. But someone will say, "You have faith, and I have works." Show me your faith apart from your works, and I by

> my works will show you my faith. You believe that God is one; you do well. Even the demons believe — and shudder. Do you want to be shown, you foolish fellow, that faith apart from works is barren? Was not Abraham our father justified by works, when he offered his son Isaac upon the altar? You see that faith was active along with his works, and faith was completed by works, and the scripture was fulfilled which says, 'Abraham believed God, and it was reckoned to him as righteousness'; and he was called the friend of God. You see that a man is justified by works and not by faith alone. And in the same way was not also Rahab the harlot justified by works when she received the messengers and sent them out another way? For as the body apart from the spirit is dead, so faith apart from works is dead" (see also Ps. 106:30-31; James 1:23-27).

When St. James uses the phrase "faith alone," he is speaking in the sense of mere intellectual assent to Christianity. St. Paul does not contradict St. James, as Luther thought, since he uses the word *faith* in the broader sense of a person's complete allegiance to God with both mind and will. But St. James also uses the word in the broader sense, as he develops his argument ("I by my works will show you my faith").

St. James is referring to that portion of justification which occurs after the initial manifestation (or what Evangelicals would specify strictly as sanctification). There is neither a contradiction between St. Paul and St. James, nor in both apostles' exposition of faith and works as organically united. The real contradiction is the one devised by Luther, whereby things that are bound together in Scripture (as we have clearly seen above) are arbitrarily separated, to the detriment of a logically and theologically consistent exegesis.

"Faith alone," or *sola fide*, could have no more indisputable and explicit refutation than this passage. Yet much more in Scripture also opposes it.

Cardinal Newman reiterates this point:

> On the whole, then, salvation is both by faith and by works. St. James says, not *dead* faith, and St. Paul, not *dead* works. St. James, "not by faith *only*," for that *would* be dead faith; St. Paul, "not by works *only*," for such *would* be dead works. Faith alone can make works living; works alone can make faith living. Take away either, and you take away both — he alone has faith who has works — he alone has works who has faith.[48]

> **1 Peter 1:2:** ". . . chosen and destined by God the Father and sanctified by the Spirit for obedience to Jesus Christ and for sprinkling with his blood . . ."

This is another remarkable verse, which incorporates so many elements together: initial justification and the resulting sanctification and obedience. Even the Trinity is implied. A Catholic motto in interpreting the Bible might be: "What therefore God [Scripture] has joined together, let no man put asunder" (Matt. 19:6).

> **1 Peter 1:17:** ". . . who judges each one impartially according to his deeds . . ."

St. Peter teaches the same concept of differential reward found in the Gospels and the Pauline epistles.

> **2 Peter 1:10:** "Therefore, brethren, be the more zealous to confirm your call and election, for if you do this you will never fall."

[48] Sermon: "The New Works of the Gospel," 1840.

St. Peter regards salvation as a process that requires diligence. The word *if* speaks volumes against "eternal security." The coexistence of human exertion ("zealous to confirm") and divine prerogative ("call and election") are especially noteworthy.

> **Revelation 22:12:** "Behold, I am coming soon, bringing my recompense, to repay everyone for what he has done."

Our Lord Jesus reiterates in the revelation to St. John his same teaching of differential reward, and by extension, the possibility of human merit though grace.

Assurance of instant salvation/salvation as a process

> **1 Corinthians 9:27:** "But I pommel my body and subdue it, lest after preaching to others I myself should be disqualified."

> **1 Corinthians 10:12:** "Therefore let anyone who thinks that he stands take heed lest he fall."

> **Galatians 5:1, 4:** "Stand fast, therefore, and do not submit again to a yoke of slavery. . . . You are severed from Christ, you who would be justified by the law; you have fallen away from grace."

> **Philippians 3:11-14:** ". . . that if possible I may attain the resurrection from the dead. Not that I have already obtained this or am already perfect; but I press on to make it my own, because Christ Jesus has made me his own. Brethren, I do not consider that I have made it my own. . . . I press on toward the goal for the prize of the upward call of God in Christ Jesus."

1 Timothy 4:1: "Now the Spirit expressly says that in later times some will depart from the Faith by giving heed to deceitful spirits and doctrines of demons."

1 Timothy 5:15: "For some have already strayed after Satan."

Hebrews 3:12-14: "Take care, brethren, lest there be in any of you an evil, unbelieving heart, leading you to fall away from the living God. But exhort one another every day . . . that none of you may be hardened by the deceitfulness of sin. For we share in Christ, if only we hold our first confidence firm to the end."

Hebrews 6:4-6: "For it is impossible to restore again to repentance those who have once been enlightened, who have tasted the heavenly gift, and have become partakers of the Holy Spirit, and have tasted the goodness of the word of God, and the powers of the age to come, if they then commit apostasy."

2 Peter 2:15, 20-21: "Forsaking the right way, they have gone astray; they have followed the way of Balaam. . . . For if, after they have escaped the defilements of the world through the knowledge of our Lord and Savior Jesus Christ, they are again entangled in them and overpowered, the last state has become worse for them than the first. For it would have been better for them never to have known the way of righteousness than, after knowing it, to turn back from the holy commandment delivered to them" (see also 1 Sam. 11:6, 18:11-12; Ezek. 18:24, 33:12-13, 18; Gal. 4:9; Col. 1:23; Heb. 6:11-12, 10:23, 26, 29, 36, 39, 12:15; Rev. 2:4-5).

The Second Council of Orange (529) and the Council of Trent (1545-1563) on the doctrine of justification

No theologian or Christian figure of any note believed in forensic, imputed justification until Luther and Calvin came onto the scene of Church history in the sixteenth century. It is simply implausible and incredible (and unbiblical: Matt. 16:18; John 14:26) to think that a theological concept considered so absolutely crucial by Protestants could have been lost immediately after the Apostles and for fifteen centuries thereafter.

The Second Council of Orange in 529[49] condemned the heresies of Pelagianism and Semi-Pelagianism (which St. Augustine had already done a century earlier). Pelagianism denied Original Sin and regarded grace as within man's natural capacities. Semi-Pelagianism made man primarily responsible for his own salvation and denigrated the necessity of God's enabling grace.

The council made many binding definitions of grace and salvation that may be quite surprising to many Protestants who are wont to accuse the Catholic Church of the same heresies that she anathematized fourteen centuries ago. The Catholic Church fully agrees with Holy Scripture that faith, the subjective condition of justification, is a gift of God (Eph. 2:8 ff.; John 6:66; Heb. 12:12; Phil. 1:6, 1:29; 1 Cor. 4:7). This was the emphasis of Second Orange. Several of its more important decrees follow:

> **Canon 3:** "If anyone says that the grace of God can be conferred in answer to man's petition, but that the petition itself is not due to the action of grace, he contradicts the prophet Isaiah and the Apostle, who both say: 'I was found by them that did not seek me, I

[49] The Second Council of Orange was not an ecumenical, or general council, but is solemnly authoritative for all Catholics due to the confirmation of Pope Boniface II (papal bull *Per Filium Nostrum*, January 25, 531).

appeared openly to them that ask not after me' " (Rom. 10:20; Isa. 15:1).

Canon 4: "If anyone contends that God waits for our will so we may be cleansed from sin — and does not admit that the very fact that we even will to be cleansed comes in us by the infusion and work of the Holy Spirit, he resists the same Holy Spirit."

Canon 5: "If anybody says that the . . . beginning of Faith and the Act of Faith itself . . . is in us naturally and not by a gift of grace that is by the inspiration of the Holy Ghost, he is opposed to Apostolic teaching."

Canon 6: "If anyone says that God has mercy on us when, without his grace, we believe, will, desire, strive, work, watch, study, ask, seek, knock, and does not confess that we believe, will, and are enabled to do all this in the way we ought, by the infusion and inspiration of the Holy Spirit within us; or makes the help of grace depend on the humility or obedience of man, rather than ascribing such humility and obedience to the free gift of grace; he goes counter to the Apostle, who says, 'What hast thou that thou hast not received?' and 'By the grace of God I am what I am' (1 Cor. 4:7 and 15:10)."

Canon 7: "If anyone asserts that we can, by our natural powers, think as we ought, or choose any good pertaining to the salvation of eternal life, that is, consent to salvation or to the message of the Gospel, without the illumination and inspiration of the Holy Spirit . . . he is misled by a heretical spirit, not understanding what the voice of God says in the Gospel,

> 'Without me you can do nothing' (John 15:5), nor the words of the Apostle, 'Not that we are sufficient to think anything of ourselves, as of ourselves, but our sufficiency is from God' (2 Cor. 3:5)."
>
> **Canon 9:** "As often as we do good, God operates in us and with us, so that we may operate."
>
> **Canon 13:** "Free will, weakened in the person of the first man, can be repaired only by the grace of Baptism. . . ." (cites John 8:36).
>
> **Canon 20:** "Man does no good except that which God brings about that man performs. . . ."
>
> **Canon 25:** "In a word, to love God is a gift of God. He, yet unloved, loves us and gave us the power to love. . . . Through the sin of the first man, the free will is so weakened and warped, that no one thereafter can either love God as he ought, or believe in God, or do good for the sake of God, unless moved, previously, by the grace of the divine mercy. . . . In every good work that we do, it is not we who have the initiative, aided, subsequently, by the mercy of God, but that he begins by inspiring faith and love towards him, without any prior merit of ours."

The Council of Trent (1545-1563) reiterated the decrees of a thousand years earlier, developing them further, and emphasizing man's free will, but adding nothing essential. Some of the more notable portions of the *Decree on Justification* (January 13, 1547) follow:

> **Chapter 5:** "The beginning of the said justification is to be derived from the prevenient grace of God through Jesus Christ; that is to say, from His vocation,

whereby, without any merits existing on their parts, they are called; that so they who by sins were alienated from God may be disposed through His quickening and assisting grace to convert themselves to their own justification by freely assenting to and cooperating with that said grace: in such sort that, while God touches the heart of man by the illumination of the Holy Ghost, neither is man himself utterly without doing anything while he receives that inspiration, for as much as he is also able to reject it; yet he is not able, by his own free-will, without the grace of God, to move himself unto justice in His sight."

Canon 2: "If anyone saith that man may be justified before God by his own works, whether done through the teaching of human nature or that of the law, without the grace of God through Jesus Christ; let him be anathema."[50]

[50] Ibid., Canon 4. See also CCC, pars. 1364, 1367, 1382. The vivid Greek term *anathema,* meaning "accursed," is directed by the Council of Trent primarily toward doctrines, rather than persons, based on the ancient practice in the Church of condemning heretical teachings — a procedure itself derived biblically from passages such as Galatians 1:8-9 and 1 Corinthians 16:22. There is nothing improper whatsoever in defining correct doctrine and rejecting contrary notions. St. Paul does this constantly. The Catholic Church, however, makes no presumption as to the eternal destiny of any individual whatsoever (not even Luther!). Most emphatically, neither *anathema* nor *excommunication* means "proclaimed damned [by the Church]," as many Protestants mistakenly suppose. The more literal meanings are "out of the Church" (in the sense of divergence from her doctrines) or "out of communion" (with the sacraments and the Christian fellowship of believers). Excommunication is perfectly in accord

Canon 4: "If anyone saith that man's free will, moved and excited by God, by assenting to God exciting and calling, no wise cooperates towards disposing and preparing itself for obtaining the grace of justification; that it cannot refuse its consent, if it would, but that, as something inanimate, it does nothing whatever and is merely passive; let him be anathema."

Canon 6: "If anyone saith that it is not in man's power to make his ways evil, but that the works that are evil God worketh as well as those that are good, not permissibly only, but properly and of Himself, in such wise that the treason of Judas is no less His own proper work than the vocation of Paul; let him be anathema."

Canon 9: "If anyone saith that men are justified, either by the sole imputation of the justice of Christ or by the sole remission of sins, to the exclusion of the grace and the charity which is poured forth in their hearts by the Holy Ghost and is inherent in them; or even that the grace, whereby we are justified, is only the favor of God; let him be anathema."

Canon 24: "If anyone saith that the justice received is not preserved and also increased before God through good works; but that the said works are merely the fruits and signs of justification obtained, but not a cause of the increase thereof; let him be anathema."

with Pauline practices and teachings as expounded in, e.g., 1 Corinthians 5:3-5; 2 Thessalonians 3:6; 1 Timothy 1:19-20; 2 Timothy 2:14-19, 4:14-15, as well as our Lord's express injunction in Matthew 18:15-18.

> **Canon 26:** "If anyone saith that the just ought not, for their good works done in God, to expect and hope for an eternal recompense from God, through His mercy and the merit of Jesus Christ, if so be that they persevere to the end in well-doing and in keeping the commandments; let him be anathema."
>
> **Canon 27:** "If anyone saith that there is no mortal sin but that of infidelity (unbelief); or that grace once received is not lost by any other sin, however grievous and enormous, save by that of infidelity; let him be anathema."
>
> **Canon 30:** "If anyone saith that, after the grace of justification has been received, to every penitent sinner the guilt is remitted, and the debt of eternal punishment is blotted out in such wise that there remains not any debt of temporal punishment to be discharged either in this world, or in the next in Purgatory, before the entrance to the Kingdom of Heaven can be opened (to him); let him be anathema."

In the *Decree on Justification* (chs. 9, 12, 15), Trent also rejects classic Protestantism's notion of subjective absolute assurance of salvation:

> But, although it is necessary to believe that sins neither are remitted, nor ever were remitted save gratuitously by the mercy of God for Christ's sake, yet it is not to be said that sins are forgiven, or have been forgiven, to anyone who boasts of his confidence and certainty of the remission of sins, and rests on that alone; seeing that it may exist, yea, does in our day exist, amongst heretics and schismatics; and with great vehemence is this vain confidence, and one alien from all godliness, preached up in opposition to the

Catholic Church. But neither is this to be asserted, that they who are truly justified must needs, without any doubting whatever, settle within themselves that they are justified, and that no one is absolved from sins and justified but he that believes for certain that he is absolved and justified; and that absolution and justification are effected by this faith alone; as though whoso has not this belief doubts of the promises of God and of the efficacy of the death and resurrection of Christ. For even as no pious person ought to doubt of the mercy of God, of the merit of Christ, and of the virtue and efficacy of the sacraments, even so each one, when he regards himself and his own weakness and indisposition, may have fear and apprehension touching his own grace; seeing that no one can know with a certainty of faith, which cannot be subject to error, that he has obtained the grace of God.

No one, moreover, so long as he is in this mortal life, ought so far to presume as regards the secret mystery of divine predestination as to determine for certain that he is assuredly in the number of the predestinate; as if it were true that he that is justified either cannot sin anymore, or, if he do sin, that he ought to promise himself an assured repentance; for except by special revelation it cannot be known whom God hath chosen unto Himself.

. . . It is to be maintained that the received grace of justification is lost not only by infidelity, whereby even faith itself is lost, but also by any other mortal sin whatever, though faith be not lost. . . .

Chapter Three

Development of Doctrine

"He will teach you"

George Salmon, an able and zealous Anglican apologist of the last century, analyzed development of doctrine in the following fashion:

> An unlearned Protestant perceives that the doctrine of Rome is not the doctrine of the Bible. A learned Protestant adds that neither is it the doctrine of the primitive Church. . . . It is at least owned that the doctrine of Rome is as unlike that of early times as an oak is unlike an acorn, or a butterfly like a caterpillar. . . . The only question remaining is whether that unlikeness is absolutely inconsistent with substantial identity. In other words, it is owned that there has been a change, and the question is whether we are to call it development or corruption. . . .[51]

Salmon frames the debate correctly. Catholics maintain that the historical growth of doctrine throughout Church history is a consistent development (which is to be expected), and not a

[51] George Salmon, *The Infallibility of the Church* (Grand Rapids, Michigan: Baker Book House), 39.

corruption of scriptural truth (or, more specifically, the "deposit of Faith," as a Catholic would put it). Contrary to Salmon's contentions, Catholics believe their doctrines are grounded both in the Bible and in the early Church.

The concept of development of doctrine provides the key for understanding why the Catholic Church today often appears on the surface as fundamentally different from the early Church. Without it, the doctrinal and historical outlook of Catholicism will, in most cases, be too difficult to comprehend fully for most Evangelicals, who have quite different presuppositions in this regard. Thoughtful and ecumenical Protestants owe it to themselves to ponder this indispensable notion before unduly criticizing the allegedly "unbiblical excesses" of Catholicism.

"Development of doctrine" is defined by Catholics as the increase in understanding — by means of the teaching of the Holy Spirit, prayer, theological study, and the reflection of the Body of Christ as a whole — of Christian doctrines that originated from the Lord Jesus himself and which have been passed down through the Apostles, the Fathers, the councils, and the Catholic Church in general.[52] The meaning of doctrines unfolds over time, but the essence or substance of any particular doctrine remains unchanged. Our extent of knowledge or subjective grasp of any given dogma is what changes. Doctrines thus achieve more clarity and depth as well as certitude in the minds and hearts of believers.[53] The Bible

[52] CCC, par. 94; see also pars. 66, 91-94, 126, 158, 171, 217, 236, 250-251, 711, 892, 1201, 1230, 1610, 2045, 2063, 2421, 2625, 2651, 2667, 2671, 2675, 2678, 2684, 2777; Second Vatican Council: *Dogmatic Constitution on Divine Revelation*, Nov. 18, 1965, ch. 2, no. 8; Dave Armstrong, *Dialogue on the Legitimacy of Catholic Development of Doctrine, With Reference to Vatican I, Vatican II, and the Catechism of the Catholic Church*, online at http://ic.net/~erasmus/RAZ372.HTM.

[53] Hardon, *PCD*, 109.

is not absolutely clear, even in the "essentials," and requires the developing interpretive wisdom of the Church.

The Catholic Church maintains that no new public revelation has been received by the Church since the time of the Apostles,[54] and "private revelations" such as Marian apparitions are not at all binding on the faithful, even though many of these have been recognized by the Church as worthy of pious belief.[55]

The description of the Christian Church as the "Body of Christ" in the Bible (e.g., Eph. 1:22-23) presupposes the ability to grow actively. The Church, according to many Protestants, resembles a statue more than a living organism. Once the biblical metaphor is consistently applied, it also makes no sense to say that growth (development) stopped in the third, fourth, or fifth century or at some other arbitrary point.

Doctrines agreed upon by virtually all Christians develop, too. The doctrine of the divinity of Jesus Christ was not formally defined until the Council of Nicaea in 325, and the divinity of the Holy Spirit was proclaimed at the Council of Constantinople in 381. The dogma of the two natures of Christ (God and man) was made official at the Council of Chalcedon in 451. We've already seen how the Canon of the New Testament was also very much a "developing doctrine," finalized only in 397. Original Sin was a slowly developed belief. Many other examples could be brought forth.

Why should Protestants accept these authoritative verdicts, but reject similar proclamations on Church government, the Real Presence of Jesus Christ in the Eucharist, Mary, the papacy, Purgatory, priestly absolution, baptismal regeneration, the Sacrifice of the Mass, the intercession of the saints, and so forth? If the answer is that these beliefs are "not biblical," then it must be

[54] CCC, par. 66.

[55] CCC, par. 67.

explained why Protestants disagree among themselves on virtually every "minor" and even "major" Christian doctrine (see Appendix One).

Corruption can just as easily consist of subtraction as addition. An automobile might be deemed corrupt if it had only half its spark plugs, watered-down gas, no rear brakes, one headlight, one quart of oil, and so forth. Thus, Protestantism's charges against Catholic "corruption," if closely scrutinized, often come back to incriminate itself with at least equal force.

The early Church, although it was obviously primitive and undeveloped, nevertheless looks like a small Catholic plant rather than a Protestant statue, whole and entire. This can be ascertained fairly easily by examining the history of doctrines.

If the early Church were Protestant in doctrinal outlook, such a Church went off the rails so astonishingly fast that such an explanation must be discarded as woefully inadequate to account for the facts of history. Furthermore, if a massive defection and apostasy took place, where was the outcry and protest from the "pure" Christian believers? We find no such thing in the historical records.

Another recurrent theme of doctrinal development throughout Church history has been a rapid increase in understanding due to the attacks of heretics who question various Christian doctrines. St. Augustine elaborates:

> While the hot restlessness of heretics stirs up questions about many things belonging to the Catholic Faith, in order to provide a defense against these heretics, we are obliged to study the points questioned more diligently, to understand them more clearly . . . and thus the question raised by the adversary becomes the occasion of instruction.[56]

[56] St. Augustine, *The City of God*, Bk. 16, ch. 2, no. 1. From Jurgens, *FEF*, Vol. 3, 103.

> There are many things that lay hidden in the Scriptures, and when heretics were cut off, they vexed the Church of God with disputes; then the hidden things were brought to light, and the will of God was made known.[57]

Obviously, then, if St. Augustine held such a view in the fifth century, development is no new "Romish" corruption of recent times. It has been present in the Church from the very beginning. Nor is it unique to Catholics. For instance, C. S. Lewis expressly affirmed it,[58] as does renowned Lutheran (more recently, Orthodox) historian of theology Jaroslav Pelikan[59] and many other Protestants. Therefore, we are left with the task of distinguishing a true development from a corruption, as Salmon stated.

For this endeavor, we must consult Cardinal Newman, who is perhaps best known for his masterpiece *An Essay on the Development of Christian Doctrine*,[60] which he completed as an Anglican in 1845, right before his conversion to Catholicism, basically convincing himself by means of rigorous and brilliant historical, ecclesiological, and analogical arguments. Jaroslav Pelikan, an expert on the history of Christian doctrine, considers the essay the quintessential work on the subject.[61] Newman is regarded by all parties as a penetrating and remarkable theological mind. The

[57] *On Psalm 54*, no. 22. From James Cardinal Gibbons, *FEF*, 11.

[58] C. S. Lewis, *God in the Dock*, Walter Hooper, ed. (Grand Rapids, Michigan: Eerdmans, 1970), 44-47. Originally from "Dogma and the Universe," *The Guardian* (March 19, 1943): 96; (March 26, 1943): 104, 107; *Mere Christianity* (New York: Macmillan, 1952), 144.

[59] Jaroslav Pelikan, *The Emergence of the Catholic Tradition (100-600)* (Chicago: University of Chicago Press, 1971), 7-10.

[60] University of Notre Dame Press, 1989.

[61] Jaroslav Pelikan, *Development of Christian Doctrine: Some Historical Prolegomena* (New Haven, Connecticut: Yale University Press, 1969), 3.

following excerpts from his book present his argument in kernel form:

> Granting that some large variations of teaching in its long course of 1800 years exist, nevertheless, these, on examination, will be found . . . to proceed on a law, and with a harmony and a definite drift, and with an analogy to Scripture revelations, which . . . constitute an argument in their favor, as witnessing to a superintending Providence and a great Design.[62]
>
> It becomes necessary . . . to assign certain characteristics of faithful developments . . . the presence of which serves as a test to discriminate between them and corruptions. . . . I venture to set down Seven Notes . . . as follows: There is no corruption if it retains one and the same type, the same principles, the same organization; if its beginnings anticipate its subsequent phases, and its later phenomena protect and subserve its earlier; if it has a power of assimilation and revival, and a vigorous action from first to last.[63]
>
> Principle is a better test of heresy than doctrine. Heretics are true to their principles, but change to and fro, backwards and forwards, in opinion; for very opposite doctrines may be exemplifications of the same principle. . . . Thus Calvinists become Unitarians from the principle of private judgment. The doctrines of heresy are accidents and soon run to an end; its principles are everlasting. . . . Protestantism, viewed in its more Catholic aspect, is doctrine without active principle; viewed in its heretical, it is active principle without doctrine.[64]

[62] Newman, *An Essay on the Development of Christian Doctrine*, vii-viii. Preface to the 1878 edition.

[63] Ibid., 170-171.

[64] Ibid., 181-182.

> A corruption is a development in that very stage in which it ceases to illustrate, and begins to disturb, the acquisitions gained in its previous history. . . . A true development . . . is an addition which illustrates . . . the body of thought from which it proceeds. . . . It is of a tendency conservative of what has gone before it.[65]
>
> Dissolution is that further state to which corruption tends. Corruption cannot, therefore, be of long standing; and thus duration is another test of a faithful development. . . . A corruption . . . is distinguished . . . by its *transitory character.*[66]
>
> If it be true that the principles of the later Church are the same as those of the earlier, then . . . the later in reality agrees more than it differs with the earlier, for principles are responsible for doctrines. Hence they who assert that the modern Roman system is the corruption of primitive theology are forced to discover some difference of principle . . . for instance, that the right of private judgment was secured to the early Church and has been lost to the later, or again, that the later Church rationalizes and the earlier went by faith. . . . As to Protestantism it is plain in how many ways it has reversed the principles of Catholic theology.[67]

Newman's arguments are highly complex and are greatly illuminated by the countless historical examples he produces in order to corroborate his "seven notes" of the characteristics of true developments, not to mention his fabulous, highly acclaimed style of English prose. Thus, the essay deserves to be read in its entirety.

To summarize, when these "notes" are applied, it is found that Protestantism fails the seven tests (that is, insofar as it differs from

[65] Ibid., 199-200, 203.

[66] Ibid., 203, 205.

[67] Ibid., 353-354.

Catholicism), whereas Catholicism is altogether consistent with them. Protestantism did not develop the doctrines that distinguish it from Catholicism (not even with reference to the beliefs of the early Church, of which it claims to be the restorer). Rather, it contains many new doctrines that had never before been present in the history of Christianity. Protestantism fails utterly in its attempts to find these in the early Church and therefore must be regarded as a corruption where it radically departs from the Christianity that preceded it for 1500 years.

On the other hand, highly developed Catholic doctrines, such as the Immaculate Conception and the full-blown papacy, can be shown to be consistent with all the marks of true developments. As Newman states:

> The Christianity of history is not Protestantism. If ever there were a safe truth, it is this. And Protestantism . . . as a whole, feels it, and has felt it. This is shown in the determination . . . of dispensing with historical Christianity altogether, and of forming a Christianity from the Bible alone. . . .[68]

Cardinal Newman was not the first major Christian figure to "invent" the notion of development of doctrine, as is often cynically supposed. In the late second century, St. Irenaeus speaks of Christian doctrine as "everywhere the same." Yet he goes on to assert that "constantly it has its youth renewed by the Spirit of God, as if it were some precious deposit in an excellent vessel; and it causes the vessel containing it also to be rejuvenated."[69]

Tertullian, writing around 206, states that "the grace of God works and perfects up to the end."[70]

[68] Ibid., 7.

[69] *Against Heresies*, Bk. 3, ch. 24, no. 1. In Jurgens, *FEF*, Vol. 1, 94.

[70] *The Veiling of Virgins*, ch. 1, no. 3. In Jurgens, *FEF*, Vol. 1, 137.

St. Vincent of Lerins, writing around 434, gave the classic exposition found in the Church Fathers:

> In the Catholic Church herself every care must be taken that we may hold fast to that which has been believed everywhere, always, and by all. For this is, then, truly and properly Catholic. . . .[71]
>
> Will there, then, be no progress of religion in the Church of Christ? Certainly there is, and the greatest. . . . But it is truly *progress* and not a *change of Faith*. What is meant by *progress* is that something is brought to an advancement within itself; by *change*, something is transformed from one thing into another. It is necessary, therefore, that understanding, knowledge, and wisdom grow and advance strongly and mightily . . . and this must take place precisely within its own kind, that is, in the same teaching, in the same meaning, and in the same opinion. The progress of religion in souls is like the growth of bodies, which, in the course of years, evolve and develop, but still remain what they were. . . . Although in the course of time something evolved from those first seeds and has now expanded under careful cultivation, nothing of the characteristics of the seeds is changed. Granted that appearance, beauty, and distinction has been added, still, the same nature of each kind remains.[72]
>
> Dogma . . . may be consolidated in the course of years, developed in the sequence of time, and sublimated by age — yet remain incorrupt and unimpaired . . . so that it does not allow of any change, or any loss of its specific character, or any variation of its inherent form.[73]

[71] In Jurgens, *FEF*, Vol. 3, 263.

[72] Ibid., 265 (emphasis added).

[73] In John Chapin, ed., *The Book of Catholic Quotations* (New York: Farrar, Straus and Cudahy, 1956), 271.

> It should flourish and ripen; it should develop and become perfect . . . but it is sinful to change them [dogmas] . . . or mutilate them. They may take on more evidence, clarity, and distinctness, but it is absolutely necessary that they retain their plenitude, integrity, and basic character. . . .
>
> The Church of Christ is a faithful and ever-watchful guardian of the dogmas which have been committed to her charge. In this sacred deposit she changes nothing, she takes nothing . . . she adds nothing to it.[74]

Here we have almost all the elements outlined by Newman fourteen centuries later, yet Protestant controversialists such as George Salmon claim that Newman's views were a radical departure from Catholic precedent![75]

Cardinal Newman points out the relative development of two doctrines in the early Church, as an example:

> Some notion of suffering . . . or other vague forms of the doctrine of *Purgatory*, has in its favor almost a *consensus* of the first four ages of the Church. . . . Whereas no one will say that there is a testimony of the Fathers, equally strong, for the doctrine of *Original Sin*. . . . In spite of the forcible teaching of St. Paul on the subject, the doctrine of Original Sin appears neither in the Apostles' nor the Nicene Creed.[76]

Finally, St. Thomas Aquinas (1225-1274) commented:

> Regarding its substance, then, Faith does not grow with the passage of time, for whatever has been believed since was

[74] Ibid.; Gibbons, *The Faith of Our Fathers*, 12.

[75] Salmon, *The Infalliblity of the Church*, 31-35.

[76] Newman, *An Essay on the Development of Christian Doctrine*, 21, 23.

> contained from the start in the Faith of the ancient fathers. As regards its explication, however, the number of articles has increased, for we moderns explicitly believe what they believed implicitly.[77]

Development of doctrine, then, has been the constant teaching of the Catholic Church from the beginning, and all through her history. Only a misunderstanding of what development entails, or ignorance of the history of Christian doctrine, could cause anyone to doubt this. Nor is the concept hostile in any way to the considerable amount of biblical data that can be brought to bear on the subject.

Development is not necessarily corruption, as so many Evangelical Protestants casually assume. Rather, it is novel innovation — according to Scripture, the early Church, the Fathers, the councils, and continuous Catholic Tradition — which is certainly a corruption of true apostolic Christianity (see Acts 2:42; 1 Cor. 11:2; 2 Thess. 3:6; Gal. 1:9, 12; Jude 3).

New Testament evidence for development of doctrine

Holy Scripture does not contain an explicit presentation of development, yet, as is the case with all Catholic doctrines (whether found "in depth" in the Bible or not), a great deal of implicit or indirect indication exists. In general, whenever Scripture refers to the increasing knowledge and maturity of Christians (especially collectively), an idea very similar to doctrinal development is present.

Furthermore, we find, clearly, that doctrine in fact develops before our eyes on the pages of Scripture — a process usually denoted as "progressive revelation" by Protestant theologians. Examples are numerous: the doctrine of the afterlife; the Trinity; the

[77] St. Thomas Aquinas, *Summa Theologica*, II-II , Q. 2, art. 7. In Chapin, *The Book of Catholic Quotations*, 271.

Messiah (who was eventually revealed in full as God the Son, the Second Person of the Trinity); the Holy Spirit (fully presented as a Divine Person in the New Testament); the acceptance of the Gentiles as equal to Jews in the eyes of God; the bodily Resurrection; aspects of the Law; sacrifice of lambs developing into the sacrifice of the Lamb of God, Jesus Christ; and many more instances.

Progressive revelation is very similar to development of doctrine insofar as, in both cases, more is learned about particular aspects of theology and spiritual life over time. Scripture is in no way hostile to development. Rather, we find that certain Protestant presuppositions wrongly preclude development for fear of "excess."

> **Matthew 13:31-32:** "The kingdom of Heaven is like a grain of mustard seed which a man took and sowed in his field; it is the smallest of all seeds, but when it has grown, it is the greatest of shrubs and becomes a tree, so that the birds of the air come and make nests in its branches."

> **John 14:26:** "But the Counselor, the Holy Spirit, whom the Father will send in my name, he will teach you all things, and bring to your remembrance all that I have said to you."

> **John 16:13:** "When the Spirit of truth comes, he will guide you into all the truth; for he will not speak on his own authority, but whatever he hears he will speak, and he will declare to you the things that are to come."

> **1 Corinthians 2:9-10:** " 'What no eye has seen, nor ear heard, nor the heart of man conceived, what God has prepared for those who love him,' God has revealed to us through the Spirit. For the Spirit

searches everything, even the depths of God" (see also 1 Cor. 2:11-16).

Ephesians 4:13-16: ". . . until we all attain to the unity of the faith and of the knowledge of the Son of God, to mature manhood, to the measure of the stature of the fullness of Christ; so that we may no longer be children, tossed to and fro and carried about with every wind of doctrine, by the cunning of men, by their craftiness in deceitful wiles. Rather, speaking the truth in love, we are to grow up in every way into him who is the head, into Christ, from whom the whole body . . . makes bodily growth and upbuilds itself in love" (see also Matthew 5:17, in which Jesus implies that he will further develop Jewish Law; St. Paul also refers to the perhaps related idea of a "fullness of time," in Galatians 4:4 and Ephesians 1:10).

Chapter Four

The Eucharist

"This is my Body"

The Council of Trent, in its *Decree Concerning the Most Holy Sacrament of the Eucharist*, of October 11, 1551, defined the following propositions — which had always been the prevailing beliefs throughout Church history — as absolutely binding on all Catholics:

> In the august sacrament of the holy Eucharist, after the consecration of the bread and wine, our Lord Jesus Christ, true God and man, is truly, really, and substantially contained under the species of those sensible things.[78]
>
> Immediately after the consecration, the veritable Body of our Lord and His veritable Blood, together with His soul and divinity, are under the species of bread and wine . . . as much is contained under either species as under both.[79]

[78] Ch. 1: On the Real Presence of Our Lord Jesus Christ in the Most Holy Sacrament of the Eucharist. See also CCC, pars. 1373-1374, 1378-1381; Hardon, *PCD*, 132-133, 360.

[79] Ch. 3: On the Excellency of the Most Holy Eucharist Over the Rest of the Sacraments. See also CCC, pars. 1377, 1390. This belief is derived largely from 1 Corinthians 11:27: "Whoever, therefore, eats the bread *or* drinks the cup of the Lord in

> By the consecration of the bread and of the wine a conversion is made of the whole substance of the bread into the substance of the Body of Christ our Lord, and of the whole substance of the wine into the substance of His Blood; which conversion is by the holy Catholic Church suitably and properly called transubstantiation.[80]

The Catholic doctrine of the Eucharist (the Greek word for "thanksgiving") is much misunderstood by non-Catholics (and many Catholics as well). Christ's substantial and physical presence in the Eucharist doesn't negate other types of spiritual presence. Rather, it is referred to as "real" because it is a presence in the fullest possible sense of the word.[81]

Therefore, the Real Presence must by its very nature be distinguished from God's omnipresence, or a merely symbolic, "spiritual" presence. The great German Catholic theologian Karl Adam lucidly described the Eucharist:

> So completely does Jesus disclose Himself to His disciples . . . that He gives Himself to them and enters into them as a personal source of grace. Jesus shares with His disciples His most intimate possession, the most precious thing that He has, His own self. . . . So greatly does Jesus love His Community,

an unworthy manner will be guilty of profaning the body *and* blood of the Lord." Most New Testament translations include the crucial word *or* (e.g., the New International Version [NIV], the New American Standard Bible [NASB], the New English Bible [NEB], the New King James Version [NKJV], and the Phillips Bible). The KJV is a notable exception, but many Protestant scholars admit that its *and* was a nonliteral, polemical mistranslation.

80 Ch. 4: On Transubstantiation. See also CCC, pars. 1375-1376, 1413; Hardon, CC, 161.

81 See Pope Paul VI's encyclical *Mysterium Fidei* (On Eucharistic Doctrine and Worship) (Glen Rock, New Jersey: Paulist Press, September 3, 1965), 42.

> that He permeates it . . . with His real self, God and Man. He enters into a real union of flesh and blood with it, and binds it to His being even as the branch is bound to the vine.[82]

The Catholic Church teaches that there are many purposes of the Eucharist and numerous spiritual benefits that accrue from partaking in Communion at Mass — provided this is undertaken in a "worthy manner" and without conscious mortal sin.[83] It is the "source and summit of the Christian life,"[84] the sign of Christian unity and of the Body of Christ, the Church, an act of thanksgiving to God, a memorial and a sacrifice, the central focus of the Liturgy and the Mass, the empowering of the faithful for ministry, a symbol of God's faithfulness and miraculous provision, an anticipation of the wedding feast of the Lamb in Heaven, a remembrance of the Last Supper and of Christ's Passion, Resurrection, and return, a sign of salvation, the "bread of Heaven," adoration and worship of God, union with Christ, the means of grace, cleansing from sin, and spiritual renewal, and an offering for the dead.[85]

[82] Karl Adam, *The Spirit of Catholicism*, Dom Justin McCann, trans. (Garden City, New York: Doubleday Image, 1954), 18.

[83] CCC, pars. 1385-1387, 1415. See 1 Corinthians 11:27-29; Vatican II: *Constitution on the Sacred Liturgy*, nos. 9, 11.

[84] Vatican II: *Dogmatic Constitution on the Church*, 11; CCC, pars. 1324, 1327.

[85] CCC: sign of Christian unity: pars. 1322-1323, 1325-1326, 1331, 1348, 1353, 1369-1370, 1396, 1398, 1416; sign of the Church: par. 1329; act of thanksgiving: pars. 1328, 1352, 1358-1361; memorial and sacrifice: pars. 1330, 1333, 1341, 1350, 1356-1357, 1362-1368, 1371-1372, 1382-1383, 1410; central focus of the Liturgy and Mass: pars. 1330, 1343, 1345-1346, 1407; empowering of the faithful for ministry: par. 1332; symbol of God's faithfulness and provision: pars. 1334-1335; anticipation of the wedding feast of the Lamb: pars. 1329, 1344, 1402; remembrance of the Last Supper: par. 1347; remembrance of Christ's Passion, Resurrection, and

The daunting word *transubstantiation* is easily understood when broken down: *trans* means "change." Therefore, the term is defined literally as the process of change of substance. The Catholic Church, in seeking to understand the Real Presence, a doctrine delivered directly by our Lord and St. Paul, gradually developed an explanation as to the exact nature of this miraculous and mysterious transformation.

Contrary to the common misconception, transubstantiation is not dependent upon Aristotelian philosophy, since some notion of the concept goes back to the earliest days of the Church, when Aristotle's philosophy was not known. The eastern Fathers, before the sixth century, used the Greek expression *metaousiosis*, or "change of being," which is essentially the same idea.

The Church did, however, draw upon prevalent philosophical categories, such as *substance* and *accidents*. In all ages, Christians have sought to defend Christianity by means of philosophy and human learning (wherever the individual intellectual categories utilized were consistent with Christian Faith). St. Paul, for instance, did this in his sermon on Mars Hill in Athens, where he made reference to pagan poets and philosophers (Acts 17:22-31). St. Augustine incorporated elements of Platonic thought into his theology, and St. Thomas Aquinas synthesized Aristotle and Christianity into a unified, consistent system of Christian thought (Scholasticism or Thomism).

Transubstantiation is predicated upon the distinction between two sorts of change: *accidental change* occurs when nonessential outward properties are transformed in some fashion. Thus, water can take on the properties of a solid (ice) or of a gas (steam), while

return: pars. 1354, 1403-1404, 1409; the "bread of Heaven": pars. 1355, 1405; adoration and worship of God: pars. 1378-1379, 1408, 1418; union with Christ: pars. 1391, 1416, 1419; means of grace, cleansing from sin, and spiritual renewal: pars. 1392-1395, 1416; offering for the dead: pars. 1371, 1414.

remaining chemically the same. A *substantial change*, on the other hand, produces something else altogether. An example of this is the metabolism of food, which becomes part of our bodies as a result of chemical and biological processes initiated by digestion. In our everyday experience, a change of substance is always accompanied by a corresponding transition of accidents, or properties.

But in the Eucharist — a supernatural transformation — substantial change occurs without accidental alteration. Thus, the properties of bread and wine continue after consecration, but their essence and substance cease to exist, replaced by the substance of the true and actual Body and Blood of Christ. It is this disjunction from the natural laws of physics which causes many to stumble (see John 6:60-69). The following chart may be helpful for understanding different types of change:

A Comparison of Accidental and Substantial Change

Type of change	**Example**	**Accidents (appearance)**	**Substance (essence)**
Natural Accidental	Water to ice or steam	Changed	Same
Natural Substantial	Metabolism of food	Changed	Changed
Supernatural Accidental	Miracles of the loaves (Matt. 14:19)	Changed (quantity)	Same
Supernatural Substantial	Transubstantiation	Same	Changed

Transubstantiation is difficult for the natural mind (especially with its modern excessively skeptical bent) to grasp and clearly requires a great deal of faith. Yet many aspects of Christianity that conservative, Evangelical, orthodox Christians have no difficulty believing transcend reason and must ultimately be accepted on faith, such as the Incarnation (in which a helpless infant in Bethlehem is God!), the Resurrection, the omniscience of God, the paradox of grace versus free will, eternity, the union of the human and divine natures in Christ (the Hypostatic Union), the Fall of Man and Original Sin, and the Virgin Birth, among many other beliefs. Transubstantiation may be considered *beyond* reason, yet it is not *opposed to* reason; suprarational, but not irrational, much like Christian theology in general.

If one accepts the fact that God became Man, then it cannot consistently be deemed impossible (as many casually assume) for him to become truly and really present under the appearances of bread and wine. Jesus, after his Resurrection, could apparently walk through walls while remaining in his physical (glorified) body (John 20:26-27). How, then, can the Real Presence reasonably be regarded as intrinsically implausible by supernaturalist Christians?

Likewise, much of the objection to this doctrine seems to arise out of a pitting of matter against spirit, or, more specifically, an *a priori* hostility toward the idea that grace can be conveyed through matter (which notion is the basis of sacramentalism). This is exceedingly curious, since precisely this concept is fundamental to the Incarnation of our Lord Jesus. If God did not take on matter and human flesh, no one would have been saved. Such a prejudice is neither logical (given belief in the miraculous and Christian precepts) nor scriptural, as we shall see.

Cardinal Newman, whom very few would accuse of being unreasonable or credulous, had this to say about the "difficulties" of transubstantiation:

> People say that the doctrine of Transubstantiation is difficult to believe. . . . It is difficult, impossible to imagine, I

> grant — but how is it difficult to believe? . . . For myself, I cannot indeed prove it, I cannot tell *how* it is; but I say, "Why should it not be? What's to hinder it? What do I know of substance or matter? Just as much as the greatest philosophers, and that is nothing at all." . . . And, in like manner . . . the doctrine of the Trinity in Unity. What do I know of the Essence of the Divine Being? I know that my abstract idea of three is simply incompatible with my idea of one; but when I come to the question of concrete fact, I have no means of proving that there is not a sense in which one and three can equally be predicated of the Incommunicable God.[86]

Once one realizes that transubstantiation is a miracle of God, any thought of impossibility vanishes, since God is omnipotent and the sovereign Lord over all creation (Matt. 19:26; Phil. 3:20-21; Heb. 1:3). If mere men can change accidental properties without changing substance (for example, turning iron into molten liquid or even vapor), then God is certainly able to change substance without outward transmutation.

Therefore, having disposed of these weak philosophical objections, we can proceed to examine the clear and indisputable biblical data that reveal to us that God does in fact perform (through the agency of priests) the supernatural act of transubstantiation.

New Testament teaching on the Real Presence

> **John 6:47-63, 66:** " 'Truly, truly, I say to you, he who believes has eternal life. I am the bread of life. Your fathers ate the manna in the wilderness, and they died. This is the bread which comes down from

[85] John Henry Cardinal Newman, *Apologia Pro Vita Sua* (Garden City, New York: Doubleday Image, 1956), 318. Newman's *Apologia* is his religious autobiography.

> Heaven, that a man may eat of it and not die. I am the living bread which came down from Heaven; if anyone eats of this bread, he will live forever; and the bread which I shall give for the life of the world is my flesh.' The Jews then disputed among themselves, saying, 'How can this man give us his flesh to eat?' So Jesus said to them, 'Truly, truly, I say to you, unless you eat the flesh of the Son of man and drink his blood, you have no life in you; he who eats my flesh and drinks my blood has eternal life, and I will raise him up at the last day. For my flesh is food indeed, and my blood is drink indeed. He who eats my flesh and drinks my blood abides in me, and I in him. As the living Father sent me, and I live because of the Father, so he who eats me will live because of me. This is the bread which came down from Heaven, not such as the fathers ate and died; he who eats this bread will live forever.' This he said in the synagogue, as he taught at Capernaum. Many of his disciples, when they heard it, said, 'This is a hard saying; who can listen to it?' But Jesus, knowing in himself that his disciples murmured at it, said to them, 'Do you take offense at this? Then what if you were to see the Son of man ascending where he was before? It is the spirit that gives life, the flesh is of no avail; the words that I have spoken to you are spirit and life.' . . . After this many of his disciples drew back and no longer went about with him."

James Cardinal Gibbons, a notable figure in American Catholicism in the late nineteenth century, commented on this passage:

> If the Eucharist were merely commemorative bread and wine, instead of being superior, it would really be inferior to

the manna; for the manna was supernatural, heavenly, miraculous food, while bread and wine are a natural, earthly food. . . .

The multitude and the disciples who are listening to Him . . . all understood the import of His language precisely as it is explained by the Catholic Church. . . .

It sometimes happened, indeed, that our Savior was misunderstood by His hearers. On such occasions He always took care to remove from their mind the wrong impression they had formed by stating His meaning in simpler language [Nicodemus — John 3:1-15; leaven of the Pharisees — Matt. 16:5-12]."[87]

Among the Jews of Jesus' time, the phrase "eat the flesh" was a metaphor for a grievous injury.[88] It is obvious that our Lord did not use the phrase in this sense (which would have been nonsensical), so it is altogether reasonable to conclude that he intended a literal meaning. When Protestants claim that Jesus meant only to "believe" in him, or to "accept" him spiritually and symbolically by faith, they are violating their own hermeneutical tenet of interpreting Scripture according to the Jewish customs, idioms, and usages of the time. The current prevailing Protestant interpretation originated only centuries afterward (basically in the sixteenth century).[89]

[87] James Cardinal Gibbons, *The Faith of Our Fathers*, 237-238.

[88] See, e.g., Job 19:22; Ps. 27:2; Eccles. 4:5; Isa. 9:20, 49:26; Mic. 3:1-3; Rev. 16:6.

[89] This historical fact is acknowledged by the reputable Protestant reference work *Oxford Dictionary of the Christian Church*, F. C. Cross and E. A. Livingstone, eds. (Oxford University Press, 1983), 475-476, 1221. It is conceded that the Real Presence was universally held from the beginning of the Church. This is also confirmed by the *New International Dictionary of the Christian Church* (J. D. Douglas, ed. [Grand Rapids, Michigan:

Surely Jesus would not condemn people to eternal punishment (John 6:53) for the neglect of something that they never even comprehended in the first place! Rather, it was the rejection of a divine revelation due to its difficulty that was the cause of the loss of eternal life (6:57-58). The hearers, it is true, did not grasp the miraculous, sacramental way in which Christ was speaking (6:60-61) and balked (somewhat understandably) at the notion of what they imagined to be some sort of grisly cannibalism (6:52). Jesus countered with a statement that his natural human body would ascend to Heaven and not remain on the earth (6:62), and that spiritual wisdom and grace are necessary in order to understand his words (6:63, 65).

But Jesus made it clear that the crucial dynamic in this situation was the willful acceptance or rejection of faith and belief in him (6:64). It is scarcely possible for anyone at that time to have intellectually grasped completely what our Lord was saying. But we know from Scripture that Jesus was repeatedly judgmentally

Zondervan, 1978], 244-245), which is openly hostile to transubstantiation, considering it unbiblical, yet honestly admits the well-nigh unanimous acceptance of the Real Presence prior to the Reformation. See also the Protestant scholarly sources: Otto W. Heick, *A History of Christian Thought* (Philadelphia: Fortress Press, 1965), Vol. 1, 221-222; Williston Walker, *A History of the Christian Church* (New York: Scribner, 1970), 90-91; Philip Schaff, *History of the Christian Church* (Grand Rapids, Michigan: Eerdmans, 1974), 492, 500, 507; Jaroslav Pelikan, *The Emergence of the Catholic Tradition (100-600)* (Chicago: University of Chicago Press, 1971), 146-147, 166-168, 170, 236-237; J. N. D. Kelly, *Early Christian Doctrines* (San Francisco: Harper and Row, 1978), 447; Carl Volz, *Faith and Practice in the Early Church* (Minneapolis: Augsburg, 1983), 107; Maurice Wiles and Mark Santar, *Documents in Early Christian Thought* (Cambridge University Press, 1975), 173. To read the relevant excerpts, see Dave Armstrong, *History of the Doctrine of the Eucharist: Nine Protestant Scholarly Sources*, online at http://ic.net/~erasmus/RAZ459.HTM.

rejected out of hand, particularly when he uttered cryptic statements (e.g., John 8:42-47; 12:35-43). Jesus should have been believed on faith, based on who he was and what he had already done to establish his divinity (Luke 11:29-36; John 20:28-29). Thus, according to Jesus, the nonacceptance of his message by many of his audience in this instance is due, not to mental noncomprehension, but rather to willful disobedience and the resisting of the Spirit (John 6:63-65; cf. Matt. 13:10-23). Fortunately for the disciples, they saved themselves by an act of more or less befuddled (but heartfelt) faith in the Lord (John 6:67-69).

Only here in the New Testament do we have an account of followers of Christ abandoning him for theological reasons (John 6:66). Certainly, if this exodus were based on a simple misunderstanding, Jesus would have assured these reluctant souls that he was speaking metaphorically, in order to get them to return. But he does no such thing. On the contrary, he reiterates his difficult teaching of eating his flesh no less than four times (6:54-58)!

Furthermore, according to the Greek in St. John's account, Jesus, after the skeptical query by the Jews (6:53), actually switches terms for "eat." At first John's Greek word (nine times in John 6:23-53) is *phago*, a generic term for eat, used accordingly (literally) throughout the New Testament. But in John 6:54-58 the word used (four times) is the more graphic and particular *trogo*, which means literally "gnaws" or "chews," as any Greek lexicon (such as Kittel or Thayer) will confirm. *Trogo* occurs only in this passage and in Matthew 24:38 and John 13:18. In those two verses, it conveys literal eating, and there are strong contextual, exegetical, and linguistic reasons to believe that it is intended literally in John 6 as well.

Therefore, Jesus, rather than softening his "rhetoric," which is to be expected if his intent was intellectually misunderstood (and after all, being God, he knew all the thoughts of men), spoke in even more physical and descriptive terms, so as to clarify and remove any remaining doubts. This is nothing unusual: Jesus often put people "on the spot" and demanded decisive, self-denying allegiance (e.g., Matt. 10:34-39; 12:30; 19:21).

Fr. Bertrand Conway, author of the enormously popular *The Question Box*, a classic of Catholic apologetics, makes some very cogent points about this important discourse:

> Catholics make a distinction between the first part of John 6 (vv. 26 to 51), wherein Christ speaks of Himself figuratively as the Bread of Heaven, a spiritual food to be received by faith, and the second part (vv. 51 to 59), wherein He speaks literally of His Flesh and Blood as a real food, and a real drink. "In the first part," writes Atzberger, "the food is of the present, in the second of the future; there it is given by the Father, here by the Redeemer Himself; there it is simply called 'bread,' here the 'Flesh of the Son of Man'; there our Lord speaks only of bread, here of His 'Flesh and Blood' "[90]
>
> Christ makes a clear-cut distinction between three kinds of breads: the bread, or manna, of the desert (Exod. 16:15; John 6:49), given by Moses to the Jews in the past to nourish the body; the Bread of Heaven, or the Bread of Life (John 6:32, 35), Christ Himself, given by the Father in the present to the Jews as an object of faith; and the Bread of Life, Christ Himself in the Eucharist, to be given in the future by Christ for the life of the world (John 6:52).
>
> Again, a figurative interpretation is impossible, according to the rules of language. If a figure of speech has a definite meaning, we cannot use it in a new sense, merely for purposes of controversy. . . .
>
> We must remember that Christ, like every good teacher, made two sorts of answers to men who objected to His

[90] *Handbuch der Kath. Dogmatik*, Vol. 4, 569.

> teaching. If they did not understand His meaning, He explained His doctrine more fully. In this way He explains . . . the possibility of the rich man being saved (Matt. 19:24-6), the fact of Lazarus's death (John 11:11-14), the idea of freedom (John 8:32-34; cf. John 4:31-34; 8:21-23). When His hearers understood His teaching but refused to accept it, He repeated His teaching with even more emphasis. Thus, He insisted upon His power to forgive sins, when the Scribes accused Him of blasphemy (Matt. 9:2-7), and insisted on His being eternal, when the Jews said He was not yet fifty years old (John 8:56-58).[91]

Conway goes on to refute the most common Protestant response — that of citing John 6:63 to the effect that when Jesus contrasts spirit and flesh, he is proclaiming the purely symbolic nature of the Eucharist:

> The words *flesh* and *spirit*, when opposed to each other in the New Testament, never mean literal and figurative, but always the corrupted dispositions of sinful human nature (flesh) contrasted with human nature enriched by the grace of God (spirit). . . .[92] Christ's meaning, therefore, is clear: My words are such as the mere carnal man cannot receive, but only the man endowed with grace. St. Chrysostom says: "Why, therefore did he say: The flesh profiteth nothing? Not of his flesh does he mean this. Far from it; but of those who would understand what he said in a carnal sense. . . . You see, there is question not of his flesh, but of the fleshly way of hearing" (*In Joan.*, 47, 2).[93]

[91] Bertrand L. Conway, *The Question Box* (New York: Paulist Press, 1929), 248-249, 251.

[92] See Matt. 26:41; Rom. 7:5-6, 25, 8:1-14; 1 Cor. 5:5; 2 Cor. 7:1; Gal. 3:3, 4:29, 5:13-26; 1 Pet. 3:18, 4:6.

[93] Conway, *The Question Box*, 251.

In conclusion, it is necessary to adopt a literal interpretation of the classic eucharistic passage in John 6 for at least eight reasons:

1. The nature of the language (such as *trogo)* used;

2. The graphic realism and intensive reiteration (for example, John 6:55);

3. The insurmountable exegetical difficulties of a figurative interpretation;

4. The absence of any correction by Christ of false interpretations by the hearers;

5. The common teaching methods of Jesus;

6. The reactions of the listeners;

7. The gravity and overriding importance of the teaching (John 6:53, 63), which Jesus, in his mercy and compassion, would not have allowed to be misunderstood;

8. The constant and unwavering interpretation of the Church up to 1517.

> **Luke 22:19-20** (the Last Supper): "And he took bread, and when he had given thanks he broke it and gave it to them, saying, 'This is my body which is given for you. Do this in remembrance of me.' And likewise the cup after supper, saying, 'This cup which is poured out for you is the new covenant in my blood' " (see also Matt. 26:26-28; Mark 14:22-24).

Jesus says, "This is my body" (in other words, that which has the appearance of bread), not "*here* is my body," which would infer more so the Lutheran view, whereby his body is present *along with* the bread and the wine ("consubstantiation"). The position that would make these words symbolic only — "this *represents* my body" — is a strained interpretation, since, as in John 6, a figure of speech not in common usage would have deceived the hearers. If the bread had been transformed into flesh with skin, bones, ligaments, and so forth, this would have been outright evidence (even though still miraculous) rather than the faith-requiring mystery that Christ intended the Eucharist to be.

Nothing in the actual text supports a metaphorical interpretation (especially given the exegetical comparison with John 6). Bread and wine are not even particularly analogous symbols of body and blood, neither for the Jews at that time nor for us. When the word *is* in Scripture has the meaning "symbolizes," this sense is readily apparent (e.g., Matt. 13:38; John 10:7, 15:1; 1 Cor. 10:4), whereas in this case, it is not. Besides, the Last Supper was the Jewish feast of Passover, which involved a literal sacrificial lamb. It is hardly possible that the disciples could have entirely missed the profound significance of what Jesus was saying. Also immediately before and after this passage, our Lord spoke of his imminent suffering (Luke 22:15-16, 18, 21-22).

Even though the disciples likely did not fully understand Jesus' meaning, they knew enough to know he was not speaking figuratively. This willing and sincere, but partial, understanding was typical of the disciples, such as in the climactic Gospel scene where St. Peter acknowledges the fact that Jesus is Messiah, the Son of God (Matt. 16:15-17) and is therefore called the "Rock" and given the "keys of the kingdom" (Matt. 16:18-19), yet goes on to rebuke Jesus for speaking of his Passion and Crucifixion (Matt. 16:21-22), thereby incurring a stern reprimand from our Lord (Matt. 16:23).

> **1 Corinthians 10:16:** "The cup of blessing which we bless, is it not a participation in the blood of Christ? The bread which we break, is it not a participation in the body of Christ?" (read 1 Cor. 10:14-22 for the context).
>
> **1 Corinthians 11: 27-30:** "Whoever, therefore, eats the bread or drinks the cup of the Lord in an unworthy manner will be guilty of profaning the body and

> blood of the Lord. Let a man examine himself, and so eat of the bread and drink of the cup. For anyone who eats and drinks without discerning the body eats and drinks judgment upon himself. That is why many of you are weak and ill, and some have died" (read 1 Cor. 11:23-26 for the context).

James Cardinal Gibbons comments on these passages:

> Could St. Paul express more clearly his belief in the Real Presence than he has done here? . . . He who receives a sacrament unworthily shall be guilty of the sin of high treason, and of shedding the blood of his Lord in vain. But how could he be guilty of a crime so enormous if he had taken in the Eucharist only a particle of bread and wine? Would a man be accused of homicide . . . if he were to offer violence to the statue or painting of the governor? Certainly not. In like manner, St. Paul would not . . . declare a man guilty of trampling on the blood of his Savior by drinking in an unworthy manner a little wine in memory of him.[94]

[94] Gibbons, *The Faith of Our Fathers*, 242-243.

Chapter Five

The Sacrifice of the Mass

"A Lamb . . . slain"

The Council of Trent, in its *Doctrine on the Sacrifice of the Mass* (September 17, 1562), authoritatively spelled out the details of this often misunderstood Catholic belief:

> Our God and Lord, though He was about to offer Himself once on the altar of the Cross unto God the Father, by means of His death, there to obtain an eternal redemption (Heb. 9:12 ff.); nevertheless, because that His priesthood was not to be extinguished by His death, in the Last Supper . . . that He might leave, to His own beloved Spouse, the Church, a visible sacrifice, such as the nature of man requires, whereby that bloody sacrifice, once to be accomplished on the Cross, might be represented, and the memory thereof remain even unto the end of the world (1 Cor. 11:24), and its salutary virtue be applied to the remission of those sins which we daily commit — declaring Himself constituted a priest forever, according to the order of Melchisedech (Ps. 110:4), He offered up to God the Father His own Body and Blood under the species of bread and wine . . . and by those words, "Do this in commemoration of me"

> (1 Cor. 11:24), He commanded them and their successors in the priesthood to offer them. . . .
>
> And this is indeed that clean oblation, which cannot be defiled by any unworthiness or malice of those that offer it; which the Lord foretold by Malachi was to be offered in every place, clean to His name (Mal. 1:11). . . . This, in fine, is that oblation which was prefigured by various types of sacrifices (Gen. 4:4; 8:20, etc.), during the period of nature and of the law; inasmuch as it comprises all the good things signified by those sacrifices, as being the consummation and perfection of them all.[95]
>
> If anyone saith that the sacrifice of the Mass is only a sacrifice of praise and of thanksgiving; or that it is a bare commemoration of the sacrifice consummated on the Cross, but not a propitiatory sacrifice; or that it profits him only who receives; and that it ought not to be offered for the living and the dead for sins, pains, satisfactions, and other necessities; let him be anathema.[96]
>
> If anyone saith that, by the sacrifice of the Mass, a blasphemy is cast upon the most holy sacrifice of Christ consummated on the Cross; or that it is thereby derogated from; let him be anathema.

Karl Adam, author of the marvelous book *The Spirit of Catholicism*, remarks upon the transcendent nature of the Mass:

> The Sacrifice of Calvary, as a great supratemporal reality, enters into the immediate present. Space and time are abolished. The same Jesus is here present who died on the Cross.

[95] Ch. 1: On the Institution of the Most Holy Sacrifice of the Mass. See also CCC, pars. 1330, 1333, 1341, 1350, 1356-1357, 1362, 1366, 1368, 1372, 1383, 1410-1411; Hardon, CC, 465-471.

[96] Ch. 9: Canons on the Sacrifice of the Mass, Canon 3. See also CCC, par. 1363, 1365, 1370-1371, 1414.

> The whole congregation unites itself with His holy sacrificial will, and through Jesus present before it, consecrates itself to the heavenly Father as a living oblation. So Holy Mass is a tremendously real experience, the experience of the reality of Golgotha.[97]

It is crucial to understand that the Sacrifice of the Mass is not a "re-sacrifice" of Christ, as is the common misconception. Jesus does not die every time a priest offers Mass, since He died once, in history, on earth. Rather, as Adam notes, the Mass lifts us into heavenly realms, where all events are eternally present (as they are with God). The Mass is thus a re-presentation of the one Sacrifice at Calvary in a sacramental, unbloody manner. One may not agree with this belief, but opponents of Catholic doctrine should at least honestly and clearly understand what it is they contest.

Furthermore, in the Mass, Jesus Christ ultimately offers the sacrifice of himself (just as at the Last Supper), with the priest merely acting in his stead, as a purely secondary, instrumental agent. In no sense, then, is the Mass some sort of magic or "hocus pocus" (this phrase itself is a caricature of the Latin words of consecration: *Hoc est enim corpus meum*). The priest and congregation are willing participants in what is God's supernatural work from beginning to end. This is the furthest thing from sorcery, which is the utilization of either demonic supernatural powers, or those thought to be natural, apart from the originating agency of a personal God (see Acts 8:17-23).

Scriptural evidence for the Sacrifice of the Mass

Genesis 14:18: "And Melchizedek, king of Salem, brought out bread and wine; he was priest of God Most High" (see also Lev. 23:13).

[97] Adam, *The Spirit of Catholicism*, 197.

> **Psalm 110:4:** "The Lord has sworn and will not change his mind, 'You are a priest forever after the order of Melchizedek.' "

This analogy between Jesus and the mysterious, majestic priest Melchizedek is made again in Hebrews (5:6, 10; 6:20; 7:1-28). The context of the entire Psalm 110 also makes it clear that Christ the Messiah is being referred to. This cross-reference must have some meaning.

We know very little about Melchizedek apart from his offering of bread and wine, his acceptance of tithes from Abraham, and his residence in "Salem," which is believed by Bible scholars to be ancient Jerusalem, as determined by verses such as Psalm 76:2. He was at once king and priest, like Christ, and unlike the practice of ancient Israel.

Judging from this scant information, Jesus must, it seems, make an offering of bread and wine, *forever*. This is obviously not identical with the Sacrifice at Calvary, yet it seems to carry some profound significance. Since Christ did make this offering at the Last Supper (significantly, at the feast of Passover: see 1 Cor. 5:7) and commanded his followers to perpetuate it, it is quite reasonable to regard the Mass as the sacramental, supernatural continuance of Christ's own self-sacrifice.

> **Malachi 1:11:** "For from the rising of the sun to its setting, my name is great among the nations, and in every place incense is offered to my name, and a pure offering; for my name is great among the nations, says the Lord of hosts" (see also Isa. 66:18, 21).

God here foretells a universally offered sacrifice that expands upon the Jewish Levitical priesthood, after the arrival of the Messiah (see, e.g., Ps. 22:27-3; Isa. 49:6). This cannot be a reference to the Sacrifice of the Cross, which occurred in one location only.

Malachi speaks of a universal "pure offering" (singular rather than plural), precisely as in Catholic teaching.

Therefore, the Mass is the straightforward fulfillment of this prophecy. Protestants, to the contrary, can only surmise that this offering is merely metaphorical — with no particular justification from the text of Malachi itself. The context of this passage, both before and after, clearly has to do with actual, physical offerings, as all would agree.

The book of Hebrews

The theme of the Epistle to the Hebrews is Christ as our High Priest. As such, the "priestly" verses are very numerous (e.g., 2:17; 3:1; 4:14-16; 5:1-10; 6:20; 7:1-28; 8:1-6; 9:11-15, 24-28; 10:19-22). The teaching here acquires much more meaning within Catholic eucharistic theology, whereas, in evangelical, nonsacramental Protestant interpretation, it is necessarily "spiritualized" away. For nearly all Protestants, Jesus Christ is a priest only insofar as he dies sacrificially as the "Lamb" and does away with the Old Testament notion of animal sacrifice. This is not false, but it is a partial truth. Generally speaking, for the Catholic, there is much more of a sense of the ever-present Sacrifice of Calvary, due to the nature of the Mass, rather than considering the Cross a past event alone.

In light of the repeated references in Hebrews to Melchizedek as the prototype of Christ's priesthood (5:6, 10; 6:20; 7:1-3, 17, 20), it follows that this priesthood is perpetual (forever), not one time only. For no one would say, for example, that Christ is King (present tense) if in fact he were King for only a short while in the past. This (Catholic) interpretation is borne out by explicit evidence in Hebrews 7:24-25: "He holds his priesthood permanently, because he continues forever. Consequently he is able for all time to save those who draw near to God through him, since he always lives to make intercession for them."

If Jesus perpetually intercedes for us, why should He not also permanently present himself as sacrifice to His Father? The connecting word, *consequently*, seems to affirm this scenario. The very notion, fundamental to all strains of Christian theology, that the Cross and the Blood are efficacious here and now for the redemption of sinners, presupposes a dimension of "presentness" to the Atonement.

Granting that premise, it only remains to deny that God could, would, or should truly and actually re-present this one Sacrifice in the Mass. God certainly *can* do this, since he is omnipotent. He *wills* to do this because Jesus commanded the observance of the Lord's Supper (Luke 22:19). Lastly, one can convincingly contend that he *should* do this in order to "bring home" graphically to Christians His Passion, Crucifixion, and Resurrection, and to impart grace in a real and profound way in Communion. The one propitiatory Atonement of Calvary is a past event, but the appropriation of its spiritual benefits to Christians is an ongoing process, in which the Mass plays a central role.

The Sacrifice of the Mass, like the Real Presence in the Eucharist, is an extension of the Incarnation. Accordingly, there is no rational *a priori* objection (under monotheistic premises) to the concept of God's transcending time and space to present himself to his disciples. Nor is there any denying that the Sacrifice of Calvary is always present to God the Father and to Jesus Christ, God the Son. How then, can anyone deny that God could make the Cross sacramentally present to us as well?

To the objection that Scripture does not teach this, and therefore it should not be believed, we reply that the scriptural data above and the evidence below are conclusive.

The book of Revelation and the altar in Heaven

It is very interesting to note that the book of Revelation (also known by Catholics as the Apocalypse) describes an altar in

Heaven (6:9; 8:3, 5; 9:13; 11:1; 14:18; 16:7). This is curious if much of Protestantism is correct about the abolition of altars, as a result of the death of Christ and cessation of the Jewish priestly system of the Old Covenant (the events in the book of Revelation all occur after Jesus' Resurrection and Ascension). In actuality, Scripture forms a continuous whole from beginning to end. There is no radical discontinuity between the Old and New Testaments, or between law and grace, as many Protestants are wont to believe.

Some verses in Revelation state that the "prayers of the saints" are being offered at the altar in the form of incense (8:3-4; cf. 5:8-9). But the climactic scene of this entire glorious portrayal of Heaven occurs in Revelation 5:1-7. Verse 6 describes "a Lamb standing as though it had been slain." Since the Lamb (Jesus, of course) is revealed as sitting in the midst of God's throne (5:6; 7:17; 22:1, 3; cf. Matt. 19:28, 25:31; Heb. 1:8), which is in front of the golden altar (Rev. 8:3), then it appears that the presentation of Christ to the Father as a sacrifice is an ongoing (from God's perspective, timeless) occurrence, precisely as in Catholic teaching. Thus, the Mass is no more than what occurs in Heaven, according to the clear revealed word of Scripture. When Hebrews speaks of a sacrifice made once (Heb. 7:27), this is from a purely human, historical perspective (which Catholicism acknowledges in holding that the Mass is a "re-presentation" of the one Sacrifice at Calvary). However, there is a transcendent aspect of the Sacrifice as well.

Jesus is referred to as the Lamb twenty-eight times throughout Revelation (compared with four times in the rest of the New Testament: John 1:29, 36; Acts 8:32; 1 Peter 1:19). Why in Revelation (of all places), if the Crucifixion is a past event, and the Christian's emphasis ought to be on the resurrected, glorious, kingly Jesus, as is stressed in Protestantism (as evidenced by a widespread disdain for crucifixes)? Obviously, the heavenly emphasis is on Jesus' Sacrifice, which is communicated by God to

John as present and "now" (Rev. 5:6; cf. Heb. 7:24). The very notion of lamb possesses inherent sacrificial and priestly connotations in the Bible.

If this aspect is of such paramount importance even in the afterlife, then certainly it should be just as real and significant to us. The Sacrifice of the Mass bridges all the gaps of space and time between our crucified Savior on the Cross and ourselves. Therefore, nothing at all in the Mass is improper, implausible, or unscriptural, which is why this doctrine was virtually unanimously accepted until the sixteenth century.

In conclusion, then, it is, I think, evident that the book of Hebrews and the scenes in Heaven in the book of Revelation are suffused with a worldview and "atmosphere" that is very "Catholic." The Mass, rightly understood, fulfills every aspect of the above passages, most particularly in the sense of Christ as the ultimate Priest for whom the earthly priest "stands in," and in the timeless and transcendent character of the Sacrifice "made present" at Mass, but never deemed to be an addition to, or duplication of, the one bloody Sacrifice of our Lord at Calvary.

Chapter Six

The Communion of Saints

"All who are in Christ"

The Council of Trent, in its Session 25 (December 3 and 4, 1563) declared the following to be the dogmatic teaching of the Catholic Church:

> The saints, who reign together with Christ, offer up their own prayers for men. . . . It is good and useful suppliantly to invoke them, and to have recourse to their prayers, aid, and help for obtaining benefits from God, through His Son, Jesus Christ, our Lord, Who is alone our Redeemer and Savior. . . . They think impiously who deny that the saints, who enjoy eternal happiness in Heaven, are to be invocated; or who assert either that they do not pray for men; or that the invocation of them to pray for each of us even in particular is idolatry; or that it is repugnant to the Word of God; and is opposed to the honor of the one mediator of God and men, Christ Jesus (1 Tim. 2:5); or that it is foolish to supplicate vocally or mentally those who reign in Heaven. . . .
>
> The holy bodies of holy martyrs, and of others now living in Christ, which bodies were the living members of Christ and the temple of the Holy Ghost (1 Cor. 3:16, 6:19;

> 2 Cor. 6:16), and which are by Him to be raised unto eternal life and to be glorified, are to be venerated by the faithful, through which (bodies) many benefits are bestowed by God on men. . . .
>
> Moreover, that the images of Christ, of the Virgin Mother of God, and of the other saints are to be had and to be retained particularly in temples, and that due honor and veneration are to be given them; not that any divinity or virtue is believed to be in them, on account of which they are to be worshiped; or that anything is to be asked of them; or that trust is to be reposed in images, as was of old done by the Gentiles who placed their hope in idols; but because the honor which is shown them is referred to the prototypes which those images represent; in such wise that by the images which we kiss, and before which we uncover the head, and prostrate ourselves, we adore Christ; and we venerate the saints whose similitude they bear. . . .[98]

Catholics believe that the one Mystical Church and Body of Christ exists on three levels: the Church Militant on earth, the Church Triumphant in Heaven, and the Church Suffering in Purgatory, and that communication can take place between all three. Those of us on earth can pray for souls in Purgatory and invoke the saints in Heaven. Saints in Heaven pray for those in the other two realms of the Church. The souls in Purgatory also invoke the saints in Heaven and pray for earthly pilgrims.[99]

We honor the saints in Heaven, who have more perfectly attained God's likeness (2 Cor. 3:18), we strive to imitate them, and we ask them for their efficacious prayers on our behalf and that of

[98] *On the Invocation, Veneration, and Relics of Saints* and *On Sacred Images*. See also Vatican II: *Dogmatic Constitution on the Church*, ch. 7, sects. 50-51; CCC, pars. 946, 955, 960.

[99] CCC, pars. 954, 958, 962; Hardon, *PCD*, 83.

others. All honor ultimately goes back to God, whose graces are the source of all that is worthy of veneration in the saints. St. Jerome said, "We show veneration to the servants so that it might radiate back from them to the Lord."[100] It is God himself whom we praise when we celebrate in music, painting, and poetry his flowers, stars, sunsets, majestic birds, forests, mountains, or oceans. It is the painter who receives the accolades when his masterpiece is praised; likewise God with his creation, including the saints.[101]

Devotion to saints no more interferes with or corrupts the unique adoration due to God than does our love for friends and relatives. A robust devotion may give rise to the language of hyperbole, just as human lovers wax eloquent in their rapturous romantic praises of each other, never intending literally to worship the object of love and affection.

Furthermore, if we cherish the memory of mere political heroes, such as Jefferson and Lincoln, and even great sports figures, such as Joe Louis, with statues, and if we honor war heroes with monuments, such as the Vietnam Memorial, why should we not honor and venerate the great Christian saints and the towering righteous men and women of the Old Testament (see Heb. 12:22-23)?

We address judges as "Your Honor" and are commanded by God to honor our mothers and fathers (Eph. 6:2), widows (1 Tim. 5:3), Christian teachers (1 Tim. 5:17), wives (1 Pet. 3:7), fellow Christians (1 Cor. 12:12-26), and governing authorities (Rom. 13:7; 1 Pet. 2:17). A spirit of honoring those who are worthy of honor is to typify the Christian (Rom. 12:10; 1 Pet. 2:17).

The saints are not only still alive, but much more vibrantly and intensely alive than we are, thoroughly able to influence and assist us, as the book of Revelation clearly testifies.[102] They are not

[100] Epistle 109, 1. In Ott, *Fundamentals of Catholic Dogma*, 319.

[101] CCC, pars. 828, 957; Hardon, *PCD*, 448.

[102] CCC, pars. 956, 2683.

preoccupied with sitting on clouds and strumming harps, as our culture's ridiculous caricatures would have it. They still think, feel, will, love, and remember — all of our attributes are theirs (and many more: see Matt. 22:30; Rom. 8:29-30, 38-39; 1 Cor. 13:9-12, 15:42-43; Phil. 3:20-21; 1 John 3:2). The invocation of saints entails much more than merely mental inspiration, although that aspect is included as well.

A sound biblical basis for the veneration of saints can be found in the Pauline passages where the apostle exhorts his followers to "imitate" him (1 Cor. 4:16; Phil. 3:17; 2 Thess. 3:7-9) as he, in turn, imitates Christ (1 Cor. 11:1; 1 Thess. 1:6). Also, we are exhorted to honor and imitate the "heroes of the faith" in Hebrews 6:12 and Chapter 11, and to take heart in the examples of the prophets and Job, who endured suffering (James 5:10-11).

The veneration of relics of saints, an aspect of the Communion of Saints, is an extension of the incarnational and sacramental principle, whereby matter itself can convey grace. Sacramentals are objects or actions that can impart grace, but the individual's disposition and the prayers of others (rather than the inherent power of the ritual itself, as with the seven sacraments) are instrumental in whatever spiritual benefit accrues.[103] They are not magic charms, since they derive all power from God. Examples of sacramentals include holy water, blessings, medals, crucifixes, exorcisms, statues, the Sign of the Cross, and relics.

Relics, too, have an explicit biblical basis: The bones of Elisha were so spiritually powerful that they caused a dead man to come back to life (2 Kings 13:20-21). Elijah's mantle parted the Jordan river (2 Kings 2:11-14). A woman was cured of a hemorrhage after she touched the fringe of Christ's garment (Matt. 9:20-22). Jesus told her that her faith had made her well, so that both the physical object and the woman's disposition worked together.

[103] CCC, pars. 1667-1670, 1677; Hardon, *PCD*, 380.

St. Peter's mere shadow healed the sick and cast out demons (Acts 5:15-16), as did "handkerchiefs or aprons" touched by St. Paul (Acts 19:11-12). The last four examples are identical to Catholic secondary relics: objects that had come into contact with a saint or with Jesus.[104]

Karl Adam sums up the Catholic position on the Communion of Saints:

> God . . . takes up into Himself the whole creation that culminates in human nature, and in a new, unheard-of supernatural manner, *lives* in it, *moves* in it, and in it *is* (see Acts 17:28). That is the basis upon which the Catholic veneration of the saints and Mary must be judged. . . . The saints are not mere exalted patterns of behavior, but living members and even constructive powers of the Body of Christ. . . .
>
> The veneration which we give to angels and saints is essentially different from the worship which we offer to God. . . . To God alone belongs the complete service of the whole man, the worship of adoration. . . . But so pervasive . . . is God's glory that it . . . is reflected also in those who in Him have become children of God. . . . We love them as countless dewdrops in which the sun's radiance is mirrored. We venerate them because we find God in them. . . . Therefore

[104] Hardon, *PCD*, 364. Concerning the Church Fathers' views on relics, renowned Protestant church historian Philip Schaff — no friend at all of these practices — concludes forlornly: "The most and the best of the church teachers of our period, Hilary, the two Gregories, Basil, Chrysostom, Isidore of Pelusium, Theodoret, Ambrose, Jerome, Augustine, and Leo . . . *gave the weight of their countenance to the worship* [i.e., veneration] *of relics*, which thus became an essential constituent of the Greek and Roman Catholic religion. They went quite as far as the Council of Trent" (*History of the Christian Church* [Grand Rapids, Michigan: Eerdmans, 1976], Vol. 3, ch. 7, sect. 87, 456; emphasis added).

> are we confident that they can and will help us only so far as creatures may. They cannot themselves sanctify us. . . .
>
> The divine blessing never works without the members, but only in and through their unity. . . . Therefore, although the veneration of saints has undergone some development in the course of the Church's history . . . yet such veneration was from the beginning germinally contained in the nature of the Church as the Body of Christ . . . the fellowship and solidarity of His members. . . . It is no pagan growth, but indigenous to Christianity. . . . Popular devotion to the saints is in line with dogma and is utterly monotheistic in character. . . . The devout Catholic . . . for the ordinary and fundamental concerns of his soul . . . practices . . . an immediate intercourse of prayer with God.[105]

Scriptural evidence for the Communion of Saints

Protestants are inclined to think that biblical evidences for the Communion of Saints and "saintly intercession" are entirely lacking, but such is assuredly not the case, as the following proofs demonstrate:

> **1 Samuel 28:12, 14-15:** "When the woman saw Samuel [who was dead], she cried. . . . And Saul knew that it was Samuel, and he bowed, with his face to the ground, and did obeisance. Then Samuel said to Saul, 'Why have you disturbed me by bringing me up?' " (Read 1 Sam. 28:7-20.)

Some commentators (for example, Tertullian and St. Jerome) have denied that this was actually Samuel, thinking that "Samuel" in this passage was an impersonating spirit of some sort, conjured up by the medium of Endor (1 Sam. 28:7). The current consensus

[105] Adam, *The Spirit of Catholicism*, 115-116, 123-125, 246.

among biblical commentators, however, appears to be that it was indeed Samuel the prophet, in an appearance after his death.[106] This was also the view of the ancient rabbis, St. Justin Martyr, Origen, and St. Augustine, among others. Sirach 46:20 reinforces the latter interpretation: "After he had fallen asleep he [Samuel] prophesied and revealed to the king his death, and lifted up his voice out of the earth in prophecy, to blot out the wickedness of the people." Samuel would have been in *Sheol* (Greek, *Hades*), the netherworld of the dead, which explains his speaking of being "brought up."

In any event, he appeared due to a miracle of God, not the magic or sorcery of a medium, and his true prophecy of Saul's impending death (1 Sam. 28:19) mitigates against the demonic interpretation, as does the medium's stunned reaction (1 Sam. 28:12-13). And Samuel prophetically speaks just as he did when alive on the earth.

> **Tobit 12:12, 15:** "I brought a reminder of your prayer before the Holy One; and when you buried the dead, I was likewise present with you. . . . I am Raphael, one of the seven holy angels who present the prayers of the saints and enter into the presence of the glory of the Holy One."

We find here a clear instance of angels interceding for us and somehow being involved in our prayers to God — an important aspect of the doctrine of the Communion of Saints (for the canonicity of Sirach, Tobit, and 2 Maccabees, see Appendix Three). The angel Raphael, it would seem, had to have some

[106] See, e.g., D. Guthrie and J. A. Motyer, eds., *The New Bible Commentary* (Grand Rapids, Michigan: Eerdmans, 1970), 301; Charles F. Pfeiffer and Everett F. Harrison, eds., *The Wycliffe Bible Commentary* (Chicago: Moody Press, 1962), 292.

knowledge of the prayers of the saints in order to present them to God. Furthermore, it appears probable that direct reference is made to this passage in both Revelation 1:4 and 8:3-4.

> **2 Maccabees 15:13-14:** "Then likewise a man appeared, distinguished by his gray hair and dignity, and of marvelous majesty and authority. And Onias spoke, saying, 'This is a man who loves the brethren and prays much for the people and the holy city, Jeremiah, the prophet of God.' "

This is an account of a vision seen by Judas Maccabeus (15:11). Onias, a deceased high priest, appears, praying with outstretched hands for the whole body of the Jews (15:12). He proceeds to introduce Judas to the prophet Jeremiah, who had been dead for centuries, yet who, according to Onias, intercedes much for the Jews. Jeremiah also speaks to Judas (15:16). Thus, we have an undeniable proof of the intercession of (dead) saints on behalf of inhabitants of the earth.

Lest someone question this evidence because it is in the so-called Apocrypha, similar information is conveyed in the Protestant Bible, in Jeremiah 15:1: "Then the Lord said to me, 'Though Moses and Samuel stood before me, yet my heart would not turn toward this people.' " Here it appears that God receives the prayers of the dead saints as a matter of course. Moses and Samuel were both known as intercessors, and Jeremiah lived centuries after both men. Also, Revelation 5:8 (in all likelihood) and 6:9-10 chronicle dead saints acting as intercessory intermediaries, as we shall see.

> **Matthew 17:1-3:** "Jesus took with him Peter and James and John his brother, and led them up a high mountain apart. And he was transfigured before them, and his face shone like the sun, and his garments became white as light. And behold, there appeared to

> them Moses and Elijah, talking with him" (see also Mark 9:4 and Luke 9:30-31).

Departed saints are again pictured as intensely interested in earthly affairs, just as angels are portrayed throughout the Bible. It is neither logical nor plausible to deny that these saints pray for us. If they are aware of our affairs, it follows that they can "hear" our petitions. If so, this is the Catholic doctrine of the invocation of the saints.

> **Matthew 18:10:** "See that you do not despise one of these little ones; for I tell you that in Heaven their angels always behold the face of my Father who is in Heaven."

This is the most straightforward biblical proof for the idea (also accepted by many Protestants) that every person has a guardian angel, who has direct access to God and in some sense "oversees" and protects the individual to whom he is assigned (see also Ps. 34:7, 91:11; Acts 12:15; Heb. 1:14).

If Jesus could have asked for the assistance of angels (Matt. 26:53) — and he certainly would not have been worshiping them in so doing — then we, who obviously need their help far more than the Lord Jesus Christ, can do the same without necessarily engaging in idolatry.

It stands to reason that if angels are so aware of our doings, as indicated in Luke 15:10, where they are said to have joy over sinners' repentance, and in 1 Corinthians 4:9, where we are told that apostles were spectacles to angels, then they certainly would be cognizant of our prayerful pleas to them. Repentance is a change of heart and will, which would suggest that angels are acquainted with our thoughts as well as with our actions.

This belief was held by the eminent Presbyterian theologian Charles Hodge, who thought that angels could act on our minds, and even "communicate with our spirits."[107] Yet he inconsistently balked at the notion of invoking their aid, since "they must not come between us and God."[108] This is an unnecessary dichotomy and false dilemma; the reasoning is as follows: If some practice can possibly become idolatrous, we must never engage in it. But anything can come between us and God and become an idol (for example, the Bible itself, our spouses, or money). So Hodge's fear is unwarranted and unreasonable — especially given the scriptural evidence — and it "proves too much." For asking an angel (or a saint) to pray for us is not that different at all from our praying for each other. In both cases, assistance is sought from a fellow creature, and (rightly understood) there is no attempt to usurp the prerogatives of God whatsoever.

The existence of guardian angels can be denied only by maintaining that intercessory requests directed to them are synonymous with either the worship due to God alone (idolatry) or the communication with evil spirits by means of a medium, or other occultic practice (necromancy or sorcery). Neither equation is biblical or logical.

If angels are powerful, benevolent beings, whose purpose is to bring us closer to God, and if they know our thoughts (Luke 15:10) and intercede for us (Tob. 12:12-15; Rev. 8:3-4), what coherent biblical reason forbids the invocation of angels, particularly guardian angels, to obtain their intercession before God on our behalf?

Misunderstandings of the doctrines and the legitimate pious devotional practices of Catholicism must give way to open-minded biblical inquiry. God revealed these avenues of grace for our spiritual well-being, and it would be foolish to ignore them.

> **Matthew 27:50, 52-53:** "And Jesus cried again with a loud voice and yielded up his spirit. . . . The tombs

[107] Hodge, *Systematic Theology*, 231-233.

[108] Ibid., 234.

> also were opened, and many bodies of the saints who had fallen asleep were raised, and coming out of the tombs after his Resurrection, they went into the holy city and appeared to many."

Appearances such as these lessen the artificial dichotomy between Heaven and earth that Protestants create out of an unfortunate, almost obsessive fear of idolatry, and unbiblical mental habit. If God wants contact between the living and the dead, who are we to forbid it in terms of prohibiting the invocation of saints and angels, which is merely the logical outcome of the belief that these beings are alive and wholly active, mentally, emotionally, volitionally, and spiritually (as suggested, for example, by Hebrews 12:1: "We are surrounded by so great a cloud of witnesses")?

> **Revelation 1:4:** "Grace to you and peace from him who is and who was and who is to come, and from the seven spirits who are before his throne" (cf. Tob. 12:15; Rev. 3:1, 4:5, 5:6).

Cardinal Newman made a fascinating comment on this scripture:

> The sacred writer goes so far as to speak of *grace* and *peace* being sent to us, not only from the Almighty, but from *the seven Spirits* . . . thus associating the Eternal with the ministers of His mercies; and this carries us on to the remarkable passage of St. Justin, one of the earliest Fathers, who, in his *Apology* (2.1), says, "To Him [God], and His Son who came from Him . . . and the host of other good Angels who follow and resemble Him, and the Prophetic Spirit, we pay veneration and homage."[109]

[109] *Letter to the Rev. E. B. Pusey, D.D.*, on *His Recent Eirenicon*, London, 1866. In Karl Keating, *Catholicism and Fundamentalism* (San Francisco: Ignatius Press, 1988), 264. St. Justin Martyr's *Apology* was written between 148 and 155.

> **Revelation 5:8:** "The four living creatures and the twenty-four elders fell down before the Lamb, each holding a harp, and with golden bowls full of incense, which are the prayers of the saints."

> **Revelation 8:3-4:** "And another angel came and stood at the altar with a golden censer; and he was given much incense to mingle with the prayers of all saints upon the golden altar before the throne; and the smoke of the incense rose with the prayers of the saints from the hand of the angel before God."

It is somewhat unclear whether the twenty-four elders in this scene are angels or men, and commentators differ on it. Early Christian Tradition associated them with the twelve patriarchs of Israel and the twelve Apostles, representing the churches of the Old and New Covenants (see Isa. 24:23; Dan. 7:9-10). References to them clad in white garments, with golden crowns (Rev. 4:4, 10) suggests the view that these elders are glorified human beings (see, e.g., 2 Tim. 4:8; James 1:12; 1 Pet. 5:4; Rev. 2:10; 3:5, 11; 6:11; 7:9, 13-14). In any event, in both examples above, creatures — whether men or angels — are involved with our prayers as intercessory intermediaries, which isn't supposed to happen if the Catholic belief in the intercession of saints and angels is untrue.

> **Revelation 6:9-10:** "I saw under the altar the souls of those who had been slain for the word of God and for the witness they had borne; they cried out with a loud voice, 'O Sovereign Lord, holy and true, how long before thou wilt judge and avenge our blood on those who dwell upon the earth?' "

Here the martyrs in Heaven are uttering what are known as "imprecatory prayers." These are not so much vengeful as they are a plea for, and recognition of, God's role as the wrathful Judge who will rescue and vindicate the righteous, either in this life or the next. Examples can be found particularly in the Psalms (35, 59, 69, 79, 109, 139) and in Jeremiah (11:18 ff., 15:15 ff., 18:19 ff., 20:11 ff.).

An angel offers up a very similar prayer in Zechariah 1:12. Jesus mentions a type of this prayer in Matthew 26:53, in which he states that he could have prayed to the Father and received legions of angels to prevent his arrest, had it been the Father's will. The idea is the same: prayer for judgment to be wrought upon the enemies of God. At the same time, imprecatory prayers often are intercessions on behalf of the righteous, as in this passage.

Therefore, unarguably, dead saints are praying for Christians on earth. If they can intercede for us, why should we not ask for their prayers? Clearly, they are aware of what is happening on earth, as indicated in this passage and, for instance, Hebrews 12:1. They are more alive, unfathomably more righteous, and obviously closer to God than we are. Omniscience is not required for them to hear our prayers, as is often charged. Rather, we have reason to believe that they are out of time, and therefore not subject to its constraints. We ought to ask for their prayers just as we would ask for the intercession of a fellow Christian on earth, and, if James 5:16 is true, their prayers will have incomparably more effect.

The well-known Protestant *New Bible Commentary* states that this plea in Heaven is indeed a prayer, which quickens the end of the age (8:1-5).[110] This admission is of immense significance for our topic. For if the prayers of dead saints have such an importance regarding the last days and the final judgment, who can

[110] Guthrie, *The New Bible Commentary*, 1289. Concurring in this opinion is Robert Jamieson, Andrew R. Fausset, and David Brown, *Commentary on the Whole Bible* (Grand Rapids, Michigan: Zondervan, 1961), 846, 1547.

deny that such prayers are valid and effective with regard to far more mundane matters (such as our everyday concerns)? The doctrine of the Communion of Saints, then, would appear to be irrefutably presented in the book of Revelation.

> **Revelation 11:3:** "And I will grant my two witnesses power to prophesy for one thousand two hundred and sixty days" (read Rev. 11:3-13).

The Protestant Jamieson, Fausset, and Brown commentary comments on the identity of these witnesses:

> The actions of the two witnesses are just those of Moses when witnessing for God against Pharaoh . . . and of Elijah . . . as Malachi 4:5-6 seems to imply (cf. Matt. 17:11; Acts 3:21). Moses and Elijah appeared with Christ at the Transfiguration. . . . As to Moses, cf. Deuteronomy 34:5-6; Jude 9. . . . Many of the early Church thought the two witnesses to be Enoch and Elijah. This would avoid the difficulty of the dying a *second* time, for these never have died [Gen. 5:24; 2 Kings 2:11]. . . . Still, the turning the water to blood, and the plagues (vs. 6), apply best to Moses.[111]

Dead saints and earthly affairs

All of these instances of miraculous appearances of long-dead figures (as opposed to other resurrections, such as those of Lazarus and Jairus's daughter), from Matthew 17 and 27, 1 Samuel 28, and Revelation 11, lead to the conclusion that God allows and approves of interaction between the saints in the next life and Christians in this one.

These biblical facts supply indisputable evidence for the Catholic doctrine of the Communion of Saints, supported partially by

[111] *Commentary on the Whole Bible*, 1556-1557.

reputable Evangelical Protestant commentaries (without acknowledging the "Catholic" implications therein). Taken as a whole, along with the other proofs above, they cast severe doubt on any notion of an unbridgeable gulf between Heaven and earth (that is, between members of the one Body of Christ: Rom. 12:4-5; Eph. 4:4; Col. 3:15).

It is interesting to note that Moses and Samuel, who together are present in two and perhaps three (Rev. 11:3) examples of extraordinary reappearances, are both renowned among Jews and Christians for their powerful intercession (Exod. 32:11-12; 1 Sam. 7:9; Ps. 99:6; Jer. 15:1 — an implied after-death prayer), thus unifying the two concepts of concern for earthly affairs and prayer for the same.

In all of these cases, much communication takes place with people on earth: Samuel talks to Saul (and Saul replies), Moses and Elijah talk to Jesus within earshot of Peter, James, and John,[112] the two witnesses prophesy for three and a half years (they must also have engaged in much conversation during all that time), and the resurrected saints of Matthew 27 "appeared to many," presumably talking with them, as did Jesus in His post-Resurrection appearances.

In light of these biblical examples, how could anyone contend that God *forbids* such interaction, allowing only that between man and God, and also, occasionally, between men and angels? God was in charge of all these occurrences, so that if they were contrary to the unique mediatorship of Christ, as Protestants put it, he could have easily disallowed them.

But God sent Moses and Elijah to the Mount of Transfiguration, Samuel to Saul (even notwithstanding an occultic context), the two witnesses (whoever they may be), and many dead saints.

[112] Luke 9:32 says they were sleepy or sleeping; whether they heard Moses and Elijah at all is unclear.

(One could plausibly contend that Christ's reappearances would have been sufficient, without all of these formerly interred saints running around Jerusalem!)

In conclusion, all the elements of the Catholic doctrine of the Communion of Saints are solidly grounded in Scripture. If this interpretation is questioned, alternative explanations ought to be produced, instead of merely unsubstantiated polemical denials of the Catholic positions (which is far too often the case).

Summary of biblical evidences

- *Prayers for the dead:* Tobit 12:12; 2 Maccabees 12:39-45; 1 Corinthians 15:29; 2 Timothy 1:16-18 (see "Purgatory" chapter).

- *Dead saints are aware of earthly affairs:* Matthew 22:30; Luke 15:10; 1 Corinthians 4:9; Hebrews 12:1.

- *Dead saints intercede for those on earth:* Jeremiah 15:1; 2 Maccabees 15:14; Revelation 6:9-10.

- *Saints are intermediaries and present our prayers to God:* Revelation 5:8.

- *Dead saints appear on earth to interact with men:* 1 Samuel 28:12-15 with Sirach 46:20; 2 Maccabees 15:13-16; Matthew 17:1-3 and 27:50-53; Revelation 11:3.

- *Guardian angels:* Psalm 34:7, 91:11; Matthew 18:10; Acts 12:15; Hebrews 1:14.

- *Angels are aware of our thoughts:* Luke 15:10; 1 Corinthians 4:9.

- *Angels participate in the giving of God's grace:* Revelation 1:4.

- *Angels are intermediaries and present our prayers to God:* Tobit 12:12, 15; Revelation 8:3-4 (cf. 5:8).

Whatever one thinks about such practices, it is clearly not the case that those who developed and defended these views intended to lessen the veneration of God. The Protestant accusation of "idolatry" and so forth, betrays an utter noncomprehension of the rationale behind the Communion of Saints. Whenever and wherever truly idolatrous excesses occur, these are not in accord with the teaching of the Catholic Church and must be thought of as aberrations, rather than sanctioned practices of Catholicism.

Except for a sizable minority faction within Anglicanism (and perhaps tiny factions here and there), the Communion of Saints, as understood in the Catholic Tradition, has been rejected outright by Protestantism, on grounds that it is either idolatrous, unbiblical, unnecessary, or quasi-occultic. But even in recent times, an "icon" of sorts among Evangelical Protestants, C. S. Lewis, maintained that the invocation of saints had a legitimate theological rationale behind it, even though he himself did not completely agree with this viewpoint. Some other prominent Protestants have also maintained some semblance of the traditional beliefs concerning the Communion of Saints.[113]

[113] C. S. Lewis, *Letters to Malcolm: Chiefly on Prayer* (New York: Harcourt Brace Jovanovich, 1964), 15-16. Lewis also makes an overt reference to the Communion of Saints in his famous *Screwtape Letters* (New York: Macmillan, 1961), 12. Other notable Protestants who stressed a sense of the "aliveness" of the saints in Heaven and their inclusion in the Body of Christ (excluding their invocation) include John Wesley *(Letter to a Roman Catholic*, Dublin, 1749), and A. W. Tozer ("The Communion of Saints," in *A Treasury of A. W. Tozer* [Grand Rapids, Michigan: Baker Book House, 1980], 168-170). The Lutheran creedal *Augsburg Confession* (1530), which was sanctioned by Martin Luther himself, in its Article 21, recommends that "saints should be kept in remembrance so that our faith may be strengthened. . . . Moreover, their good works are to be an example for us" (from John H. Leith, ed., *Creeds of the Churches* [Garden City, New York: Doubleday Anchor, 1963], 77).

Chapter Seven

Purgatory

"Saved, but only as through fire"

The Second Ecumenical Council of Lyons in 1274 defined Purgatory for the Catholic faithful:

> Those who, after Baptism, lapse into sin must not be rebaptized, but obtain pardon for their sins through true penance; that if, being truly repentant, they die in charity before having satisfied by worthy fruits of penance for their sins of commission and omission, their souls are cleansed after death by purgatorial and purifying penalties . . . and that to alleviate such penalties, the acts of intercession of the living faithful benefit them, namely the sacrifices of the Mass, prayers, alms, and other works of piety. . . .
>
> As for the souls of those who, after having received holy Baptism, have incurred no stain of sin whatever, and those souls who, after having contracted the stain of sin, have been cleansed, either while remaining still in their bodies or after having been divested of them as stated above, they are received immediately into Heaven.[114]

[114] *Profession of Faith of Michael Palaeologus*, Pt. 2. From J. Neuner and J. Dupuis, eds., *The Christian Faith: Doctrinal Documents of*

The word *Purgatory* is derived from the Latin *purgatorio* ("cleansing," "purifying"). The Catholic Church has not defined whether Purgatory is a place or a process, or whether it contains real fire. The sufferings correspond to the degree of sin present for each individual. This purifying pain, although assuredly intense, does not exclude the presence of much peace and joy. These souls love God deeply, and they have the assurance of eventual entrance into Heaven; therefore, they do not despair, but always possess hope. Purgatory is the vestibule of Heaven, not the anteroom of Hell. It is the mountain-climb to the glorious summit of the Beatific Vision of God, rather than a "second Hell," as much popular mythology would have it. Purgatory will cease to exist after the general judgment.

The necessity of Purgatory flows from infused (actual, transforming) justification, and the doctrine is consistent with penance, merit, the Communion of Saints, sanctification, and indulgences. All Christians should seek after purity, perfection, and righteousness. Catholicism merely approaches this goal with the utmost seriousness by maintaining that some purification will be necessary after death for most of us, since holiness is a prerequisite for entering into the presence of God (Rev. 21:27).

Protestants agree that real (not merely declared or imputed) holiness is a requirement for Heaven, but disagree with the purification process, believing instead in some sort of *instantaneous* transformation at death for the redeemed. Thus, in Protestantism, both salvation and ultimate glorification are essentially one-time events, whereas in Catholicism, they are durational *processes* (both belief-systems are logically consistent with their premises).

the Catholic Church (New York: Alba House, 1990), 18. See also CCC, pars. 1030-1032; Vatican II: *Dogmatic Constitution on the Church*, ch. 7, sects. 50-51; Hardon, *PCD*, 356-357; Hardon, CC, 274-275, 278-280.

Karl Adam, penetrating and astute as usual, offers an illuminating explanation of Purgatory:

> The poor soul, having failed to make use of the easier and happier penance of this world, must now endure all the bitterness and all the dire penalties which are necessarily attached by the inviolable law of God's justice to even the least sin, until she has tasted the wretchedness of sin to its dregs and has lost even the smallest attachment to it, until all that is fragmentary in her has attained completeness, in the perfection of the love of Christ. It is a long and painful process, "so as by fire." Is it real fire? We cannot tell; its true nature will certainly always remain hidden from us in this world. But we know this: that no penalty presses so hard upon the "poor souls"as the consciousness that they are by their own fault long debarred from the blessed Vision of God. The more they are disengaged gradually in the whole compass of their being from their narrow selves, and the more freely and completely their hearts are opened to God, so much the more is the bitterness of their separation spiritualized and transfigured. It is homesickness for their Father; and the further their purification proceeds, the more painfully are their souls scourged with its rods of fire. . . .
>
> Purgatory is only a thoroughfare to the Father, toilsome indeed and painful, but yet a thoroughfare, in which there is no standing still and which is illuminated by glad hope. For every step of the road brings the Father nearer. Purgatory is like the beginning of spring. Warm rays commence to fall on the hard soil and here and there awaken timid life. . . . Countless souls are already awakening to the full day of eternal life. . . .[115]

[115] Adam, *The Spirit of Catholicism*, 110-111.

Cardinal Newman, in his Anglican period, preached with fascinating insight on this subject:

> In one sense, all Christians die with their work unfinished. Let them have chastened themselves all their lives long, and lived in faith and obedience, yet still there is much in them unsubdued — much pride, much ignorance, much unrepented, unknown sin, much inconsistency, much irregularity in prayer, much lightness and frivolity of thought. Who can tell, then, but, in God's mercy, the time of waiting between death and Christ's coming, may be profitable to those who have been His true servants here, as a time of maturing that fruit of grace, but partly formed in them in this life — a school-time of contemplation, as this world is a discipline of active service? Such, surely, is the force of the Apostle's words, that "He that hath begun a good work in us, will perform it *until* the day of Jesus Christ," *until*, not *at*, not stopping it with death, but carrying it on to the Resurrection. And this, which will be accorded to all Saints, will be profitable to each in proportion to the degree of holiness in which he dies. . . .
>
> It will be found, on the whole, that death is not the object put forward in Scripture for hope to rest upon, but the *coming of Christ*, as if the interval between death and His coming was by no means to be omitted in the process of our preparation for Heaven.[116]

The Bible itself — closely examined — doesn't compel us to think that God's work of grace in each soul is instantaneously completed at the moment of physical death. If approached without an ultimately groundless bias against any process of sanctification after death, the biblical data is sufficient to establish the

[116] Sermon: "The Intermediate State," 1836.

Catholic position, or at least make it plausible enough to accept on the basis of a Tradition very well-attested throughout the history of the Church up to the Protestant Reformation, when it was first rejected outright.

Scriptural evidence for Purgatory

> **Psalm 66:12:** "Thou didst let men ride over our heads; we went through fire and through water; yet thou hast brought us forth to a spacious place."

This verse was considered a proof of Purgatory by Origen[117] and St. Ambrose,[118] who posits the water of Baptism and the fire of Purgatory.

> **Ecclesiastes 12:14:** "For God will bring every deed into judgment, with every secret thing, whether good or evil."

> **Isaiah 4:4:** "When the Lord shall have washed away the filth of the daughters of Zion and cleansed the bloodstains of Jerusalem from its midst by a spirit of judgment and by a spirit of burning" (see also Isa. 1:25-26).

St. Francis de Sales, the great Catholic apologist of the sixteenth century, commented on this verse as follows:

> This purgation made in the spirit of judgment and of burning is understood of Purgatory by St. Augustine, in the twentieth book of the *City of God*, Chapter 25. And in fact this interpretation is favored by the words preceding, in which mention is made of the salvation of men, and also by the end of the chapter, where the repose of the blessed is

[117] Homily 25 on Numbers.

[118] *In Ps. 36*; Sermon 3 on Ps. 118.

spoken of; wherefore that which is said — "the Lord shall wash away the filth" — is to be understood of the purgation necessary for this salvation. And since it is said that this purgation is to be made in the spirit of heat and of burning, it cannot well be understood save of Purgatory and its fire.[119]

> **Isaiah 6:5-7:** "And I said: 'Woe is me! for I am lost; for I am a man of unclean lips, and I dwell in the midst of a people of unclean lips; for my eyes have seen the King, the Lord of hosts.' Then flew one of the seraphim to me, having in his hand a burning coal which he had taken with tongs from the altar. And he touched my mouth, and said: 'Behold, this has touched your lips; your guilt is taken away, and your sin forgiven.' "

This passage is a noteworthy example of what happens when men experience God's presence directly. An immediate recognition of one's own unholiness occurs, along with the corresponding feeling of inadequacy. Like Isaiah, we must all undergo a self-conscious and voluntary purging upon approaching God more closely than in this present life.

Few doctrines are clearer in Scripture than the necessity of absolute holiness in order to enter Heaven. On this, Protestants and Catholics are in total agreement. Therefore, the fundamental disagreement on this subject is: how *long* does this purification upon death take? Certainly, it cannot be logically denied as a *possibility* that this purging might involve duration.

> **Micah 7:8-9:** "Rejoice not over me, O mine enemy; when I fall, I shall rise; when I sit in darkness, the

[119] St. Francis de Sales, *The Catholic Controversy* (*CON*), Henry B. Mackey, trans. (Rockford, Illinois: TAN Books, 1989), 358.

> Lord will be a light to me. I will bear the indignation of the Lord because I have sinned against him, until he pleads my cause and executes judgment for me. He will bring me forth to the light; I shall behold his deliverance" (see also Lev. 26:41, 43; Job 40:4-5; Lam. 3:39).

St. Jerome (d. 420) considered this a clear proof of Purgatory.[120] Cardinal Newman (not yet Catholic at this point) offered lucid commentary on this passage:

> There are a very great many cases, I fear, where persons, religious and well-meaning, according to the ordinary standard, are little or not at all impressed with the notion that their past sins, whether from their moral consequences, or as remembered by God, are a present disadvantage to them . . .
>
> Nothing surely is more common among persons of the most various characters of mind than thus to think that God forgets sin as soon as we forget it. . . .
>
> It is clear that men commonly think a sin to be canceled when it is done and over, or, in other words, that *amendment is an expiation*. . . .
>
> Now it will be answered that the merits of our Lord Jesus Christ are sufficient to wash out all sin, and that they really do wash it out. Doubtless; but the question to be decided is, whether He has promised to apply His all-sufficient merits at once on persons doing nothing more than changing their mode of living. . . . Men in general . . . think that the state of grace in which they are is such as to absorb (as it were) and consume all sin as fast as it springs up in the heart — or they think that faith has this power of obliterating and annihilating sin, so that in fact there is nothing on their

[120] Ibid.

conscience to repent of. They consider faith as superseding repentance. . . .

Regret, vexation, sorrow, such feelings seem to this busy, practical, unspiritual generation as idle; as something despicable and unmanly — just as tears may be. . . .

However, it may be objected . . . that little indeed is said in the New Testament about . . . the necessity of such deprecation on the part of Christians. In answer, I allow that there is very little in the New Testament concerning the punishment of Christians; but then there is as little said about their sins; so that if Scripture negatives everything which it is silent about, it would be as easy to show that the Gospel does not belong at all to those who have lapsed into sin, as that punishments are not their portion, and penitential acts not their duty. As the sins of Christians are beyond the ordinary contemplation of Scripture, so are their remedies.[121]

> **Malachi 3:2-4:** "But who can endure the day of his coming, and who can stand when he appears? For he is like a refiner's fire, and like fullers' soap; he will sit as a refiner and purifier of silver, and he will purify the sons of Levi, and refine them like gold and silver, till they present right offerings to the Lord. Then the offering of Judah and Jerusalem will be pleasing to the Lord as in the days of old and as in former years."

St. Francis de Sales recounts the patristic views on this passage:

This place is expounded of a purifying punishment by Origen *(Hom. 6 on Exodus)*, St. Ambrose *(On Ps. 36)*, St.

[121] Sermon: "Chastisement Amid Mercy," 1838 (on Mic. 7:8-9).

Augustine (*City of God*, Bk. 20, ch. 25), and St. Jerome (on this place). We are quite aware that they understand it of a purgation which will be at the end of the world by the general fire and conflagration, in which will be purged away the remains of the sins of those who will be found alive; but we still are able to draw from this a good argument for our Purgatory. For if persons at that time have need of purgation before receiving the effects of the benediction of the supreme Judge, why shall not those also have need of it who die before that time, since some of these may be found at death to have remains of their imperfections. . . . St. Irenaeus in this connection, in Chapter 29 of Book 5, says that because the Militant Church is then to mount up to the heavenly palace of the Spouse, and will no longer have time for purgation, her faults and stains will there and then be purged away by this fire which will precede the judgment.[122]

> **2 Maccabees 12:39-42, 44-45:** "Judas and his men went to take up the bodies of the fallen. . . . Then under the tunic of every one of the dead they found sacred tokens of the idols of Jamnia, which the law forbids the Jews to wear. . . . So they all . . . turned to prayer, beseeching that the sin which had been committed might be wholly blotted out. . . . For if he were not expecting that those who had fallen would rise again, it would have been superfluous and foolish to pray for the dead. But if he was looking to the splendid reward that is laid up for those who fall asleep in godliness, it was a holy and pious thought. Therefore he made atonement for the dead, that they might be delivered from their sin."

[122] St. Francis de Sales, *CON*, 359-360.

The Jews offered *atonement* and *prayer* for their deceased brethren, who had clearly violated Mosaic Law. Such a practice presupposes Purgatory, since those in Heaven would not need any help, and those in Hell are beyond it. The Jewish people, therefore, believed in prayer for the dead (whether or not this book is scriptural; Protestants deny that it is). Christ did not correct this belief, as He surely would have done if it were erroneous (see Matt. 5:22, 25-26, 12:32; Luke 12:58-59, 16:9, 19-31). When our Lord and Savior talks about the afterlife, he never denies that there is a third state, and the overall evidence of his utterances in this regard strongly indicates that he accepted the existence of Purgatory.

> **Matthew 5:22:** "But I say to you that everyone who is angry with his brother shall be liable to judgment; whoever insults his brother shall be liable to the council, and whoever says, 'You fool!' shall be liable to the Hell of fire."

St. Francis de Sales elucidates the implications of this statement of Christ:

> It is only the third sort of offense which is punished with Hell; therefore in the judgment of God after this life there are other pains which are not eternal or infernal — these are the pains of Purgatory. One may say that the pains will be suffered in this world; but St. Augustine and the other Fathers understand them for the other world. And again may it not be that a man should die on the first or second offence which is spoken here? And when will such a one pay the penalty due to his offense? . . . Do then as the ancient Fathers did, and say that there is a place where they will be purified, and then they will go to Heaven above.[123]

[123] Ibid., 373-374.

Matthew 5:25-26: "Make friends quickly with your accuser, while you are going with him to court, lest your accuser hand you over to the judge, and the judge to the guard, and you be put in prison; truly, I say to you, you will never get out till you have paid the last penny" (see also Luke 12:58-59).

St. Francis de Sales:

Origen, St. Cyprian, St. Hilary, St. Ambrose, St. Jerome, and St. Augustine say that the way which is meant in the *whilst thou art in the way* [*while you are going with him to court*] is no other than the passage of the present life: the *adversary* [*accuser*] will be our own conscience . . . as St. Ambrose expounds, and Bede, St. Augustine, St. Gregory [the Great], and St. Bernard. Lastly, the judge is without doubt our Lord. . . . The *prison*, again, is . . . the place of punishment in the other world, in which, as in a large jail, there are many buildings; one for those who are damned, which is as it were for criminals, the other for those in Purgatory, which is as it were for debt. The *farthing* [*penny*] . . . [represents] little sins and infirmities, as the farthing is the smallest money one can owe.

Now let us consider a little where this repayment . . . is to be made. And we find from most ancient Fathers that it is in Purgatory: Tertullian,[124] Cyprian,[125] Origen,[126] . . . St. Ambrose,[127] St. Jerome.[128] . . . Who sees not that in St. Luke the comparison is drawn, not from a murderer or some

[124] *The Soul*, 100, 10.

[125] Epistle 4, 2.

[126] Homily 35 on Luke 12.

[127] Commentary on Luke 12.

[128] Commentary on Matthew 5.

criminal, who can have no hope of escape, but from a debtor who is thrown into prison till payment, and when this is made is at once let out?

This then is the meaning of our Lord, that whilst we are in this world, we should try by penitence and its fruits to pay, according to the power which we have by the blood of the Redeemer, the penalty to which our sins have subjected us; since if we wait till death, we shall not have such good terms in Purgatory, when we shall be treated with severity of justice.[129]

> **Matthew 12:32:** "And whoever says a word against the Son of man will be forgiven; but whoever speaks against the Holy Spirit will not be forgiven, either in this age or in the age to come."

If sins can be pardoned in the "age to come" (the afterlife), again, in the nature of things, this must be in Purgatory. We would laugh at a man who said that he would not marry in this world or the next (as if he could in the next — see Mark 12:25). If this sin cannot be forgiven after death, it follows that there are others which *can be*. Accordingly, this interpretation was held by St. Augustine,[130] St. Gregory the Great,[131] Bede,[132] and St. Bernard,[133] among others.

> **Luke 16:9:** "And I tell you, make friends for yourselves by means of unrighteous mammon, so that when it fails they may receive you into the eternal habitations" (read Luke 16:1-13 for the context).

[129] St. Francis de Sales, *CON*, 372-373.

[130] *City of God*, Bk. 21, ch. 24.

[131] *Dialogues*, 4, 39.

[132] Commentary on Mark 3.

[133] Homily 66 in Cant.

St. Francis de Sales:

To *fail* — what is it but to die? — and the *friends* — who are they but the Saints? The interpreters all understand it so; whence two things follow — that the Saints can help men departed, and that the departed can be helped by the Saints. . . . Thus is this passage expounded by St. Ambrose and by St. Augustine.[134] But the parable our Lord is using is too clear to allow us any doubt of this interpretation; for the similitude is taken from a steward who, being dismissed from his office and reduced to poverty [16:2], begged help from his friends, and our Lord likens the dismissal unto death, and the help begged from friends unto the help one receives after death from those to whom one has given alms. This help cannot be received by those who are in Paradise or in Hell; it is then by those who are in Purgatory.[135]

Luke 16:19-31: "There was a rich man who was clothed in purple and fine linen and who feasted sumptuously every day. And at his gate lay a poor man named Lazarus, full of sores, who desired to be fed with what fell from the rich man's table. . . . The poor man died and was carried by the angels to Abraham's bosom. The rich man also died and was buried; and in Hades, being in torment, he lifted up his eyes, and saw Abraham far off and Lazarus in his bosom.

"And he called out, 'Father Abraham, have mercy upon me, and send Lazarus to dip the end of his finger in water and cool my tongue; for I am in anguish in this flame.' But Abraham said, 'Son, remember that you in your lifetime received your good things,

[134] *City of God*, 12:27.

[135] St. Francis de Sales, *CON*, 374-375.

and Lazarus in like manner evil things, but now he is comforted here, and you are in anguish. And besides all this, between us and you a great chasm has been fixed, in order that those who would pass from here to you may not be able, and none may cross from there to us.'

"And he said, 'Then I beg you, father, to send him to my father's house, for I have five brothers, so that he may warn them, lest they also come into this place of torment.' But Abraham said, 'They have Moses and the prophets; let them hear them.'

"And he said, 'No, father Abraham; but if some one goes to them from the dead, they will repent.' He said to him, 'If they do not hear Moses and the prophets, neither will they be convinced if some one should rise from the dead.' "

Zechariah 9:11: "As for you also, because of the blood of my covenant with you, I will set your captives free from the waterless pit."

Ephesians 4:8-10: " 'When he ascended on high, he led a host of captives, and he gave gifts to men.' (In saying, 'he ascended,' what does it mean but that he had also descended into the lower parts of the earth? He who descended is he who also ascended far above all the heavens, that he might fill all things.)"

1 Peter 3:19-20: "He went and preached to the spirits in prison, who formerly did not obey, when God's patience waited in the days of Noah, during the building of the ark, in which a few, that is, eight persons, were saved through water" (see also 1 Pet. 4:6).

Catholic commentator George Leo Haydcock states:

> Abraham's bosom — the place of rest, where the souls of the saints resided, till Christ had opened Heaven by his death. . . . The bosom of Abraham (the common Father of all the faithful) was the place where the souls of the saints, and departed patriarchs, waited the arrival of their Deliverer. It was thither that Jesus went after his death; as it is said in the Creed, he descended into hell, to deliver those who were detained there, and who might at Christ's Ascension enter into Heaven (see 1 Pet. 3:19; Matt. 8:11). . . .
>
> [On 1 Peter 3:19-20:] These spirits in prison, to whom Christ went to preach after his death, were not in Heaven, nor yet in the Hell of the damned; because Heaven is no prison, and Christ did not go to preach to the damned. . . . In this prison souls would not be detained unless they were indebted to divine justice, nor would salvation be preached to them unless they were in a state that was capable of receiving salvation.[136]

At the very least, these passages prove that there can and does exist a third, intermediate state after death besides Heaven and Hell. Thus, Purgatory is not *a priori* unthinkable from a biblical perspective (as many Protestants casually assume). True, the Hebrew Sheol is not identical to Purgatory (both righteous and unrighteous go there), but it is nevertheless strikingly similar. Sheol is referred to frequently throughout the Old Testament (Deut. 32:22; 2 Sam. 22:6; Ps. 16:10, 18:5, 55:15, 86:13, 116:3, 139:8; Prov. 9:18, 23:14; Isa. 5:14, 14:9,15; Ezek. 31:16-17, 32:21, 27). In Jewish apocalyptic literature (in the few hundred years before Christ), the notion of divisions in Sheol is found (e.g., Enoch 22:1-14).

[136] *Haydcock's Catholic Family Bible and Commentary* (Monrovia, California: Catholic Treasures, 1991), 1376-1377, 1611.

The Christian Hell is equivalent to the New Testament Gehenna, or Lake of Fire. Gehenna was literally the burning ash-heap outside Jerusalem and was used as the name for Hell by Christ (Matt. 5:22, 29-30, 10:28, 18:9, 23:15, 33; Mark 9:43, 45, 47; Luke 12:5; cf. James 3:6). "Lake of fire" occurs only in Revelation as a chilling description of the horrors of Hell into which the damned would be thrown (Rev. 19:20, 20:10, 14-15, 21:8).

We know from Scripture that a few Old Testament saints went to Heaven before Christ went to Sheol and led (presumably) the majority of the pre-Christian righteous there (Eph. 4:8-10; 1 Pet. 3:19-20). Elijah went straight to Heaven by a whirlwind, as we are informed in 2 Kings 2:11. It is also generally thought by all sides that Enoch went directly to Heaven as well (Gen. 5:24). Moses came with Elijah to the Mount of Transfiguration to talk with Jesus (Matt. 17:1-3; Mark 9:4; Luke 9:30-31). By implication, then, it could be held that he, too, had been in Heaven, and by further logical inference, other Old Testament saintly figures.

It follows that, even before Christ, there was a "two-tiered" afterlife for the righteous: some, such as Elijah, Enoch, and likely Moses and others, went to Heaven, whereas a second, larger group went temporarily to Sheol. Likewise, now the elect of God can go straight to Heaven if sufficiently holy, or to Purgatory as a necessary stopping-point to attain to the proper sanctity that is becoming of inhabitants of heavenly glory. Therefore, it is neither true that all righteous dead before Christ went solely to Sheol, nor that all after his Resurrection went, and go, to Heaven. On the other hand, the reprobate dead in Sheol (or Hades) eventually are sentenced to Hell (Rev. 20:13-15).

Cardinal Newman comments:

> Our Savior, as we suppose, did not go to the abyss assigned to the fallen angels, but to those mysterious mansions where the souls of all men await the judgment. That He

went to the abode of blessed spirits is evident, from His words addressed to the robber on the cross, when He also called it Paradise; that He went to some other place besides Paradise may be conjectured from St. Peter's saying, 'He went and preached to the spirits in prison, who had once been disobedient' (1 Pet. 3:19-20). The circumstances, then, that these two abodes of disembodied good and bad, are called by one name, Hades . . . seems clearly to show that Paradise is not the same as Heaven, but a resting-place at the foot of it. Let it be further remarked, that Samuel, when brought from the dead, in the witch's cavern, said, 'Why hast thou disquieted me, to bring me up?' (1 Sam. 28:15), words which would seem quite inconsistent with his being then already in Heaven.[137]

> **1 Corinthians 3:11-15:** "For no other foundation can anyone lay than that which is laid, which is Jesus Christ. Now, if anyone builds on the foundation with gold, silver, precious stones, wood, hay, stubble — each man's work will become manifest; for the Day will disclose it, because it will be revealed with fire, and the fire will test what sort of work each one has done. If the work which any man has built on the foundation survives, he will receive a reward. If any man's work is burned up, he will suffer loss, though he himself will be saved, but only as through fire."

This is a clear and obvious allusion to Purgatory, or at least, even for the most skeptical person, something exceedingly similar to it. Thus thought the Church Fathers, such as St. Cyprian,[138] St.

[137] Sermon: "The Intermediate State," 1836.

[138] Bk. 4, epistle 2.

Ambrose,[139] St. Jerome,[140] St. Gregory the Great,[141] Origen,[142] and St. Augustine:

> Lord, rebuke me not in Your indignation, nor correct me in Your anger [Ps. 38:1]. . . . In this life may You cleanse me and make me such that I have no need of the corrective fire, which is for those who are saved, but as if by fire. . . . For it is said: "He shall be saved, but as if by fire" [1 Cor. 3:15]. And because it is said that he shall be saved, little is thought of that fire. Yet plainly, though we be saved by fire, that fire will be more severe than anything a man can suffer in this life.[143]

St. Francis de Sales observes:

> The Apostle uses two similitudes. The first is of an architect who with solid materials builds a valuable house on a rock; the second is of one who on the same foundation erects a house of boards, reeds, straw. Let us now imagine that a fire breaks out in both houses. That which is of solid material will be out of danger, and the other will be burnt to ashes. And if the architect be in the first, he will be whole and safe; if he be in the second, he must, if he would escape, rush through fire and flame, and shall be saved yet so that he will bear the marks of having been in fire. . . . The fire by which the architect is saved can only be understood of the fire of Purgatory. . . .
>
> When he . . . speaks of him who has built on the foundation, wood, straw, stubble, he shows that he is not speaking

139 Commentary on 1 Cor. 3; Sermon 20; Commentary on Ps. 116.

140 Commentary on Amos 4.

141 *Dialogues*, 4, 39.

142 Sixth homily on Exodus.

143 Explanations of the Psalms, 37, 3. From Jurgens, *FEF*, Vol. 3, 17.

of the fire which will precede the day of judgment, since by this will pass not only those who have built with these light materials, but also those who shall have built in gold, silver, etc. All this interpretation, besides that it agrees very well with the text, is also most authentic, as having been followed with common consent by the ancient Fathers.[144]

> **1 Corinthians 15:29:** "Otherwise, what do people mean by being baptized on behalf of the dead? If the dead are not raised at all, why are people baptized on their behalf?"

St. Francis de Sales:

This passage properly understood evidently shows that it was the custom of the primitive Church to watch, pray, and fast for the souls of the departed. For, firstly, in the Scriptures, to be baptized is often taken for afflictions and penances; as in Luke 12:50 . . . and in St. Mark 10:38-9 . . . in which places our Lord calls "pains and afflictions" baptism [cf. Matt. 3:11, 20:22-3; Luke 3:16].

This, then, is the sense of that Scripture: if the dead rise not again, what is the use of mortifying and afflicting oneself, of praying and fasting for the dead? And indeed this sentence of St. Paul resembles that of 2 Maccabees 12:44 [cited above]: "It is superfluous and vain to pray for the dead if the dead rise not again." . . . Now, it was not for those in Paradise [Heaven], who had no need of it, nor for those in Hell, who could get no benefit from it; it was, then, for those in Purgatory. Thus did St. Ephraim [d. 373] expound it.[145]

[144] St. Francis de Sales, *CON*, 360-362.

[145] Ibid., 368-369.

The "penance" interpretation is supported contextually by the next three verses, where the apostle speaks of being in peril every hour and dying every day. St. Paul certainly doesn't condemn the practice, whatever it is (his question being merely rhetorical). Given these facts, and the striking resemblance to 2 Maccabees 12:44, the traditional Catholic interpretation seems the most plausible.

In any event, Protestants are at almost a complete loss in coherently explaining this verse — one of the most difficult in the New Testament for them to interpret. It simply does not comport with their theology, which utterly disallows any penitential or prayerful efforts on behalf of the deceased.

> **2 Corinthians 5:10:** "For we must all appear before the judgment seat of Christ, so that each one may receive good or evil, according to what he has done in the body."

Our sins are judged here rather than forgiven, and this takes place in the next life. The standard Protestant theology of the judgment seat of Christ is not dissimilar to the notion of the chastising purifications of Purgatory. There is a direct relation between judgment and the purging of sin. We are punished, in some fashion — or so St. Paul tells us in this verse — for evil deeds done. The pains of Purgatory are roughly identical, or else highly akin, to this punishment, since they are the taking away of those sinful habits, tendencies, and affinities to which we have become attached. Conversely, we are rewarded for good deeds. As there are differential rewards for righteousness, so there are differential sufferings in Purgatory for unrighteousness, so that a certain parallelism exists between the two concepts.

This passage is a sort of liaison between the theological categories of justification and Purgatory (and penance) — the former being the "positive" establishment of sanctity, and the latter being the "negative" removal of unholiness. This congruity between reward and punishment is even more clearly seen in 1 Corinthians 3:11-15, where St. Paul freely intermingles rewards and punishments, in the context of purgatorial fire. Given the obvious affinity of that passage with this one, each can be legitimately interpreted in light of the other. In doing so, the Catholic interpretation, with its distinctive understanding of faith and works, penance and Purgatory, is more satisfactory exegetically than the usual Protestant interpretations, which are uncomfortable, by and large, with differential rewards and punishments (seeing these as somewhat incompatible with faith alone).

> **2 Corinthians 7:1:** "Let us cleanse ourselves from every defilement of body and spirit, and make holiness perfect in the fear of God" (see also 1 Thess. 3:13; 4:7).

Here is a description of that analogous process of sanctification in this life which will be greatly intensified and made completely efficacious in the next, in Purgatory.

> **Philippians 2:10-11:** "At the name of Jesus, every knee should bow, in Heaven and on earth and under the earth, and every tongue confess that Jesus Christ is Lord, to the glory of God the Father."

> **Revelation 5:3, 13:** "And no one in Heaven or on earth or under the earth was able to open the scroll or to look into it. . . . And I heard every creature in Heaven and on earth and under the earth and in the sea, and all therein, saying, 'To him who sits upon the throne and to the Lamb be blessing and honor and glory and might forever and ever!' "

If God refuses to receive prayer, praise, and worship from the unrepentant sinner (Ps. 66:18; Prov. 1:28-30; Isa. 1:15, 59:2; Jer.

6:20; Amos 5:21-24; Mic. 3:4; Mal. 1:10; John 9:31; Heb. 10:38), why would he permit the damned to undertake this practice?

Furthermore, if God does not compel human beings to follow him and to enjoy his presence for eternity contrary to their free will, then it seems that he would not — as far as we can tell from Scripture — compel them to praise Him, as this would be meaningless, if not repulsive.

Therefore, "under the earth" must refer to Purgatory. Revelation 5:13 especially makes sense under this interpretation, as the praise spoken there does not in any way appear forced, but rather, heartfelt and seemingly spontaneous, which would not be at all expected of persons eternally consigned to Hell (see Matt. 8:29; Luke 4:34, 8:28; James 2:19).

Some Protestant commentators readily admit that "under the earth" is a reference to those in Sheol, or Hades. Granting this interpretation for the sake of argument, most Protestants would presumably regard Hades in this instance (after Christ's death — see Revelation 5:12) as simply the "holding tank" for those ultimately destined for Hell (the elect having been taken to Heaven by Christ). But this leads straight back to the exegetical problem of God's neither desiring nor accepting such praise from even the obstinate sinner, let alone the damned.

The acceptance of a third, intermediate state in the afterlife for the righteous as well as the reprobate, even after Christ's Resurrection, is a seriously troublesome position if one holds to the tenets of mainstream Reformational eschatological theology. For, given the Protestant view on justification, why would (or should) there be a second state for the "saved" once the road to Heaven was paved by Christ? This state of affairs leads inexorably to considerations of differential merit and reward, such that a whole class is relegated to continued separation from Christ in some partial sense, and by implication, punishment, since these children of God have not yet attained to full union with God in eternal happiness and bliss.

Once it is conceded that (dead) righteous men praise God from "under the earth," the standard Protestant position of all the saved "going straight to Heaven at death" crumbles, for the simple reason that this group is contrasted with those in Heaven. Furthermore, a position that "under the earth" refers metaphorically to merely all dead righteous (who, according to Protestantism are in Heaven), makes the phraseology of Philippians 2:10 and Revelation 5:3, 13 absurdly redundant, since St. Paul and St. John would be saying, "Those in Heaven, and on earth, and in Heaven . . ."

Again, the only reasonable alternate interpretation, given all the above data, is to posit the existence of Purgatory, from which praise to God emanates — it being that portion of the Church stationed for a time in the portico of Heaven, so to speak.

> **2 Timothy 1:16-18:** "May the Lord grant mercy to the household of Onesiphorus, for he often refreshed me; he was not ashamed of my chains, but when he arrived in Rome, he searched for me eagerly and found me — may the Lord grant him to find mercy from the Lord on that Day — and you well know all the service he rendered at Ephesus."

Onesiphorus appears to be dead at the time St. Paul writes this letter to Timothy. If that is true, then Paul is praying for the dead. A well-known Protestant commentary[146] admits that Onesiphorus is likely dead, citing the cross-reference of 2 Timothy 4:19, yet takes the remarkably incoherent position that St. Paul is praying for his conduct in life and reward at the Judgment. Thus, the admitted prayer (2 Tim. 1:18), since it supposedly refers to the earthly life of the intended recipient, somehow thereby ceases to

[146] *The New Bible Commentary*, 1178. The Lutheran Johannes Bengel (1687-1752) and the Anglican Henry Alford (1810-1871) who were both highly respected expositors, also held that Onesiphorus was dead.

be a prayer for the dead, even though it is pleading for mercy on the Day of Judgment for one who has indeed departed!

Now, of course, St. Paul could also pray for a living person to be recompensed justly by God, but this is missing the point and is an example of the classic logical fallacy of proposing a "distinction without a difference." For what distinguishes prayers for a living or a dead man, where the final judgment is concerned?

Protestants say that it is impermissible to pray for the dead on this score, since their fate is already sealed and it will be to no avail. The error here lies in the fact that the person's fate had always been known (God being omniscient and out of time, foreordaining in a mysterious way the beginning and end of all things). In both cases, our knowledge is paltry and altogether insufficient as to the person's destiny. We pray out of charity (or "desire," as it were), and because we are commanded to, having been assured by the inspired biblical revelation that it has an effect.

The Jamieson, Fausset, and Brown commentary, another respected Evangelical reference, takes a different position: "His household would hardly retain his name after the master was dead. . . . Nowhere has Paul prayers for the dead, which is fatal to the theory . . . that he was dead."[147]

But *Word Pictures in the New Testament*, a linguistic commentary by the great Greek scholar A. T. Robertson, states: "Apparently Onesiphorus is now dead as is implied by the wish in 1:18."[148]

On the face of it, why couldn't St. Paul be referring to the house of Onesiphorus in the same sense in which we speak of a deceased person's "surviving wife and children"? His statement in 1:18 is similar to our spontaneous utterances at funerals, such as "May God rest his soul," etc. (sometimes spoken or thought,

[147] *Commentary on the Whole Bible*, 1376.

[148] A. T. Robertson, *Word Pictures in the New Testament* (Nashville: Broadman Press, 1930), Vol. 4, 615.

despite theologies to the contrary). And if Paul is "wishing" for benefits for the soul of a dead man, as Robertson holds, how is this essentially any different from praying for the dead?

To conclude, of the three prominent Evangelical Protestant commentaries surveyed, two hold that St. Paul is "praying," and one that he is "wishing." Two conclude that Onesiphorus is probably dead, with a third denying this. It might be supposed with good reason that if reputable, scholarly Protestant commentators are more or less forced into (for them) uncomfortable positions due to the inescapable clarity of a text, perhaps the Catholic interpretation is the best one, as it requires no unnatural straining. All that is necessary is the willingness to accept the practice of prayers for the dead, for which there is ample scriptural warrant, Jewish precedent, and abundant support in the early Christian Church, as will be demonstrated subsequently.

> **Hebrews 12:14:** "Strive for peace with all men, and for the holiness without which no one will see the Lord" (see also Heb. 12:1, 5-11, 15, 23; Eph. 5:5; 1 Thess. 4:3; 1 John 3:2-3).

Cardinal Newman writes:

> The truth itself is declared in one form or another in every part of Scripture. It is told us again and again, that to make sinful creatures holy was the great end which our Lord had in view in taking upon Himself our nature, and thus none but the holy will be accepted for His sake at the last day. The whole history of redemption, the covenant of mercy in all its parts and provisions, attests the necessity of holiness in order to salvation; as indeed even our natural conscience bears witness also. . . .
>
> Even supposing a man of unholy life were suffered to enter Heaven, he would not be happy there; so that it would

> be no mercy to permit him to enter. . . . We conclude that any man, whatever his habits, tastes, or manner of life, if once admitted into Heaven, would be happy there. . . . [But] here every man can do his own pleasure, but there he must do God's pleasure. . . . "Let us alone! What have we to do with Thee?" is the sole thought and desire of unclean souls, even while they acknowledge His majesty. None but the holy can look upon the Holy One; without holiness no man can endure to see the Lord. . . .
>
> Heaven is not Heaven, is not a place of happiness except to the holy. . . . There is a moral malady which disorders the inward sight and taste; and no man laboring under it is in a condition to enjoy what Scripture calls the fullness of joy in God's presence, and pleasures at His right hand forevermore.[149]

Newman explains (in effect) why Purgatory (which he accepts elsewhere, even before his conversion to Catholicism in 1845) is a necessary and, indeed, ultimately desirable process for all of us imperfect sinners to undergo, in order to approach God properly in his unfathomable majesty and holiness.

> **Hebrews 12:29:** "Our God is a consuming fire" (see also Exod. 3:2-6, 19:18, 24:17; Num. 31:23; Deut. 4:24, 9:3; Ps. 66:10-12; Mal. 3:2, 4:1; Heb. 10:27, 31).

> **Revelation 21:27:** "But nothing unclean shall enter it, nor anyone who practices abomination or falsehood, but only those who are written in the Lamb's book of life."

The relevance of this biblical data in terms of its analogy to the idea of Purgatory is very clear. The abundance of such scriptural

[149] Sermon: "Holiness Necessary for Future Blessedness," 1834.

evidence for Purgatory led to a consensus among the Church Fathers as well. Protestant church historian Philip Schaff, who can definitely be considered a "hostile witness" as pertains this topic, summarized the belief of the early Christian Church:

> These views of the middle state in connection with prayers for the dead show a strong tendency to the Roman Catholic doctrine of Purgatory. . . . There are traces of the purgatorial idea of suffering the temporal consequences of sin, and a painful struggle after holiness. . . . The common people and most of the fathers understood it of a material fire; but this is not a matter of faith. . . . A material fire would be very harmless without a material body.[150]

Despite all this, Protestantism rejected the beliefs in Purgatory and prayers for the dead, with the exception of Anglicans, many of whom have retained some form of these. C. S. Lewis was one of these traditional Anglicans. In one of his last books, *Letters to Malcolm: Chiefly on Prayer,* he stated that he prayed for the dead, among whom were many of his loved ones, and that he believed in Purgatory, comparing it to an intense rinsing of the mouth at the dentist's office. He thought no one would want to enter Heaven unclean, as this would be downright embarrassing.[151]

[150] Philip Schaff, *History of the Christian Church,* Vol. 2, ch. 12, sects. 156, 604-606.

[151] Lewis, *Letters to Malcolm: Chiefly on Prayer,* 107-109.

Chapter Eight

Penance

"Share Christ's sufferings"

The doctrine of penance was dogmatically defined at the Council of Trent in its Session 14, November 25, 1551:

> Finally, as regards satisfaction — which as it is, of all the parts of penance, that which has been at all times recommended to the Christian people by our Fathers . . . the holy synod declares that it is wholly false, and alien from the word of God, that the guilt is never forgiven by the Lord without the whole punishment also being therewith pardoned. For clear and illustrious examples are found in the Sacred Writings (Gen. 3:16 ff.; Num. 12:14 ff., 20:11 ff.; 2 Sam. 12:13 ff., etc.), whereby, besides by divine tradition, this error is refuted in the plainest manner possible. . . .
>
> For, doubtless, these satisfactory punishments greatly recall from sin and check, as it were, with a bridle and make penitents more cautious and watchful for the future; they are also remedies for the remains of sin, and, by acts of the opposite virtues, they remove the habits acquired by evil living. Neither indeed was there ever in the Church of God any way accounted surer to turn aside the impending chastisement

of the Lord than that men should, with true sorrow of mind, practice these works of penitence (e.g., Matt. 3:8; 4:17; 11:21). Add to these things that, whilst we thus, by making satisfaction, suffer for our sins, we are made conformable to *Jesus Christ,* who satisfied for our sins (Rom. 5:10; 1 John 2:1 ff.), *from whom all our sufficiency is* (2 Cor. 3:5); having also thereby a most sure pledge that, *if we suffer with Him, we shall also be glorified with Him* (Rom. 8:17). But *neither is this satisfaction,* which we discharge for our sins, so our own as not to be through Jesus Christ. For we who can do nothing of ourselves, *as of ourselves, can do all things, He cooperating who strengthens us* (Phil. 4:13). Thus, man has not wherein to glory, but *all our glorying is in Christ* (1 Cor. 1:31; 2 Cor. 10:17; Gal. 6:14): in whom we live; *in whom we merit* (cf. Acts 17:28); in whom we satisfy; bringing forth fruits worthy of penance (Luke 3:8), which *from Him have their efficacy;* by Him are offered to the Father; and *through Him are accepted by the Father. . . .*

For the ancient Fathers . . . teach that the keys of the priests were given, not to loose only, but also to bind (Matt. 16:19, 18:18; John 20:23). But not, therefore, did they imagine that the Sacrament of Penance is a tribunal of wrath or of punishments; even as *no Catholic ever thought that, by this kind of satisfactions on our parts, the efficacy of the merit and of the satisfaction of our Lord Jesus Christ is either obscured or in any way lessened;* which when the innovators seek to understand, they in such wise maintain a new life to be the best penance as to take away the entire efficacy and use of satisfaction.[152]

[152] *On the Most Holy Sacrament of Penance and Extreme Unction,* Ch. 8: "On the Necessity and on the Fruit of Satisfaction" (emphasis added). In the same session, the Council produced several Canons on the Most Holy Sacrament of Penance, among which are the following:

Catholic apologist Bertrand Conway elaborates:

Not only must the sinner be truly sorry for his sins; he must also make satisfaction for them. Even when sins have been pardoned by God, there often remains the liability to temporal punishment to atone for the injury done Him, and to bring about the sinner's reformation. God often requires satisfaction of the sinner for the transgression of His laws, both natural and supernatural. The impure man may be forgiven his sin, and yet be punished for his immorality by ill health; the murderer may be pardoned his crime, and yet have to expiate it in the electric chair.

The Scriptures tell us that God pardoned Adam his disobedience, the Israelites in the desert their murmuring and idolatry, Moses his lack of faith, and David his murder, adultery, and pride; but they were all severely punished by Him

Canon III: "If anyone saith that those words of the Lord the Savior: 'Receive ye the Holy Ghost, whose sins you shall forgive, they are forgiven them, and whose sins you shall retain, they are retained' (John 20:22 ff.), are not to be understood of the power of forgiving and of retaining sins in the sacrament of Penance, as the Catholic Church has always from the beginning understood them; but wrests them, contrary to the institution of this sacrament, to the power of preaching the Gospel; let him be anathema."

Canon XII: "If anyone saith that God always remits the whole punishment together with the guilt, and that the satisfaction of penitents is no other than the faith whereby they apprehend that Christ has satisfied for them; let him be anathema."

Canon XIV: "If anyone saith that the satisfactions by which penitents redeem their sins through Jesus Christ are not a worship of God, but traditions of men, which obscure the doctrine of grace and the true worship of God and the benefit itself of the death of Christ; let him be anathema."

See also CCC, pars. 1422-1429, 1436, 1446, 1448, 1450, 1470, 1472-1473, 1480, 1496; Hardon, *PCD*, 271, 320, 382, 396; and Hardon, CC, 481-500, 555-561.

(Gen. 3:19; Exod. 22:14, 27; Num. 14:20-23, 20:12; Deut. 32:51-52; 2 Sam. 12:13-14, ch. 24). St. Paul also speaks of sickness and death as temporal punishments for unworthy Communions (1 Cor. 11:30-32).[153]

Catholic theologian Ludwig Ott further explains:

The virtue of penance, which is insistently recommended in both the Old and New Testaments (cf. Ezek. 18:21 ff., 33:11; Jer. 18:11, 25:5 ff.; Joel 2:12 ff.; Matt. 3:2, 4:17; Acts 2:38), and which at all times was a necessary precondition for the forgiveness of sins, is that moral virtue, which inclines the will to turn away inwardly from sin, and to render atonement to God for it. . . .

External manifestations of the virtue of penance are the confession of sins, the performance of penitential works of every kind; for example, prayer, fasting, almsgiving, mortifications, and the patient bearing of all trials sent by God. . . .

The faithful on earth can, by their good works performed in the state of grace, render atonement for one another. The effect of the atonement is the remission of temporal punishment for sin. The possibility of vicarious atonement is founded in the unity of the Mystical Body. As Christ, the Head, in His expiatory sufferings, took the place of the members, so also one member can take the place of another. The doctrine of indulgences is based on the possibility and reality of vicarious atonement. . . .

Even in the Old Testament the idea of vicarious atonement by innocent persons for guilty is known. The innocent person takes on himself responsibility for the displeasure of God which the guilty person has merited, in order by sacrifice to win again the divine favor for the latter. Moses

[153] Conway, *The Question Box*, 293.

> offers himself to God as a sacrifice for the people who sinned (Exod. 32:32). Job brings God a burnt offering, in order to expiate the sins of his children (Job 1:5). . . .
>
> The Apostle Paul teaches that also the faithful can rend expiation for one another (Col. 1:24; 2 Cor. 12:15; 2 Tim. 4:6). . . .
>
> The possibility of meriting for others is based on the friendship of God for the just, and on the Communion of Saints. More effective than such merit is prayer for others. Cf. James 5:16: "Pray for one another, that you may be saved, for the continual prayer of a just man availeth much" (cf. 1 Tim. 2:1-4).[154]

In the sacrament of Penance, it is required for a Catholic who commits a mortal sin to repent (express contrition),[155] confess the sin to a priest,[156] and be absolved by the priest (absolution)[157] in the name of Christ (Matt. 18:18; John 20:23).[158] Grace is received

[154] Ott, *Fundamentals of Catholic Dogma,* 416, 317, 269.

[155] CCC, pars. 1430-1433, 1439, 1451-1454, 1490, 1492.

[156] CCC, pars. 1455-1457, 1484, 1491, 1493, 1495, 1497, 2490.

[157] CCC, pars. 1449, 1463, 1484, 1495.

[158] CCC, pars. 1441-1442, 1444-1445, 1461-1462, 1465-1467, 1485. G. K. Chesterton, the famous writer and convert to Catholicism, wrote of Confession:

"When people ask me, or indeed anyone else, 'Why did you join the Church of Rome?' the first essential answer, if it is partly an elliptical answer, is, 'To get rid of my sins.' For there is no other religious system that does really profess to get rid of people's sins. It is confirmed by the logic, which to many seems startling, by which the Church deduces that sin confessed and adequately repented is actually abolished; and that the sinner does really begin again as if he had never sinned. . . .

"When a Catholic comes from Confession, he does truly, by definition, step out again into that dawn of his own beginning and look with new eyes across the world. . . . He believes that in that dim corner, and in that brief ritual, God has really

in absolution that will help to prevent future sin. The priest also assigns a penance to be performed to remove the temporal punishment due to sin.[159] This expiation of moral transgressions is called satisfaction.[160] Venial sins may be confessed to a priest also (as the Church recommends), but this is not a binding requirement for a Catholic.[161] These sins can be confessed directly to God, with whatever penance the contrite believer deems appropriate.

As penance is the imposition of (and, it is hoped, voluntary acceptance of) temporal punishment or penalties for sin, so indulgences are the remission or relaxation of these same temporal penalties, by virtue of the prayer and penitence (of various sorts) of others in the Church.[162] The doctrine of indulgences presupposes both the Communion of Saints[163] and the treasury of merits, ultimately derived from the Person and work of Jesus Christ, secondarily through the holiness of the saints, especially the Blessed Virgin.[164]

remade him in His own image. He is now a new experiment of the Creator. He is as much a new experiment as he was when he was really only five years old. . . .

"The Sacrament of Penance gives a new life, and reconciles a man to all living, but it does not do it as the optimists and the hedonists and the heathen preachers of happiness do it. The gift is given at a price, and is conditioned by a confession. In other words, the name of the price is Truth, which may also be called Reality; but it is facing the reality about oneself. When the process is only applied to other people, it is called Realism" (*Autobiography* [New York: Sheed and Ward, 1936], 340-342).

159 CCC, pars. 1460, 1494.

160 CCC, pars. 1032, 1434-1435, 1437-1438, 1459.

161 CCC, pars. 1458, 1464, 1493.

162 CCC, pars. 1471, 1498; Hardon, CC, 560-570; Hardon, *PCD*, 193-194; Council of Trent, Session 25 (December 3-4, 1563), *Decree Concerning Indulgences*.

163 CCC, pars. 1474-1475, 1479.

164 CCC, pars. 1476-1477.

The Church has the jurisdiction mercifully to dispense these accumulated merits to those who possess less merit (see 1 Cor. 12:26).[165] Indulgences are a logical extension of infused justification and penance, and are essentially the same as any spiritual or temporal benefit applied to a person due to the prayer of another. In both cases, one Christian is assisted by the loving act of another.

The Council of Trent forbade the selling of indulgences, since abuses had become scandalous in the preceding period, thus agreeing with Luther and the Protestants on this point, while retaining the doctrine itself (not wanting to "throw the baby out with the bath water").[166] In recent decrees on this doctrine, the Church has

[165] CCC, par. 1478.

[166] In *The Question Box* (pp. 296-297), Bertrand Conway writes of the controversial history of indulgences:

"Catholic historians . . . have frequently mentioned the abuses connected with the preaching of Indulgences in the Middle Ages. The medieval pardoner . . . was often an unscrupulous rascal, whose dishonesty and fraud were condemned by the Bishops of the time. We find orders for their arrest in Germany at the Council of Mainz in 1261, and in England by order of the Bishop of Durham in 1340. To indict the Church for these abuses . . . is manifestly dishonest. . . .

"It is comparatively easy today to get monies for any charitable enterprise, for we can appeal to thousands by letter, post, radio, or the daily press. In the Middle Ages, when men wished to build a church or support a worthy charity, the Bishop or Pope granted an Indulgence, which first of all called upon the people to approach the Sacraments of Penance and the Eucharist, and then 'to lend a helping hand' in some special work of charity. The Council of Trent, following the Councils of Fourth Lateran [1215], Lyons [1245 and 1274], and Vienne [1311-1312], condemned in express terms 'the wicked abuse of quaestors of alms,' and, because of the great scandal they had given, 'abolished their name and use' (Session 24).

"While Catholics believe that the building of St. Peter's in Rome was a matter of interest to the whole Catholic world, they heartily condemn with Grisar and Janssen [Catholic

stressed that the pious disposition of the receiver of an indulgence is of foremost and primary importance (similar to the use of sacramentals, such as holy water).[167]

To summarize, Catholics believe that sin causes a cosmic disturbance and is a direct insult to God, our Creator, and that it also perpetuates destructive tendencies and practices in the individual

historians] the manner of financing the Indulgence, and the exaggerations of the preachers in extolling unduly its effects and privileges.

"No one believes today the calumnies against Tetzel's character. Luther did not speak the truth when he asserted that 'Tetzel sold grace for money at the highest price.' As both Pastor and Grisar point out, we must carefully distinguish between Tetzel's teaching with regard to Indulgences for the living, and Indulgences applicable to the dead. With regard to Indulgences for the living, his teaching, as we know from his Vorlegung and his Frankfort Theses, was perfectly Catholic. . . .

" 'As regards Indulgences for the dead,' Pastor writes, 'there is no doubt that Tetzel did, according to what he considered his authoritative instructions, proclaim as Christian doctrine that nothing but an offering of money was required to gain the Indulgence for the dead, without there being any question of contrition or confession. He also taught, in accordance with an opinion then held, that an Indulgence could be applied to any given soul with unfailing effect. . . . The Papal Bull of Indulgence gave no sanction whatever to this proposition. It was a vague scholastic opinion, rejected by the Sorbonne in 1482, and again in 1518, and certainly not a doctrine of the Church' (*History of the Popes*, Vol. 7, 349). Cardinal Cajetan at the time condemned Tetzel's opinion, and taught that 'while we may presume in a general way that God is willing to accept Indulgences for the dead, we have no certainty whatever that He does so in any particular case. That is the secret of God alone.' In 1477 Pope Sixtus IV had expressly taught that the Church applies Indulgences for the dead 'by way of suffrage,' for the souls in Purgatory are no longer subject to her jurisdiction. They receive Indulgences not directly, but indirectly, through the intercession of the living."

[167] Pope Paul VI, *Apostolic Constitution on the Revision of Indulgences* (1967).

and disastrous results within the Church and the human community.[168] Sin effects a breach in our "friendship" with God, which requires some sort of reparation.[169]

Penance and indulgences are complementary aspects of the thoroughly biblical and harmonious Catholic system of theology wherein actual, infused justification (as opposed to merely imputed, forensic, or declared justification) takes place. If indeed, God's goal is to free us of sin in this life — as Catholics believe — then the expiation and elimination of sin is of the utmost importance: hence the doctrine and practice of penance.

Scriptural evidence for Penance

> **Exodus 32:30:** "Moses said to the people, 'You have sinned a great sin. And now I will go up to the Lord; perhaps I can make atonement for your sin' " (read also 32:31-32).

Here we have an example of vicarious atonement, whereby one member of the chosen people (analogous, of course, to the Church), sought to atone for others. This concept is essentially no different from intercessory prayer. The Catholic Church simply takes it further by stating that various works of charity, as well as voluntary and involuntary suffering, are efficacious for the purpose of blessing others and atoning for their sins. Furthermore, the notion of ritual blood atonement is common throughout the Old Testament (e.g., Exod. 29, 30; Lev. 4, 14, 16).

Such sacrifices were certainly but shadows of the great Atonement of Christ on the Cross. Yet they also prefigured vicarious atonement between and among Christians, since Moses, the priests, etc., were mere men who atoned for the Israelites in the sense of participating in the rituals foreordained and empowered by God.

[168] CCC, pars. 980, 1440, 1443-1445, 1469, 1488.

[169] CCC, pars. 980, 1440, 1468.

> **Numbers 14:19-23:** " 'Pardon the iniquity of this people, I pray thee, according to the greatness of thy steadfast love, and according as thou hast forgiven this people, from Egypt even until now.' Then the Lord said, 'I have pardoned, according to your word; but truly, as I live, and as all the earth shall be filled with the glory of the Lord, none of the men who have seen my glory and my signs which I wrought in Egypt and in the wilderness, and yet have put me to the proof these ten times and have not hearkened to my voice, shall see the land which I swore to give to their fathers; and none of those who despised me shall see it.' "

God forgave the Israelites (14:20), due, at least in part to Moses' intercession (14:19). Yet punishment, or penance, remained (14:23) because of their exceedingly great disobedience, despite seeing signs and wonders (14:22). Thus, forgiveness is not complete in the sense that it removes all the ramifications of sin, or "cancels out" any further need for satisfaction and penitential acts, either undertaken voluntarily, ordered by legitimate Church authority, or ordained by God Himself by means of trials and tribulations.

> **Numbers 16:46-48:** "And Moses said to Aaron, 'Take your censer, and put fire therein from off the altar, and lay incense on it, and carry it quickly to the congregation, and make an atonement for them; for wrath has gone forth from the Lord; the plague has begun.' So Aaron took it as Moses said, and ran into the midst of the assembly; and, behold, the plague had already begun among the people; and he put on the incense, and made atonement for the people. And he stood between the dead and the living; and the plague was stopped."

This is another clear example of vicarious atonement, as in Exodus 32:30-32.

> **Numbers 25:11-13:** "Phinehas the son of Eleazar, son of Aaron the priest, has turned back my wrath from the people of Israel, in that he was jealous with my jealousy among them, so that I did not consume the people of Israel in my jealousy. Therefore say, 'Behold, I give to him my covenant of peace; and it shall be to him, and to his descendants after him, the covenant of a perpetual priesthood, because he was jealous for his God, and made atonement for the people of Israel' " (read also Num. 25:6-10).

It is no more foolish to believe that God's wrath can be ameliorated by acts (works) of obedience to his laws (in this case, the prevention of fornication and idolatry; see Numbers 25:1-5) than to believe the same is accomplished by intercessory prayer (as in Exodus 32:31-32). Both penitential acts exemplify unselfish love for others and are qualitatively equivalent. Such good works bring about a better relationship with God and improve the spiritual state of others in the Body of Christ, thus maintaining the communal nature of Christianity and the Church.

> **2 Samuel 12:13-14:** "David said to Nathan, 'I have sinned against the Lord.' And Nathan said to David, 'The Lord also has put away your sin; you shall not die. Nevertheless, because by this deed you have utterly scorned the Lord, the child that is born to you shall die.' "

Again, the sinner David was forgiven, but the temporal punishment was not obliterated (his child was to die; particular sins often harm the innocent who have nothing to do with them), as in Catholic teaching.

> **Proverbs 16:6:** "By loyalty and faithfulness iniquity is atoned for, and by the fear of the Lord a man avoids evil."

This principle is not unlike Catholic penance, in which sin is atoned for. Such penance and the sanctification resulting therefrom is not inconsistent with the Atonement of Christ, from which all these benefits flow as a stream from the ocean. In Protestantism, Christ's Atonement makes all lesser participatory atonements null and void. Neither Scripture nor logic, however, requires such a false dichotomy.

> **Matthew 10:38:** "And he who does not take his cross and follow me is not worthy of me."

> **Matthew 16:24:** "Then Jesus told his disciples, 'If any man would come after me, let him deny himself and take up his cross and follow me' " (see also Mark 8:34-35).

The disciple of Christ is called to suffer (Matt. 10:22; Mark 10:37-39; Luke 6:22; Acts 14:22; Rom. 5:3-5; 2 Cor. 12:7-10; Phil. 1:29; 1 Thess. 3:3; 2 Tim. 1:8, 2:3, 3:12; Heb. 5:8; James 1:2-4, 12; 1 Pet. 1:6-7, 2:20-21, 4:12-19; Rev. 1:9). No biblically informed Christian would dispute that. Controversy arises only over whether such sufferings can improve one's estate vis-à-vis salvation, or help anyone else in the Body of Christ. Catholics believe that all our sufferings can be a source of grace for the one experiencing them, as well as helpful with regard to the spiritual graces of another (Rom. 15:1; 1 Cor. 12:24-26), to whom these penitential sufferings are applied (as in intercessory prayer), thus giving suffering the highest possible purpose and meaning.

Furthermore, the painful experience of being corrected by God, as parents discipline their children (Lev. 26:23-24; Deut. 8:2, 5; 2 Sam. 7:14; Job 5:17-18; Ps. 89:30-34, 94:12, 103:9,

118:18, 119:67, 71, 75; Prov. 3:11-12; Isa. 48:10; Jer. 10:24, 30:11, 31:18; Zech. 13:9; Mal. 3:3; 1 Cor. 11:32; Heb. 12:5-11; Rev. 3:19), is quite similar to the Catholic notion of temporal punishments for sin, which can be lessened by penance.

St. Paul explicitly expounds the Catholic doctrine of penance, suffering, and vicarious atonement in the following passages:

> **Romans 8:13, 17:** "For if you live according to the flesh, you will die, but if by the Spirit you put to death the deeds of the body, you will live. . . . And if [we are] children, then heirs, heirs of God and fellow heirs with Christ, provided we suffer with him in order that we may also be glorified with him" (see also 1 Cor. 15:31; 2 Cor. 6:9, 1 Pet. 4:1, 13).

> **1 Corinthians 11:27, 30:** "Whoever, therefore, eats the bread or drinks the cup of the Lord in an unworthy manner will be guilty of profaning the body and blood of the Lord. . . . That is why many of you are weak and ill, and some have died" (see also 1 Cor. 5:5; 11:31-32).

> **2 Corinthians 4:10:** ". . . always carrying in the body the death of Jesus, so that the life of Jesus may also be manifested in our bodies" (see also 2 Cor. 1:5-7).

> **Philippians 2:17:** "Even if I am to be poured out as a libation upon the sacrificial offering of your faith, I am glad and rejoice with you all" (see also 2 Cor. 6:4-10).

> **Philippians 3:10:** "That I may know him and the power of his Resurrection, and may share his sufferings, becoming like him in his death" (see also Gal. 2:20).

> **2 Timothy 4:6:** "For I am already on the point of being sacrificed; the time of my departure has come" (see also Rom. 12:1).

In this verse and in Philippians 2:17, the Greek word for "libation" and "sacrifice" is *spendomai*. In the Septuagint, the Greek translation of the Old Testament, which was the Bible of the early Christians, this term is used for a variety of offerings and sacrifices commanded by the Mosaic Law (e.g., Gen. 35:14; Exod. 29:12, 38 ff.; Lev. 4:7 ff., 23:37). Most intriguing is its occurrence with reference to the Messiah, Jesus, in Isaiah 53:12: "He poured out his soul to death." It appears, then, that St. Paul is stressing a mystical, profound identification with Jesus even in his death (as also in 2 Cor. 4:10 and Phil. 3:10 above).

This comparison leads inexorably to the Catholic doctrine of vicarious atonement among members of the Body of Christ. In some mysterious, glorious way, God chooses to involve us in the very Redemption (always in a secondary and derivative sense, but actual nonetheless), just as he voluntarily involves us in his providence by means of prayer and evangelism, and in his creation by our procreation and childbirth. Our sufferings become identified with those of Christ. (Instances of the stigmata, whereby saintly persons — such as St. Francis of Assisi — actually receive the wounds of Christ in their bodies, are an extremely graphic image of this scriptural teaching.)

Since we are the Body of Christ (1 Cor. 12:27; Eph. 1:22-23, 5:30; Col. 1:24 below), such a "radical" convergence is not to be unexpected. For instance, when St. Paul was converted to Christ, Jesus said to him, "I am Jesus, whom you are persecuting" (Acts 9:5). This couldn't literally refer to Jesus the Divine Person, since he had already ascended to Heaven (Acts 1:9-11). Rather, Jesus meant that Christ's Church really was his Body, whom Paul (Saul) was persecuting (Acts 8:1, 3; 9:1-2). Jesus also identifies the

Church with himself in Matthew 25:34-45 (25:40 — "brethren"; cf. Matt. 12:50, 28:1; John 20:17). Thus, Jesus' sufferings are ours, and ours are his in a very real sense, as St. Paul unmistakably teaches, particularly and most strikingly in Colossians 1:24:

> **Colossians 1:24:** "Now I rejoice in my sufferings for your sake, and in my flesh I complete what is lacking in Christ's afflictions for the sake of his body, that is, the church" (see also 2 Cor. 11:23-30; Gal. 6:17).

A *Catholic Commentary on Holy Scripture* offers a precise explanation of the two traditional Catholic interpretations of this extraordinary verse:[170]

> What are the sufferings, or afflictions, of Christ to which Paul brings (along with the operation of Christ) completeness? . . . There are two opinions, each of which has Catholic supporters. First, the afflictions are those endured by Christ. The Passion is complete, infinite in its atoning or satisfactory power. To this power neither St. Paul nor anyone else could add anything. But the application of the merits of Christ's Passion to individual souls involves a toll of suffering, especially on the part of those chosen by Christ as his ministers (cf. 1 Cor. 3:9). . . . His sufferings are in union with those of Christ. They are the vehicle for conveying the Passion to the hearts and souls of men, and in this way they bring completeness to the Passion in an external way. . . .
>
> The other opinion regards the sufferings of Christ as those of the Mystical Body (cf. Acts 9:14). St. Augustine (*Enarr. in Ps.* 62, 4): "Thou [member of Christ's Body] sufferest so much as was to be contributed out of thy sufferings to the whole sufferings of Christ, that hath suffered in

[170] Dom Bernard Orchard, ed. (London: Thomas Nelson and Sons, 1953), 1135.

our Head, and doth suffer in his members, that is, in our own selves." The Passion of Christ, then, is continued in the members of his Body, the Church. This fits in with the truth that the Church is in a real though mystical sense Christ himself. . . .

The first opinion seems preferable; it gives the ordinary sense of the phrase "the sufferings of Christ." In either opinion, we are presented with an important lesson: suffering can be, not a terrifying enigma in our eyes, but something very precious, since it is the instrument God chose to redeem us, and we can make our sufferings serve in the cause of Christ's Passion (cf. Rom. 8:18, 28).

Biblical evidence for indulgences

Matthew 16:19: "I will give you the keys of the kingdom of Heaven, and whatever you bind on earth shall be bound in Heaven, and whatever you loose on earth shall be loosed in Heaven."

Matthew 18:18: "Whatever you bind on earth shall be bound in Heaven, and whatever you loose on earth shall be loosed in Heaven."

John 20:23: "If you forgive the sins of any, they are forgiven; if you retain the sins of any, they are retained."

These passages form the biblical basis for priestly absolution (forgiveness), and broadly speaking, for both papal and Church jurisdiction (by extension, for the power to impose penance — binding, retaining — and to grant indulgences — loosing, forgiving). Matthew 16:19 was spoken by our Lord to St. Peter alone and is the primary foundation for the concept of the papacy (along with the preceding verse). Matthew 18:18 and John 20:23 were directed toward the twelve disciples. From these verses, among others, the Catholic Church deduces the power and governing jurisdiction of the bishops (in agreement with the Pope), especially in an ecumenical council, such as Trent or Vatican II.

Karl Adam, in his marvelously insightful book *The Spirit of Catholicism*, comments on the Catholic belief in indulgences:

> The Church in virtue of her power of binding and loosing may supplement the poverty of one member out of the wealth of another. . . . All the main ideas upon which the doctrine of indulgences is based — the necessity of expiation for sin, the cooperative expiation of the members of the Body of Christ, the Church's power so to bind and loose on earth that her action is valid in Heaven — all these ideas are contained in holy Scripture.
>
> So that although the historical form of the indulgence has undergone some change . . . and may in the future undergo further change, and although the theology of indulgences has only been gradually elaborated, yet in its substance the doctrine is in line with the pure thought of the Scriptures. Here, as in no other practice of the Church, do the members of the Body of Christ cooperate in loving expiation. All the earnestness and joyfulness, humility and contrition, love and fidelity, which animate the Body are here especially combined and manifested.[171]

1 Corinthians 5:3-5: "I have already pronounced judgment in the name of the Lord Jesus on the man who has done such a thing. When you are assembled, and my spirit is present, with the power of our Lord Jesus, you are to deliver this man to Satan for the destruction of the flesh, that his spirit may be saved in the day of the Lord Jesus" (see 1 Cor. 5:1-2).

[171] Adam, *The Spirit of Catholicism*, 127-128.

> **2 Corinthians 2:6-8, 10-11:** "For such a one this punishment by the majority is enough; so you should rather turn to forgive and comfort him, or he may be overwhelmed by excessive sorrow. So I beg you to reaffirm your love for him. . . . Anyone whom you forgive, I also forgive . . . in the presence of Christ, to keep Satan from gaining the advantage over us; for we are not ignorant of his designs."

St. Paul in his commands and exhortations to the Corinthians is in entire agreement with the Catholic tenets of penance and indulgences. He binds in 1 Corinthians 5:3-5 and looses in 2 Corinthians 2:6-7, 10, acting as a type of papal figure in 2 Corinthians 2:10, much like St. Peter among the Apostles. He forgives, and bids the Corinthian elders to forgive also, even though the offense was not committed against them personally. Clearly, both parties are acting as God's representatives in the matter of the forgiveness of sins and the remission of sin's temporal penalties (an indulgence). In this, as in all other doctrinal matters, the Catholic Church is grounded in the Bible, takes seriously all that she teaches, and grapples with all the implications and deepest wellsprings of Truth to be found within the pages of God's holy Scriptures.

Cardinal Gibbons elaborates:

> Here we have all the elements that constitute an Indulgence. First, a penance, or temporal punishment proportioned to the gravity of the offense, is imposed on the transgressor. Second, the penitent is truly contrite for his crime. Third, this determines the Apostle to remit the penalty. Fourth, the Apostle considers the relaxation of the penance ratified by Jesus Christ, in whose name it is imparted.[172]

[172] Gibbons, *The Faith of Our Fathers*, 308-309.

The doctrine of penance was indisputably believed and practiced by the early Church, as reputable Protestant Church history reference works admit.[173] It was firmly established in the early Church and did not substantially change in the Middle Ages, but was only *developed*, like all Catholic doctrines. It was the subject of much reasoned speculation and discussion among the Scholastics (such as St. Thomas Aquinas), but it was neither invented nor distorted at this time, as the biblical evidence we have examined proves conclusively.

[173] *The Oxford Dictionary of the Christian Church*, 762.

Chapter Nine

The Blessed Virgin Mary

"Hail, full of grace"

Karl Adam commented on the proper Catholic understanding of the Virgin Mary:

> Mary . . . like every creature . . . was called into existence out of nothingness. An infinite distance separates her from the Infinite, from Father, Son, and Holy Ghost. And she has no grace, no virtue, no privilege, which she does not owe to the divine Mediator. Both in her natural and in her supernatural being, she is wholly the gift of God, "full of grace" (Luke 1:28). There is nothing, therefore, so misguided and so preposterous as to decry the Mother of God as some "mother goddess," and to talk of Catholicism having a polytheistic character. There is but one God, the Triune God, and every created thing lives in awe of His mystery.[174]

Jesuit Nicholas Russo defended the Catholic view in 1886:

> In honoring Mary, what else are we doing but imitating the heavenly messenger who saluted her as full of grace, united

[174] Adam, *The Spirit of Catholicism*, 113-114.

> to God ["the Lord is with thee"], blessed among women? What are all the praises which the Church offers to Mary . . . but a faint commentary on the words of the archangel? What is the veneration we have for her but the fulfillment of the prophecy made by our heavenly Mother herself when, filled with the Holy Ghost, magnifying the Lord and extolling His mercy, she exclaimed: "All generations shall call me blessed"? (Luke 1:43). To suppress our feelings, therefore, would not only be inconsistent with the filial love we should have for her, but would also contradict the clear teaching of the Gospel.[175]

Archbishop Fulton Sheen, well known for his 1950s television sermons, eloquently wrote:

> There is, actually, only one person in all humanity of whom God has one picture, and in whom there is a perfect conformity between what He wanted her to be and what she is, and that is His own Mother. Most of us are a minus sign, in the sense that we do not fulfill the high hopes the Heavenly Father has for us. But Mary is the equal sign. The ideal that God had of her — that she *is*, and in the flesh. The model and the copy are perfect; she is all that was foreseen, planned, and dreamed. The melody of her life is played, just as it was written. Mary was thought, conceived, and planned as the equal sign between ideal and history, thought and reality, hope and realization. . . .
>
> As Eden was the Paradise of Creation, Mary is the Paradise of the Incarnation, and in her as a Garden was celebrated the first nuptials of God and man. The closer one gets to fire, the greater the heat; the closer one is to God, the greater

[175] Nicholas Russo, *The True Religion* (New York: P. J. Kenedy and Sons, 1886), 270-271.

the purity. But since no one was ever closer to God than the woman whose human portals He threw open to walk this earth, then no one could have been more pure than she. . . .

She is the one whom every man loves when he loves a woman — whether he knows it or not. She is what every woman wants to be, when she looks at herself. . . . She is the secret desire every woman has to be honored and fostered; she is the way every woman wants to command respect and love because of the beauty of her goodness of body and soul. . . . This Dream Woman . . . is the one of whom every heart can say in its depth of depths: "She is the Woman I love!" . . .[176]

The key to understanding Mary is this: We do not start with Mary. We start with Christ, the Son of the living God! The less we think of Him, the less we think of her; the more we think of Him, the more we think of her; the more we adore His Divinity, the more we venerate her Motherhood; the less we adore His Divinity, the less reason we have for respecting her. . . .

No one . . . who thinks logically about Christ can understand such a question as: "Why do you speak so often of His Mother?" . . .

It may be objected: "Our Lord is enough for me. I have no need of her." But *He* needed her, whether we do or not. And what is more important, Our Blessed Lord gave us His Mother as *our* Mother. . . .

Mary is a window through which our humanity first catches a glimpse of Divinity on earth. Or perhaps she is

[176] Fulton Sheen, *The World's First Love* (New York: McGraw-Hill Book Co., 1952), 5, 8, 11-12. C. S. Lewis also makes a noteworthy observation about different perspectives on Mary in his masterpiece of basic Christian apologetics, *Mere Christianity* (New York: Macmillan, 1952), 7-8.

> more like a magnifying glass that intensifies our love of her Son, and makes our prayers more bright and burning.
>
> God, Who made the sun, also made the moon. The moon does not take away from the brilliance of the sun. The moon would only be a burnt-out cinder floating in the immensity of space, were it not for the sun. All its light is reflected from the sun. The Blessed Mother reflects her Divine Son; without Him, she is nothing. With Him, she is the Mother of Men.[177]

Protestants (and many Catholics as well) are often concerned about abuses in the practice of Marian devotion. Wholly apart from the question of the exact nature of the Catholic Church's teaching about Mary, it must be admitted (and is, by many Catholic writers) that excesses in language and practice have indeed regrettably occurred too often among individual Catholics. Granting this, at the same time, much of the veneration and verbal praises directed toward Mary have to be understood as poetic utterances — not usually to be interpreted literally, just as the love letters of those in the midst of new romance have their own unique language, which everyone understands and accordingly takes into account.

Furthermore, it is also true that insufficient attention is paid to the many instances through the centuries of papal and conciliar censures of such abuses. For example, in our own time, both the Second Vatican Council[178] and Pope Paul VI[179] have addressed this issue frankly and directly, often with Protestant perceptions and objections in mind.

[177] Sheen, *The World's First Love*, 51, 58-59, 61, 63.

[178] Second Vatican Council, *Dogmatic Constitution on the Church*, ch. 8, "Our Lady," IV, 67.

[179] Pope Paul VI, *Apostolic Exhortation Devotion to the Blessed Virgin Mary* (Washington: U.S. Catholic Conference, February 2, 1974), 24.

In any event, an ecumenical and scriptural understanding of the Blessed Virgin Mary and her place within Catholicism and Christianity must begin with the actual dogmas of Catholicism, which are "in the books" to be examined by one and all. These beliefs are often misunderstood, and it is the Catholic apologist's task to clarify painstakingly the Marian doctrines of his Church and to rectify the common, longstanding misconstructions of them.

Definition: Mary the "Mother of God" (Theotokos)

The official, dogmatic proclamation of this dogma was made at the Ecumenical Council of Ephesus in 431, in response to the heresy of Nestorianism, which expressly denied that Mary was *Theotokos* (literally, "God-bearer"), and held, rather, that Mary was only the mother of the man Jesus *(Christotokos)*. The term *Theotokos* had been used at least as early as Origen (d. c. 254) and was in common use soon after his lifetime. The Council of Ephesus officially approved the *Second Letter of Cyril of Alexandria to Nestorius* as its definition on this matter. It reads in part as follows:

> It was not that an ordinary man was born first of the holy Virgin, on whom afterward the Word descended; what we say is that, being united with the flesh from the womb, [the Word] has undergone birth in the flesh, making the birth in the flesh His own. . . . Thus [the holy Fathers] have unhesitatingly called the holy Virgin "Mother of God" *[Theotokos]*. This does not mean that the nature of the Word or His divinity received the beginning of its existence from the holy Virgin, but that, since the holy body, animated by a rational soul, which the Word united to Himself according to the hypostasis, was born from her, the Word was born according to the flesh.[180]

[180] From Neuner and Dupuis, *The Christian Faith*, 160-161. See also CCC, pars. 484-486, 494-495, 509, 721, 963, 972,

Scriptural evidence: Mary the "Mother of God" (Theotokos)

Ludwig Ott, in his systematic summary of Catholic dogma, contends:

> Scripture implicitly affirms Mary's Divine motherhood by attesting, on the one hand, the true Divinity of Christ, and on the other hand, Mary's true motherhood. Thus Mary is called: "Mother of Jesus" (John 2:1) . . . "Mother of the Lord" (Luke 1:43). Mary's true motherhood is clearly foretold by the Prophet Isaiah: "Behold a virgin shall conceive and bear a Son, and his name shall be called Emmanuel" (Isaiah 7:14). . . . The woman who bore the Son of God is the Progenitress of God, or the Mother of God [see also Matt. 1:18, 12:46, 13:55; Luke 1:31, 35; Gal. 4:4].[181]

The doctrine of Mary as *Theotokos* flows consistently and straightforwardly from the doctrine of the Holy Trinity and the Incarnation of the Second Person of the Trinity, the Son, Jesus. Cardinal Gibbons explains:

> We affirm that the Second Person of the Blessed Trinity, the Word of God, who in His divine nature is from all eternity begotten of the Father, consubstantial with Him, was in the fullness of time again begotten, by being born of the Virgin, thus taking to Himself, from her maternal womb, a human nature of the same substance with hers.
>
> But it may be said the Blessed Virgin is not the Mother of the Divinity. She had not, and she could not have, any part in the generation of the Word of God, for that generation is eternal; her maternity is temporal. He is her Creator; she is His creature. Style her, if you will, the Mother of the

975; Hardon, *PCD*, 272-273, 432-433; Hardon, CC, 132-138.

[181] Ott, *Fundamentals of Catholic Dogma*, 196-197.

man Jesus or even of the human nature of the Son of God, but not the Mother of God.

I shall answer this objection by putting a question. Did the mother who bore us have any part in the production of our *soul?* Was not this nobler part of our being the work of God alone? And yet who would for a moment dream of saying "the mother of my body," and not "*my* mother"? . . .

In like manner . . . the Blessed Virgin, under the overshadowing of the Holy Ghost, by communicating to the Second Person of the Adorable Trinity, as mothers do, a true human nature of the same substance with her own, is thereby really and truly His Mother.

It is in this sense that the title "Mother of God," denied by Nestorius, was vindicated to her by the General Council of Ephesus, in 431; in this sense, and in no other, has the Church called her by that title.

Hence, by immediate and necessary consequence, follow her surpassing dignity and excellence.[182]

Cardinal Newman elaborates:

There was in the first ages no public and ecclesiastical recognition of the place which St. Mary holds in the Economy of grace; this was reserved for the fifth century, as the definition of our Lord's proper Divinity had been the work of the fourth. . . . In order to do honor to Christ, in order to defend the true doctrine of the Incarnation, in order to secure a right faith in the manhood of the Eternal Son, the Council of Ephesus determined the Blessed Virgin to be the Mother of God. . . .

But the spontaneous or traditional feeling of Christians had in great measure anticipated the formal ecclesiastical

[182] Gibbons, *The Faith of Our Fathers*, 137-138.

decision. Thus the title *Theotokos*, or "Mother of God," was familiar to Christians from primitive times, and had been used, among other writers, by Origen, Eusebius, St. Alexander, St. Athanasius, St. Ambrose, St. Gregory Nazianzen, St. Gregory Nyssen, and St. Nilus.[183]

Definition: the Immaculate Conception of Mary

Pope Pius IX (in the papal bull *Ineffabilis Deus*) infallibly defined this doctrine as binding upon all Catholics on December 8, 1854:

> We declare, pronounce, and define: the doctrine which holds that the most Blessed Virgin Mary was, from the first moment of her conception, by the singular grace and privilege of almighty God and in view of the merits of Christ Jesus the Savior of the human race, preserved immune from all stain of Original Sin, is revealed by God and, therefore, firmly and constantly to be believed by all the faithful.[184]

Scriptural evidence: the Immaculate Conception of Mary

Genesis 3:15 (known as the "Protoevangelion"): "I will put enmity between you and the woman, and between your seed and her seed; he shall bruise your head, and you shall bruise his heel."

[183] *An Essay on the Development of Christian Doctrine*, Pt. 1, ch. 4, sect. 2, no. 10. The Lutheran scholar Jaroslav Pelikan concurs completely (*The Emergence of the Catholic Tradition* [Chicago: University of Chicago Press, 1971], 241-242). Virtually all of the original Protestant Reformers (e.g., Luther, Calvin, Zwingli) used this title as well, with the same understanding.

[184] See CCC, pars. 411, 490-494, 508, 721-722, 966; Hardon, CC, 150-160; Hardon, *PCD*, 187-188.

Ludwig Ott expounds this verse:

> The *literal sense* of the passage is possibly the following: Between Satan and his followers on the one hand, and Eve and her posterity on the other hand, there is to be constant moral warfare. The posterity of Eve will achieve a complete and final victory over Satan and his followers, even if it is wounded in the struggle. The posterity of Eve includes the Messiah, in whose power humanity will win a victory over Satan. Thus the passage is indirectly messianic.
>
> The seed of the woman was understood as referring to the Redeemer, and thus the Mother of the Redeemer came to be seen in the woman. Since the second century, this direct messianic-marian interpretation has been expounded by individual Fathers, for example, St. Irenaeus, St. Epiphanius . . . St. Cyprian . . . St. Leo the Great. However, it is not found in the writings of the majority of the Fathers. . . . According to this interpretation, Mary stands with Christ in a perfect and victorious enmity toward Satan and his following. Many of the later scholastics and a great many modern theologians argue, in the light of this interpretation . . . that Mary's victory over Satan would not have been perfect, if she had ever been under his dominion. Consequently she must have entered this world without the stain of Original Sin.[185]

> **Luke 1:28:** "And he [the angel Gabriel — Luke 1:26-27] came to her, and said, 'Hail, O favored one, the Lord is with you!' "

Most Protestant Bible translations follow the King James, or Authorized, Version's lead in rendering *kecharitomene*, the Greek

[185] Ott, *Fundamentals of Catholic Dogma*, 200.

word, as "favored," as indeed also some recent Catholic versions (New American, Jerusalem). The favored (no pun intended!) traditional Catholic rendering (actually the more literal rendering) is "Hail, full of grace" (for example, Douay, Confraternity, Knox). The word *Mary* (after *hail)* is not in the text, but strongly implied, as the angel is addressing her by title; thus we arrive at the phrase "Hail, Mary, full of grace," the beginning of the quintessential Catholic devotional prayer (another portion of it can be found at Luke 1:42).

In responding to the Protestant charge, often put forth, that "full of grace" is impermissible and indicative of Catholic bias, we cite two reputable Protestant linguistic sources to the contrary:

An Expository Dictionary of New Testament Words, by W. E. Vine, makes a very interesting observation:

> *Charitoo:* akin to *charis*, to endow with *charis*, primarily signified to make graceful or gracious, and came to denote, in Hellenistic Greek, to cause to find favor, Luke 1:28, "highly favored" (margin, "endued with grace"). . . . Grace implies more than favor; grace is a free gift, favor may be deserved or gained.[186]

Vine has here given a thoroughly Catholic view on this verse and what it tells us about Mary. For by saying that "grace is a free gift," he shows that the traditional Catholic rendering clearly makes Mary's Immaculate Conception entirely unmerited on her part — a sheer act of mercy and grace performed solely by God. "Favor," on the other hand, the preferred Protestant translation, may imply something "deserved or gained." Thus, by a great irony, the Protestant Bibles are more likely to be misinterpreted in the

[186] W. E. Vine, *An Expository Dictionary of New Testament Words* (Old Tappan, New Jersey: Fleming H. Revell, 1940), Vol. 2, 84.

sense that Mary has *earned* this gift, a notion expressly denied by Catholic theology and dogmatic pronouncements.

Whichever translation one prefers (this is not necessarily an either-or proposition), it is certain that *kecharitomene* is directly concerned with the idea of "grace," since, as Vine noted, it is derived from the root word *charis*, whose literal meaning is "grace." *Charis* is translated by the King James Version, for example, 129 times (out of 150 total appearances) as "grace."

Likewise, *Word Pictures in the New Testament* expounds Luke 1:28 as follows:

> "Highly favored" *(kecharitomene)*. Perfect passive participle of *charitoo* and means endowed with grace *(charis)*, enriched with grace as in Ephesians 1:6. . . . The Vulgate *gratiae plena* "is right, if it means 'full of grace *which thou hast received*'; wrong, if it means 'full of grace *which thou hast to bestow*' " (Plummer).[187]

The Catholic belief is precisely the former option, which Robertson's approved source has deemed "right."

Another important aspect of Luke 1:28 should be noted. The angel is here, in effect, giving Mary a new name ("full of grace"). As was mentioned earlier, the word *Mary* does not appear in the text. It was as if the angel were addressing Abraham "Hail, full of faith," or Solomon "Hail, full of wisdom" (characteristics for which they were particularly noteworthy). The biblical and Hebraic understanding of one's name was quite profound. God was very particular in naming individuals himself (e.g., Gen. 17:5, 15, 19; Isa. 45:3-4; Matt. 1:21). God renamed persons to indicate regeneration (as in Gen. 17:5, 15; 32:28) or condemnation (as in Jer. 20:3). For the ancient Hebrews, names signified the character, nature, and qualities of a person and were much more

[187] Robertson, *Word Pictures in the New Testament*, Vol. 2, 13.

than mere identifying labels. Thus, God chose his Son's name (Matt. 1:21).

As a passing speculation, it is interesting that the meaning of the Hebrew *Miriam* (Greek, *Mariam*, or "Mary") is very uncertain, according to etymologists. It may be that the angel is giving the name its definitive meaning in Luke 1:28: one who is characterized as being "full of grace."

It is permissible, on Greek grammatical and linguistic grounds, to paraphrase *kecharitomene* as completely, perfectly, enduringly endowed with grace.[188] Thus, in just this one verse, pregnant with meaning and far-reaching implications, the uniqueness of Mary is strongly indicated, and the Immaculate Conception can rightly be deemed entirely consistent with the meaning of this passage.

The Bible speaks only implicitly of many things that Protestants strongly believe, such as the proper mode of Baptism (immersion, sprinkling, or pouring?). The Immaculate Conception is entirely possible within scriptural presuppositions.

> **Luke 1:35** (The Annunciation; Mary as a type of the ark of the covenant): "And the angel said to her, 'The Holy Spirit will come upon you, and the power of the Most High will overshadow you; therefore the child to be born will be called holy, the Son of God.' "

Overshadow is derived from the Greek, *episkiasei*, which denotes a bright cloud or cloud of glory. It is used in reference to the cloud at the transfiguration of Jesus (Matt. 17:5; Mark 9:7; Luke 9:34) and hearkens back to instances of the *Shekinah* glory of God in the Old Testament (Exod. 24:15-16, 40:34-38; 1 Kings 8:10).

[188] Blass and DeBrunner, *Greek Grammar of the New Testament* (Chicago: University of Chicago Press, 1961), 166; H. W. Smyth, *Greek Grammar* (Cambridge: Harvard University Press, 1968), sect. 1852:b.

The Septuagint uses *episkiasei* in Exodus 40:34-35. Mary, as *Theotokos*, becomes, in effect, the new temple and holy of holies, where God dwelt in a special, spatially located fashion. In particular, Scripture seems to be making a direct symbolic parallelism between Mary and the ark of the covenant. She is the bearer and ark of the New Covenant, which Jesus brings about (Heb. 8:6-13; 12:24).

The ark of the old covenant was constructed according to meticulous instructions from God (Exod. 25:9; 39:42-43). How much more perfect must the "God-bearer" be, who would carry in her womb God made flesh, the eternal *Logos*, or "Word" of God, the Second Person of the Blessed Trinity?

Thus, when the ark and its surrounding sacred items were completed, the glory cloud of God descended and "covered" the tabernacle, in which the ark was kept, and Moses could not even enter (Exod. 40:34-35). This a direct parallel to Luke 1:35. A very similar occurrence can be found in 1 Kings 8:4-11 (especially 8:10-11), when the ark is brought to the newly completed temple.

Another parallel is seen in the comparison of King David's words upon seeing the recently regained ark (2 Sam. 6:9) and Elizabeth's exclamation upon seeing Mary (Luke 1:43). Also, the people of Jerusalem shouted with joy on the same occasion (2 Sam. 6:15), while Elizabeth also reacted with a "loud cry" to Mary (Luke 1:42), saying, "Blessed are you among women, and blessed is the fruit of your womb!"

Furthermore, as David leapt for joy when the ark was brought to Jerusalem (2 Sam. 6:14-16; cf. 1 Chron. 15:29), so did John the Baptist in Elizabeth's womb when the ark of the New Covenant was near (Luke 1:44). It was what each ark contained (the written and incarnated Word of God) that caused the joy in each case, and that is the whole point of the Catholic veneration of Mary.

Finally, there is another parallel of three-month stays in the hill country of Judea, of the ark of the old covenant (2 Sam. 6:10-12) and of Mary, the ark of the New Covenant (Luke 1:39-45, 56).

Perhaps a bit more reflection on the nature of the ark, the tabernacle, and the temple will be helpful at this point, to reveal the profundity of the parallelism between these "holy places," where God is "specially" present (after all, he is omnipresent), and the Blessed Virgin, in whom God in the flesh first chose to take up his earthly abode.

By analyzing the similarities, one can see how Mary's Immaculate Conception is altogether in keeping with the typology of Scripture in this regard, and quite appropriate and fitting for one who was granted the unfathomable honor of being chosen as the Mother of God.

The temple site was very sacred and holy (1 Chron. 29:3; Isa. 11:9, 56:7, 64:10), as were its various rooms and areas and all its sacred objects (Ezek. 42:13, 46:19; Isa. 62:9), and the city of Jerusalem itself (Neh. 11:1,18; Isaiah 48:2). Of course, the ground of Mt. Sinai was holy due to God's peculiar presence (Exod. 3:5), and God's presence in the Israelite camp rendered it holy (Deut. 23:14).

The presence of God always imparted holiness (Deut. 7:6, 26:19; Jer. 2:3). Even God's "holy name" was thought by the Jews to constitute his actual presence with them (Lev. 20:3, 22:2; 1 Chron. 16:10). When something was holy, it then partook of God's own holiness. Angels are called "holy ones" precisely because of their proximity to God (Job 5:1; Ps. 89:6-7).

The furnishings of the tabernacle, a portable sacred tent that prefigured and preceded the temple, were not to be touched by the Levites (or anyone else, save for a select few priests), on pain of death (Num. 1:51-53; 2:17; 4:15). Likewise, the ark, which was carried on poles inserted through rings on its edges, was so holy that it could not be touched.

On one occasion, the ark was about to fall over when being transported, and one Uzziah (seemingly with the purest motives) reached out to steady it. He was immediately struck dead (2 Sam.

6:2-7). The men of Beth-shemesh also died when they merely looked inside the ark (1 Sam. 6:19; cf. Exod. 33:20).

The Temple in Jerusalem (actually, three in succession) was simply the permanent structure based on the plan of the tabernacle, with outer courts, priest's courts, an altar, and the innermost holy sanctuary, the "holy of holies." The ark of the covenant was placed inside the holy of holies in the first (Solomon's) Temple, but was lost after the destruction of Jerusalem and the Temple by the Babylonians, led by Nebuchadnezzar, in 587 B.C.

Israelite priests were subject to very strict demands regarding marriage and ritual purity (Lev. 21-22), especially the high priest (Lev. 21:10-15). The holy of holies could be entered only by the high priest, and only on the yearly Day of Atonement (Yom Kippur), with appropriate reverential precautions (Lev. 16; Num. 29:8).

In Leviticus 16:2, 13, the high priest is warned properly to observe instructions "that he die not." The Jews used to tie a rope to the ankle of the high priest on Yom Kippur, so that they could safely pull him out if he was disobedient in some respect and died in the holy of holies. God dwelt above the mercy seat on top of the ark, between the two cherubim (Exod. 25:22).

Just before the Israelites were to receive the Ten Commandments, God made a spectacular appearance at Mt. Sinai (Exod. 19-20), accompanied, as usual in Scripture, by fire and a cloud ("smoke," Exod. 19:18). He warned the people not even to touch the mountain, or its "border," under penalty of death (Exod. 19:12-13). Even animals were included in the restriction.

The point of all this digression is to illustrate how God regards people and also inanimate objects that are to come in close contact with Him. Cruel as it may seem from our vantage point, the severity of death as the consequence of disrespect or disobedience was necessary to make absolutely clear how awesome and majestic God's holiness is.

The strictness of the ceremonial Law was to change, of course, with the arrival of the Messiah and the New Covenant, but the Old Testament principle of "holiness/separate unto the Lord" remained. Mary, because of her ineffable physical and spiritual relationship with God the Son, the Holy Spirit (as "spouse," so to speak), and God the Father ("the Daughter of Zion" typology), necessarily had to be granted the grace of sinlessness from conception, just as all of us must be cleansed utterly in order to be present with God in all his fullness in Heaven (see, e.g., 1 Cor. 3:13-17; 1 John 3:3-9; Rev. 21:27).

The Immaculate Conception is merely the supreme, glorious realization of the notion that leaps out from practically every page of Scripture from beginning to end: that God is holy, and the closer we get to him, the more *we* must be holy.

Lest anyone wrongly think that arguments such as the above, from "types and shadows," are a peculiar form of "Romish excess," the biblical examples in the table on the opposite page should suffice to show the commonness of such types in Scripture.

Many factors can be deduced, when considering all of the above scriptural indications of the Immaculate Conception. Cardinal Gibbons pointed out many parallels between the sinless Blessed Virgin Mary and other biblical figures:

> Whenever God designs any person for some important work, He bestows on that person the graces and dispositions necessary for faithfully discharging it. . . .
>
> The Prophet Jeremiah was sanctified from his very birth because he was destined to be the herald of God's law to the children of Israel: "Before I formed thee in the bowels of thy mother, I knew thee, and before thou camest forth out of the womb I sanctified thee" (Jer. 1:5). . . .
>
> John the Baptist was "filled with the Holy Ghost even from his mother's womb" (Luke 1:15). He was "a burning

Type/Shadow/Figure	Fulfillment/Parallel
Colossians 2:16-17: Food, Sabbath	"Shadow of things to come"
Hebrews 9:8-12, 24: High Priest and the tabernacle	Christ as High Priest/Heaven
Hebrews 10:1: the Law	The New Covenant
Romans 5:14/ 1 Corinthians 15:45-49: Adam	Christ (the second Adam)
Galatians 4:22-31: Isaac and Ishmael (sons of Abraham)	Children of "the flesh" and of "promise"/"after the Spirit"
1 Peter 3:19-21: Noah's Ark and the flood	The Church and Baptism
Exodus 12:21-28: Passover lamb slain for Israel's sins	Christ the Lamb slain for the sins of mankind (Revelation 5:6, 9; John 1:29)
Moses (delivered Israel from the bondage of slavery)	Jesus Christ (delivers mankind from the bondage of sin)
Circumcision (infant rite for initiation as one of God's "chosen people")	Baptism (infant rite for initiation into God's family)
The creation before the Fall, the ark of the Covenant, and Eve	Mary as Immaculate, "bearer of God," and as "spiritual mother" and representative of the human race

and a shining light" (John 5:35) because he was chosen to prepare the way of the Lord.

The Apostles received the plenitude of grace; they were endowed with the gift of tongues and other privileges (Acts 2) before they commenced the work of the ministry. Hence St. Paul says: "Our sufficiency is from God, who hath made

> us fit ministers of the New Testament" (2 Cor. 3:5-6) [other translations have *able*, *competent*, *qualified]*. . . .
>
> There is none who filled any position so exalted, so sacred, as is the incommunicable office of Mother of Jesus; and there is no one, consequently, that needed so high a degree of holiness as she did.
>
> For, if God thus sanctified His Prophets and Apostles as being destined to be the bearers of the Word of life, how much more sanctified must Mary have been, who was to bear the Lord and "Author of life" (Acts 3:5)? . . . If God said to His Priests of old: "Be ye clean, you that carry the vessels of the Lord" (Isa. 3:2); nay, if the vessels themselves used in the divine service and churches are set apart by special consecration, we cannot conceive Mary to have been ever profaned by sin, who was the chosen vessel of election, even the Mother of God.[189]

It is clearly untrue to maintain — as many do — that God is the only sinless being. Adam and Eve were created sinless and would and could have remained so — but for their disobedience and the Fall. Likewise, the angels in Heaven began their existence without sin and have even remained so. Saints in Heaven are made completely sinless (Rev. 14:5; 21:27).

And Mary needed a Savior just as much as the rest of us. She was fully aware of that necessity (Luke 1:47). The difference between Mary and other ultimately saved persons is that they had all fallen into the filthy pit of sin, whereas she had not. But she certainly *would* have, too, if it were not for God's special act of grace whereby she was conceived immaculate and spared from the inheritance of Original Sin. God redeemed us from the pit, but prevented her from falling into it. In both cases, it is proper to speak

[189] Gibbons, *The Faith of Our Fathers*, 135-137.

of God as having "saved" his creatures "from the pit." As the proverb goes, "Prevention is the best cure."

In fact, Mary was saved more out of absolute grace than anyone ever was, so that it is altogether unfounded to charge the Catholic Church with undermining the doctrine of free grace by virtue of her Marian beliefs. For all the Church is saying with regard to Mary's Immaculate Conception is what Calvinists and many other Protestants claim for all saved individuals: grace that is efficacious wholly apart from our cooperation.

In Mary's case, the grace began without any possibility whatever of her own merit, since it was from the moment of conception, when she had not as yet a free will to choose one way or the other! Later on, she did indeed truly cooperate with God (Luke 1:38)[190] and was free of actual sin by choice,[191] but at first, the grace came with no possibility of her even accepting or rejecting it. Thus, Protestant objections on this score are utterly unfounded, for everything that Mary is, derives entirely from God's free grace and providential will.[192] Far from being idolatry, the veneration accorded Mary by the Catholic is merely an acknowledgment of the glory promised by God (through the work of Jesus Christ) to all his redeemed creatures.[193]

Cardinal Newman was puzzled by some of the objections to the Immaculate Conception. He wrote, with characteristically brilliant, rhetorical prose, a piece intended as a counterargument:

> Does not the objector consider that *Eve* was created, or born, *without* Original Sin? Why does not *this* shock him? Would he have been inclined to *worship* Eve in that first estate of hers? Why, then, Mary?

[190] CCC, pars. 488, 490, 494, 511, 967, 973.

[191] CCC, pars. 411, 493-494, 508, 721.

[192] CCC, pars. 487, 492, 722, 964, 970.

[193] CCC, par. 971.

Does he not believe that St. John the Baptist had the grace of God, i.e., was regenerated, even before his birth? What do we believe of Mary, but that grace was given her at a still earlier period? *All* we say is that grace was given her from the first moment of her existence.

We do not say that she did not owe her salvation to the death of her Son. Just the contrary, we say that she, of all mere children of Adam, is in the truest sense the fruit and purchase of His Passion. He has done for her more than for anyone else. To others He gives grace and regeneration at a *point* in their earthly existence; to her, from the very beginning.

We do not make her *nature* different from others. . . . Certainly she *would* have been a frail being, like Eve, *without* the grace of God. . . . It was not her *nature* which secured her perseverance, but the excess of grace which hindered Nature acting as Nature ever will act. There is no difference in *kind* between her and us, though an inconceivable difference of *degree*. She and we are both simply saved by the grace of Christ.

Thus, sincerely speaking, I really do not see *what* the difficulty is. . . . The above statement is no private statement of my own. I never heard of any Catholic who ever had any other view. . . .

Consider what I have said. Is it, after all, *certainly* irrational? Is it *certainly* against Scripture? Is it *certainly* against the primitive Fathers? Is it *certainly* idolatrous? I cannot help smiling as I put the questions. . . .

Many, many doctrines are far harder than the Immaculate Conception. The doctrine of Original Sin is indefinitely harder. Mary just has *not* this difficulty. It is *no* difficulty to believe that a soul is united to the flesh *without* Original Sin; the great mystery is that any, that millions on

> millions, are born with it. Our teaching about Mary has just one difficulty less than our teaching about the state of mankind generally.[194]

Finally, the English bishop William Ullathorne (1806-1889), a friend of Newman, wrote eloquently in a book on this subject that was published originally a year after the dogma was proclaimed:

> It is the divine maternity of Mary which explains both her perfect excellence and her perfect holiness. It is the key to all her gifts and privileges. For the excellence of each creature is to be found in the degree in which it resembles its Creator. . . .
>
> Mary was made as like to Him [Christ], as being a mere creature, she could be made. For, having no earthly father, our Lord bore the human likeness of His mother in all His features. Or rather, she bore His likeness. And as, for thirty years of His life, her mind was the law which directed His obedience, and her will the guide which regulated His actions, her soul was the perfect reflection of His conduct.
>
> And as all created holiness is derived from Jesus, and from the degree of our union with Jesus, of which union His sacred and life-giving flesh is the great instrument; we may understand something of the perfect holiness of the Mother of God, from the perfection of her union with her Son. For He was formed by the Holy Ghost of her flesh. And His blood, that saving blood which redeemed the world, was taken from her heart. And whilst the Godhead dwelt bodily in Him, He, for nine months, dwelt bodily in her. And all

[194] John Henry Cardinal Newman, *Meditations and Devotions* (Harrison, New York: Roman Catholic Books, n.d.), 151-152, 155-156.

that time . . . the stream which nourished the growth of life in Jesus flowed from the heart of Mary, and, at each pulsation, flowed back again, and re-entered His Mother's heart, enriching her with His divinest spirit. How pregnant is that blood of His with sanctifying grace, one drop of which might have redeemed the world. . . . Next to that union by which Jesus is God and man in one person, there is no union so intimate as that of a mother with her child. . . .

Certainly, He who preserved the three children from being touched by the fire in the midst of which they walked uninjured, and who preserved the bush unconsumed in the midst of a burning flame, could preserve Mary untouched from the burning fuel of concupiscence. He who took up Elijah in the fiery chariot, so that he tasted not of death, could, in the chariot of His ardent love, set Mary on high above the law of sin. . . . And He who held back the waves of that Jordan, that the ark of the Old Testament might pass untouched and honored through its bed, could hold back the wave of Adam, lest it overflow the ark of the New Testament beneath its defiling floods. For that we are born in the crime of Adam and with Original Sin, is not the result of absolute necessity, but of the divine will. And if He who ordained this penalty, had already solved it in part, when ere His birth, He sanctified the holy Precursor of His Coming; much more could he solve it altogether when He sanctified His holy Mother.

For He who could have limited Adam's sin unto himself, can ward off that sin from Mary. And what He could, that He willed to do. For why should He not have willed it?[195]

[195] William Ullathorne, *The Immaculate Conception of the Mother of God* (Westminster, Maryland: Christian Classics, 1988), 6-7, 32-33.

Definition: the Assumption of Mary

Pope Pius XII, in his Apostolic Constitution, *Munificentissimus Deus*, of November 1, 1950, proclaimed this dogma in the following carefully selected words:

> By the authority of our Lord Jesus Christ, of the blessed apostles Peter and Paul, and by our own authority, we proclaim, declare, and define as a dogma revealed by God: the Immaculate Mother of God, Mary ever Virgin, when the course of her earthly life was finished, was taken up body and soul into the glory of Heaven.[196]

Scriptural evidence: the Assumption of Mary

Ludwig Ott presents some of the biblical indications of the Assumption:

> Direct and express scriptural proofs are not to be had. The possibility of the bodily assumption before the second coming of Christ is not excluded by 1 Corinthians 15:23, as the objective Redemption was completed with the sacrificial death of Christ, and the beginning of the final era foretold by the prophets commenced. Its probability is suggested by Matthew 27:52-53: "And the graves were opened: and many bodies of the saints that had slept arose, and coming out of the tombs after His Resurrection came into the holy city and appeared to many." According to the more probable explanation, which was already expounded by the Fathers, the awakening of the "saints" was a final resurrection and transfiguration. If, however, the justified of the Old Covenant were called to the perfection of salvation immediately

[196] CCC, pars. 966, 974; Hardon, CC, 154-155, 160-163; Hardon, *PCD*, 32.

> after the conclusion of the redemptive work of Christ, then it is possible and probable that the Mother of the Lord was called to it also.
>
> From her fullness of grace spoken of in Luke 1:28, Scholastic theology derives the doctrine of the bodily assumption and glorification of Mary. Since she was full of grace, she remained preserved from the three-fold curse of sin (Gen. 3:16-19), as well as from her return to dust. . . .
>
> Modern theology usually cites Genesis 3:15 in support of the doctrine. Since by "the seed of the woman" it understands Christ, and by "the woman," Mary, it is argued that as Mary had an intimate share in Christ's battle against Satan and in His victory over Satan and sin, she must also have participated intimately in His victory over death. It is true that the literal reference of the text is to Eve and not Mary, but already since the end of the second century (St. Justin), Tradition has seen in Mary the new Eve.[197]

Lest one think that a bodily ascent into Heaven (of a creature, as opposed to Jesus) is impossible and "biblically unthinkable," Holy Scripture contains the examples of Enoch (Heb. 11:5; cf. Gen. 5:24), Elijah (2 Kings 2:1, 11), St. Paul's being caught up to the third heaven (2 Cor. 12:2-4), possibly bodily, and events during the Second Coming (1 Thess. 4:15-17), believed by many Evangelicals to constitute the "Rapture," an additional return of Christ for believers only. All of these occur by virtue of the power of God, not the intrinsic ability of the persons.

The Assumption of the Blessed Virgin flows of necessity from the Immaculate Conception and Mary's actual sinlessness. Bodily death and decay are the result of sin and the Fall (Gen. 3:19; Ps. 16:10). Thus, the absence of actual sin and Original Sin "breaks

[197] Ott, *Fundamentals of Catholic Dogma*, 208-209. For the "New Eve" typology, see CCC, pars. 411, 494, 511, 726, 975.

the chain" and allows for instant bodily resurrection and also immortality, just as God intended for all human beings.

Christ achieved a triple victory over the Devil (Heb. 2:14-18). Mary (as foretold in Gen. 3:15) shared in this triumph of her Son, Jesus: over sin, through her Immaculate Conception; over concupiscence and inordinate sexual desire, by her virginal motherhood; and over death, by her glorious Assumption.

Jesus' Resurrection brings forth the possibility of universal resurrection (1 Cor. 15:13, 16), which is why he is called the "first fruits" (1 Cor. 15:20-23). Mary's Assumption is the "first fruits," sign, and type of the general resurrection of all mankind, so that she represents the age to come, in which death and sin will be conquered once and for all (1 Cor. 15:26). The Assumption is, therefore, directly the result of Christ's own victory over sin and death. It, too, has a Christocentric meaning, in the same way as the Immaculate Conception and the designation *Theotokos*.

Cardinal Newman made several remarkable observations concerning the Assumption of the Blessed Virgin Mary:

> Not till the end of the fourth century did the Church declare the divinity of the Holy Ghost. . . . *Of course* it was held by implication, since the Holy Trinity was believed from the first — but I mean the bare absolute proposition "The Holy Ghost is God." . . . The Assumption of our Lady is more pointedly and in express words held by all Catholics, and has been for a thousand years, than the proposition "The Holy Ghost is God" was held by the Catholic world in St. Basil's time. There has been a gradual evolution of Apostolic doctrine or dogma, as delivered from our Lord to the Church. If the Assumption of our Blessed Lady were now defined at the Vatican Council [1870], I should say that plainly it, as the Immaculate Conception, is contained in the dogma "Mary the Second Eve." . . .

If Mary is like Eve but greater, then, as Eve would not have seen death or corruption, so while Mary underwent death because she was a child of fallen Adam, she did not see corruption because she had more than the prerogatives of Eve.[198]

Who can conceive, my brethren, that God should so repay the debt, which He condescended to owe to His Mother, for the elements of His human body, as to allow the flesh and blood from which it was taken to molder in the grave? . . . Or who can conceive that that virginal frame, which never sinned, was to undergo the death of a sinner? Why should she share the curse of Adam who had no share in his fall? . . . She died, then, as we hold, because even our Lord and Savior died. . . . She died . . . not . . . because of sin, but to submit herself to her condition, to glorify God, to do what her Son did. . . .

She, the Lily of Eden, who had always dwelt out of the sight of man, fittingly did she die in the garden's shade, and amid the sweet flowers in which she had lived. Her departure made no noise in the world. . . . They sought for her relics, but they found them not. . . . Her tomb could not be pointed out, or if it was found, it was open.[199]

Finally, Archbishop Fulton Sheen movingly sums up the profundity of Mary's glorious Assumption into Heaven:

Shall she, as the garden in which grew the lily of divine sinlessness and the red rose of the passion of redemption, be

[198] Letter of September 10, 1869, in Alberic Stacpoole, ed., *Mary's Place in Christian Dialogue* (Wilton, Connecticut: Morehouse-Barlow, 1982), 240.

[199] Sermon for the Assumption (1849), in *Discourses to Mixed Congregations*, 1849, 371-373, in Stacpoole, *Mary's Place in Christian Dialogue*, 240-241.

delivered over to the weeds and be forgotten by the Heavenly Gardener? . . .

Neither would Omnipotence, Who tabernacled Himself within Mary, consent to see His fleshly home subjected to the dissolution of the tomb. . . .

Eat the food of earth, and one dies; eat the Eucharist, and one lives eternally. She, who is the mother of the Eucharist, escapes the decomposition of death. . . .

Mary always seems to be the Advent of what is in store for man. She anticipates Christ for nine months, as she bears Heaven within her; she anticipates His Passion at Cana, and His Church at Pentecost. Now, in the last great Doctrine of the Assumption, she anticipates heavenly glory, and the definition comes at a time when men think of it least.[200]

Definition: the perpetual virginity of Mary

Pope Paul IV, in his Constitution, *Cum Quorumdam Hominum*, of 1555, expressed the constant teaching of the Catholic Church concerning both the virgin birth of Jesus Christ and the perpetual virginity of Mary:

> We question and admonish all those who . . . have asserted, taught, and believed . . . that our Lord . . . was not conceived from the Holy Spirit according to the flesh in the womb of the Blessed Mary ever Virgin but, as other men, from the seed of Joseph . . . or that the same Blessed Virgin Mary is not truly the mother of God and did not retain her virginity intact before the birth, in the birth, and perpetually after the birth.[201]

[200] Sheen, *The World's First Love*, 118-119, 121.

[201] In Neuner and Dupuis, *The Christian Faith*, 217. See CCC, pars. 484-486, 496-498, 502-506, 510, 723 (for the virgin

Scriptural evidence: the perpetual virginity of Mary

The Greek word for *brother* in the New Testament is *adelphos*. The well-known Protestant linguistic reference *An Expository Dictionary of New Testament Words* defines it as follows:

> *Adelphos:* denotes a brother, or near kinsman; in the plural, a community based on identity of origin or life. It is used of:
>
> 1. male children of the same parents . . .
>
> 2. male descendants of the same parents, Acts 7:23, 26; Hebrews 7:5 . . .
>
> 4. people of the same nationality, Acts 3:17, 22; Romans 9:3 . . .
>
> 5. any man, a neighbor, Luke 10:29; Matthew 5:22, 7:3;
>
> 6. persons united by a common interest, Matthew 5:47;
>
> 7. persons united by a common calling, Revelation 22:9;
>
> 8. mankind, Matthew 25:40; Hebrews 2:17;
>
> 9. the disciples, and so, by implication, all believers, Matthew 28:10; John 20:17;
>
> 10. believers, apart from sex, Matthew 23:8; Acts 1:15; Romans 1:13; 1 Thessalonians 1:4; Revelation 19:10 (the word *sisters* is used of believers, only in 1 Timothy 5:2). . . .[202]

It is evident, therefore, from the range of possible definitions of *adelphos*, that Jesus' "brothers" need not necessarily be siblings of Jesus on linguistic grounds, as many commentators, learned and unlearned, seem to assume uncritically. By examining the use of *adelphos* and related words in Hebrew, and by comparing Scripture with Scripture ("exegesis"), one can determine the most sensible explanation of all the biblical data taken collectively. Many examples prove that *adelphos* has a very wide variety of meanings:

birth); pars. 499-501, 507, 510, 721 (for the perpetual virginity of Mary).

[202] Vine, *An Expository Dictionary of New Testament Words*, Vol. 1, 154-155.

• In the King James Version, Jacob is called the "brother" of his Uncle Laban (Gen. 29:15; 29:10). The same thing occurs with regard to Lot and Abraham (Gen. 14:14; 11:26-27). The Revised Standard Version uses "kinsman" at 29:15 and 14:14.

• Use of *brother* or *brethren* for mere kinsmen: Deuteronomy 23:7; 2 Samuel 1:26; 1 Kings 9:13, 20:32; 2 Kings 10:13-14; Jeremiah 34:9; Amos 1:9.

• Neither Hebrew nor Aramaic has a word for *cousin*. Although the New Testament was written in Greek, which does have such a word, the literal rendering of the Hebrew word *ach*, which was used by the first disciples and Jesus, is indeed *adelphos*, the literal equivalent of the English "brother." But even in English, *brother* has multiple meanings as well.

Moving on to more direct biblical evidences of the perpetual virginity of Mary, we discover the following facts:

• In Luke 2:41-51, the story of Mary and Joseph's taking Jesus to the Temple at the age of twelve, it is fairly obvious that Jesus is the only child. Since everyone agrees he was the first child of Mary, if there were up to five or more siblings, as some maintain (arguing, for example, from Matthew 13:55), they were nowhere to be found at this time. This passage alone furnishes a strong argument for the implausibility of the "literal brothers" theory.

• Jesus himself uses *brethren* in the larger sense. In Matthew 23:8 he calls the "crowds" and his "disciples" (23:1) "brethren." In other words, they are *each other's* "brothers" (that is, the brotherhood of Christians). In Matthew 12:49-50 he calls his disciples and all who do the will of his Father "my brothers."

• By comparing Matthew 27:56, Mark 15:40, and John 19:25, we find that James and Joseph — mentioned in Matthew 13:55 with Simon and Jude as Jesus' "brothers" — are also called sons of Mary, wife of Clopas. This other Mary (Matthew 27:61, 28:1) is called our Lady's *adelphe* in John 19:25 (it isn't likely that there were two women named "Mary" in one family — thus even this usage apparently means "cousin" or more distant relative). Matthew 13:55-56 and Mark 6:3 mention Simon, Jude, and "sisters" along with James and Joseph, calling all *adelphoi*. Since we know for sure that at least James and Joseph are not Jesus' blood brothers, the most likely interpretation of Matthew 13:55 is that all these "brothers" are cousins, according to the linguistic conventions discussed above. At the very least, the term *brother* is not determinative in and of itself.

• *Firstborn:* the use of this term to assert that Mary had "second-borns" and "third-borns" proves nothing, since the primary meaning of the Greek *prototokos* is "pre-eminent." To illustrate: David is described by God as the firstborn, the highest of the kings of the earth (Ps. 89:27). Likewise, God refers to Ephraim (Jer. 31:9) and the nation Israel (Exod. 4:22) as "my firstborn." Jesus is called "the firstborn of all creation" in Colossians 1:15, meaning, according to all reputable Greek lexicons, that he was pre-eminent over creation, that is, the Creator. The Jewish rabbinical writers even called God the Father *Bekorah Shelolam*, meaning "firstborn." Similarly, God is called the "first" in Scripture (Isa. 41:4, 44:6, 48:12; cf. Rev. 1:8, 21:6-7). Christians are called "the firstborn" in Hebrews 12:23. Literally speaking, however, among the Jews, the firstborn was ordinarily the child who was first to open the womb (Exod. 13:2), whether there were other children or not. This is probably the meaning of Matthew 1:25, in which case, hypothetical younger children of Mary are not implied at all, contrary to the standard present-day Protestant assertions.

• Mary is committed to the care of the apostle John by Jesus from the Cross (John 19:26-27). Many Protestant interpreters agree with the Catholic view that Jesus likely would not have done this if he had had brothers (who would all have been younger than he was). Many Church Fathers held this interpretation, including St. Athanasius, St. Epiphanius, St. Hilary, St. Jerome, and St. Ambrose, and used it in the defense of Mary's perpetual virginity.

• Catholics believe that Mary's reply to the angel Gabriel's announcement that she would bear the Messiah, at the Annunciation — "How can this be, since I have no husband?" (Luke 1:34) — indicates a prior vow of perpetual virginity. St. Augustine, in his work *Holy Virginity* (4, 4), wrote: "Surely, she would not say, 'How shall this be?' unless she had already vowed herself to God as a virgin. . . . If she intended to have intercourse, she wouldn't have asked this question!"

These conclusions are not merely the result of "Catholic bias" and special pleading, as many charge. For example, the prominent Protestant *Commentary on the Whole Bible* comments on Matthew 13:55:

> An *exceedingly difficult question* here arises: What were these "brethren" and "sisters" to Jesus? Were they, first, His full brothers and sisters? Or, secondly, were they His step-brothers and step-sisters, children of Joseph by a former marriage? Or, thirdly, were they His cousins, according to a common way of speaking among the Jews respecting persons of collateral descent? On this subject an immense deal has been written, *nor are opinions yet by any means*

> *agreed. . . .* In addition to other objections, *many of the best interpreters . . . prefer the third opinion. . . .* Thus dubiously we prefer to leave *this vexed question, encompassed as it is with difficulties.*[203]

Matthew 1:24-25: "Joseph . . . knew her not until she had borne a son."

This verse has been used as an argument that Mary did not remain a virgin after the birth of Jesus, but the same Protestant source also comments:

> The word *till* does not necessarily imply that they lived on a different footing afterward (as will be evident from the use of the same word in 1 Samuel 15:35; 2 Samuel 6:23; Matthew 12:20); nor does the word *firstborn* decide the *much-disputed question*, whether Mary had any children to Joseph after the birth of Christ; for, as Lightfoot says, "The law, in speaking of the firstborn, regarded not whether any were born *after* or no, but only that none were born before."[204]

John Calvin used this very argument to establish the fact of Mary's perpetual virginity, which he believed (based primarily on Scripture alone), as did Luther, Zwingli, Bullinger, and many later prominent, theologically conservative, and scholarly Protestants (such as John Wesley). No one had ever denied this doctrine until the late fourth century, when one Helvidius tangled unsuccessfully with St. Jerome. Calvin appealed to St. Jerome in his own commentary on this issue, and the issue of Jesus' supposed blood

[203] *Commentary on the Whole Bible*, 928 (emphasis added).

[204] Ibid., 882 (first emphasis added). Romans 8:22, 1 Timothy 4:13, 6:14, and Revelation 2:25 furnish four further examples of a similar meaning of *until*.

brothers did not come up again until the last few centuries, in which "higher criticism" has often been employed to question traditional interpretations of the Bible.

Scriptural evidence: Mary the intercessor, Mediatrix, and spiritual Mother

> **John 19:26-27:** "He said to his mother, 'Woman, behold your son!' Then he said to the disciple, 'Behold your mother!' "

It is quite reasonable to assume that in this utterance of Jesus on the Cross, more is involved than simply asking John to look after his mother. For Jesus addresses Mary first, which is odd if in fact no spiritual meaning is to be found here. John, like Nicodemus (John 3:1-15), is a representative figure in this instance: the disciple of Christ, in relationship to the Mother of the Church. As he would care for her physical needs, so she was to be to him (and to all Christians) a spiritual Mother.[205]

Neither Mary nor John are called by their proper names. Rather, they are the archetypes of "Mother Church"[206] and the faithful follower of Christ. The double phraseology recalls the covenantal formula of the Old Testament: "I will be his father, and he shall be my son" (2 Sam. 7:14; cf. 2 Cor. 6:16, 18; Heb. 1:5; Rev. 21:7). The motherhood of the Church is seen in passages such as Galatians 4:26: "But the Jerusalem above is free, and she is our mother."

> **Revelation 12:1, 5, 17:** "And a great portent appeared in Heaven: a woman clothed with the sun, with the moon under her feet, and on her head a crown of twelve stars. . . .

[205] CCC, pars. 501, 507, 963, 968-970, 972-973, 975.

[206] CCC, pars. 507, 722, 967.

> She brought forth a male child, one who is to rule all the nations with a rod of iron, but her child was caught up to God and to his throne. . . .
>
> Then the dragon was angry with the woman, and went off to make war on the rest of her offspring, on those who keep the commandments of God and bear testimony to Jesus. . . .

Cardinal Newman comments:

> What I would maintain is this, that the Holy Apostle would not have spoken of the Church under this particular image, *unless* there had existed a blessed Virgin Mary, who was exalted on high and the object of veneration to all the faithful. No one doubts that the "man-child" spoken of is an allusion to our Lord; why then is not "the Woman" an allusion to His mother?[207]

This passage has traditionally had a double interpretation, which is not unusual in Scripture. The primary application is to the Church, or the people of God. But a secondary reference can legitimately be made to the Blessed Virgin Mary, according to the literal meaning of 12:5, in which she bears the Messiah, Jesus (see Ps. 2:9). As such, the passage echoes the Mary/Eve symbolism of John 19:26-27.

Furthermore, the war with the dragon (identified as Satan in 12:9) recalls the Protoevangelion of Genesis 3:15 ("her seed"/"her offspring" battle the Devil) and supports the notion of the spiritual motherhood of Mary. The symbolism of Mary as the Church and the New Eve was already prevalent in the early centuries of the Church. The "woman" here gives birth "in anguish" (12:2), which hearkens back to Genesis 3:16, and is perhaps an anticipation of Calvary.

[207] John Henry Newman, "Letter to Pusey," in *Difficulties of Anglicans*, Vol. 2, 1875.

Mary as intercessor

As the pre-eminent saint and "all-holy one," Mary has a singular role in Heaven as an intercessor for us (James 5:16) and, as such, is venerated due to her unique attributes and privileges. This aspect has been dealt with generally with regard to the Communion of Saints. Mary is unique in this regard because she is the Mother of God and without sin, and is, therefore, the very highest and most exalted of all God's creatures.

Cardinal Newman exclaims:

> I consider it impossible, then, for those who believe the Church to be one vast body in Heaven and on earth, in which every holy creature of God has his place, and of which prayer is the life, when once they recognize the sanctity and dignity of the Blessed Virgin, not to perceive immediately that her office above is one of perpetual intercession for the faithful militant, and that our very relation to her must be that of clients to a patron, and that . . . the weapon of the Second Eve and Mother of God is prayer.[208]

Mary as a type of the Church

Mary is the first Christian, and is the Mother of believers in the same way that Abraham is known as the Father of believers. Abraham brought about the Old Covenant (humanly speaking) by an act of faith, and Mary, as the New Eve, assents obediently at the Annunciation, thus undoing the disobedience of Eve, the mother of the human race. As the sterile and aged Sarah was to be a mother to Israel, so the Virgin Mary would become the Mother of God and of Christians.

There is also a fascinating type in the Old Testament of which Mary, again, appears to be the fulfillment: the Daughter of Zion,[209]

[208] Ibid.

[209] CCC, pars. 489, 722.

who is the personification of Israel (the Church is the "new Israel"). The following verses are a representative sample of this typology: Lamentations 1:15, 2:13; Isaiah 62:5, 62:11; Jeremiah 4:31; Micah 4:10; Zechariah 2:10, 9:9; Zephaniah 3:14; cf. Revelation 21:2-3. In Lamentations 1:15 and Isaiah 62:5, the "Daughter of Zion" is described as a virgin.

In Zephaniah 3:14 and Zechariah 9:9, the Greek word *chaire* ("hail") appears in the Septuagint — the same word as that in Luke 1:28 ("Hail, full of grace"). *Chaire* is used in prophecies regarding the messianic deliverance of the Jews. The parallelism is seen to be more profound by a verse-by-verse comparison of Zephaniah 3:14-17 with Luke 1:28-31.

Mary as Mediatrix

Ludwig Ott explains this greatly misunderstood doctrine:

> Mary is designated Mediatrix of all graces in a double sense: 1) Mary gave the Redeemer, the Source of all graces, to the world, and in this way she is the channel of all graces; 2) Since Mary's Assumption into Heaven, no grace is conferred on man without her actual intercessory cooperation. . . .
>
> Mary freely and deliberately cooperated in giving the Redeemer to the world. . . . The Incarnation . . . and the Redemption . . . were dependent on her assent. In this significant moment in the history of Salvation Mary represented humanity. . . .
>
> The title Co-redemptrix, which has been current since the fifteenth century . . . must not be conceived in the sense of an equation of the efficacy of Mary with the redemptive activity of Christ, the sole Redeemer of humanity (1 Tim. 2:5). . . . Her cooperation in the objective redemption is an indirect, remote cooperation, and derives from this, that she voluntarily devoted her whole life to the service

> of the Redeemer, and under the Cross, suffered and sacrificed with Him. . . .
>
> Christ alone truly offered the sacrifice of atonement on the Cross; Mary merely gave Him moral support in this action. . . .
>
> Since her assumption into Heaven, Mary cooperates in the application of the grace of Redemption to man. She participates in the distribution of grace by her maternal intercession, which is far inferior in efficacy to that of the intercessory prayer of Christ, the High Priest, but surpasses far the intercessory prayer of all the other saints.
>
> According to the view of the older, and of many of the modern theologians Mary's intercessory cooperation extends to all graces, which are conferred on mankind, so that no grace accrues to men without the intercession of Mary. The implication of this is not that we are obliged to beg for all graces through Mary, nor that Mary's intercession is intrinsically necessary for the application of the grace, but that, according to God's positive ordinance, the redemptive grace of Christ is conferred on nobody without the actual intercessory cooperation of Mary.[210]

Mary's secondary (to Christ) and wholly derivative function as the Mediatrix[211] is no more a violation of his unique mediatorship than any number of functions he sanctions and allows among his Body, the Church. We pray for each other, thus acting as mediators. One could just as easily say, "Why ask your fellow Christians to pray for you when you can ask Jesus?" as "Why do you ask for Mary's prayers when you can go directly to Jesus?" Yet God commands us to pray for one another. God is Creator, but he gives us the privilege of procreation, in childbirth and parenthood. Jesus is

[210] Ott, *Fundamentals of Christian Dogma*, 212-213.

[211] CCC, pars. 964-965, 968-970, 975.

the "chief" Shepherd of his flock (John 10:11-16; 1 Pet. 5:4), yet he assigns lesser shepherds to watch over his own (John 21:15-17; Eph. 4:11). And he is the supreme Judge, but he bids us to judge as well (Matt. 19:28; 1 Cor. 6:2-3; Rev. 20:4). Many other similar examples can be found in the Bible.

The Mariology of the founders of Protestantism

The founders of Protestantism, or Reformers, as they are known, who believed in "Scripture alone" as the highest Christian authority, nevertheless continued in the sixteenth century to retain a surprising number of Marian dogmas (particularly the perpetual virginity and the use of *Theotokos*). In many respects they were closer in belief to their Catholic opponents than they are to present-day Protestants. Martin Luther himself was startlingly "Catholic" in this regard. The views of these men are of considerable historical interest and deserve to be detailed at some length.

Martin Luther taught the traditional understanding of the title "Mother of God" in the following passage:

> God did not derive his divinity from Mary; but it does not follow that it is therefore wrong to say that God was born of Mary, that God is Mary's Son, and that Mary is God's mother. . . . She is the true mother of God and bearer of God. . . . Mary suckled God, rocked God to sleep, prepared broth and soup for God, etc. For God and man are one person, one Christ, one Son, one Jesus, not two Christs . . . just as your son is not two sons . . . even though he has two natures, body and soul, the body from you, the soul from God alone.[212]

[212] *On the Councils and the Church* (1539). From Jaroslav Pelikan and Helmut T. Lehmann, eds., *Luther's Works* (St. Louis: Concordia Publishing House [Vols. 1-30], Philadelphia: Fortress Press [Vols. 31-55], 1955), Vol. 41, 99-100.

Luther also thought it altogether proper to venerate Mary:

> The veneration of Mary is inscribed in the very depths of the human heart.[213]
>
> She is nobility, wisdom, and holiness personified. We can never honor her enough. Still honor and praise must be given to her in such a way as to injure neither Christ nor the Scriptures.[214]

The perpetual virginity of Mary is expressly upheld by Luther:

> Christ, our Savior, was the real and natural fruit of Mary's virginal womb. . . . This was without the cooperation of a man, and she remained a virgin after that.[215]
>
> Christ . . . was the only Son of Mary, and the Virgin Mary bore no children besides Him. . . . I am inclined to agree with those who declare that *brothers* really mean "cousins" here, for Holy Writ and the Jews always call cousins brothers.[216]

Luther even accepted the Immaculate Conception:

> It is a sweet and pious belief that the infusion of Mary's soul was effected *without Original Sin;* so that in the very *infusion of her soul* she was also purified from Original Sin and adorned with God's gifts, receiving a pure soul infused by God; thus from the first moment she began to live, she was free from all sin.[217]

[213] William J. Cole, "Was Luther a Devotee of Mary?" *Marian Studies*, Vol. 21, 1970: 131 (Sermon, September 1, 1522).

[214] Ibid. (Christmas sermon, 1531).

[215] "Sermons on John, chs. 1-4" (1537-1539). In Pelikan, *Luther's Works*, Vol. 22, 23.

[216] Ibid., 214-215. Pelikan asserts that this was Luther's lifelong belief.

[217] Sermon: "On the Day of the Conception of Mary, the Mother of God" (December 1527). From Grisar, Hartmann, *Luther*,

> She is *full of grace;* so that she may be recognized as without any sin. That is a high and great thing, for God's grace fills her with all gifts and frees her from all evil.[218]

The Lutheran scholar Arthur Carl Piepkorn (1907-1973), of Concordia Seminary in St. Louis, after intense study, confirmed Luther's lifelong (barring two "lapses") acceptance of the Immaculate Conception.[219] Although he made no unequivocal statements concerning it, Luther never denied the Assumption.[220] Additionally, he upheld the spiritual motherhood of Mary, the usefulness of the Rosary, and the propriety of the phrase "Queen of Heaven":

> Mary is the Mother of Jesus and the Mother of all of us. . . . If he is ours, we ought to be in his situation; there where he is, we ought also to be and all that he has ought to be ours, and his mother is also our mother.[221]
>
> Our prayer should include the Mother of God. . . . What the Hail Mary says is that all glory should be given to God, using these words: "Hail Mary, full of grace. The Lord is with thee; blessed art thou among women and blessed is the fruit of thy womb, Jesus Christ. Amen!" You see that these words are not concerned with prayer, but purely with giving praise and honor. . . . We can use the Hail Mary as a meditation in which we recite what grace God has given her.

trans., E. M. Lamond, ed. Luigi Cappadelta (London: Kegan Paul, Trench, Trubner, and Co., 1917), Vol. 4, 238 (emphasis added). See also, e.g., House Sermon for Christmas, 1533.

[218] Cole, "Was Luther a Devotee of Mary?" 185; *Little Prayer Book* (1522).

[219] "Mary's Place within the People of God According to Non-Roman Catholics," *Marian Studies*, Vol. 18, 1967: 46-83 (see page 76).

[220] Cole, "Was Luther a Devotee of Mary?" 123-124.

[221] Ibid., 128 (Sermon, Christmas, 1529; emphasis added).

> Second, we should add a wish that everyone may know and respect her. . . . He who has no faith is advised to refrain from saying the Hail Mary. . . .[222]
>
> Although she was without sin, yet that grace was far too great for her to deserve it in any way. How should a creature deserve to become the Mother of God? . . . It is necessary also to keep within bounds and not to make too much of calling her "Queen of Heaven," which is a *true-enough name*. . . .[223]

Even John Calvin, who was much less traditional than Luther in many ways, makes several "Catholic-sounding" comments about Mary:

> We cannot give praise for the blessing which Christ has given to us without remembering at the same time the glorious privilege which God bestowed on Mary by choosing her to be the mother of his only Son. . . . Now she is called Blessed because, receiving by faith the blessing which is offered to her, she opened the way for God to accomplish his work.[224]
>
> Let us learn to praise the holy Virgin. When we confess with her that we are nothing . . . and that we owe all to the pure goodness of God, see how we will be disciples of the Virgin Mary?[225]

[222] *Little Prayer Book* (1522). In Pelikan, *Luther's Works*, Vol. 43, 39-41.

[223] "Magnificat" (1521). In Pelikan, *Luther's Works*, Vol. 21, 327 (emphasis added).

[224] Commentary on Luke 1:42, 45. In Max Thurian, *Mary: Mother of All Christians*, Neville B. Cryer, trans. (New York: Herder and Herder, 1963), 186.

[225] Ross MacKenzie, "Mariology as an Ecumenical Problem," *Marian Studies*, Vol. 26, 1975: 206-207 (*Harmony of Matthew, Mark, and Luke*, sect. 39 [Geneva, 1562]).

> There has been some ignorance in that they have reproved this fashion of speaking of the Virgin Mary as the mother of God.[226]
>
> Helvidius displayed excessive ignorance in concluding that Mary must have had many sons, because Christ's "brothers" are sometimes mentioned.[227]
>
> [On Matthew 1:25:] The inference he [Helvidius] drew from it was that Mary remained a virgin no longer than till her first birth, and that afterwards she had other children by her husband. . . . No just and well-grounded inference can be drawn from these words . . . as to what took place after the birth of Christ. He is called "firstborn"; but it is for the sole purpose of informing us that he was born of a virgin. . . . What took place afterward the historian does not inform us. . . . No man will obstinately keep up the argument, except from an extreme fondness for disputation.[228]

Heinrich Bullinger, another historically significant Protestant Reformer, made an extraordinary proclamation which appears to uphold virtually all of the Catholic Marian dogmas:

> Elijah was transported, body and soul, in a chariot of fire; he was not buried in any Church bearing his name, but mounted up to Heaven, so that . . . we might know what immortality and recompense God prepares for his faithful

[226] Letter to French community in London, Sept. 27, 1552. In Thurian, *Mary: Mother of All Christians*, 77.

[227] Calvin, *Harmony*, Vol. 2. From *Calvin's Commentaries*, William Pringle, trans. (Grand Rapids, Michigan: Eerdmans, 1949), 215; on Matthew 13:55.

[228] *Calvin's Commentaries*, Vol. 1, 107. Calvin, in his commentary on Luke 1:34 in his *Harmony*, affirms the perpetual virginity of Mary, while at the same time denying that Mary had made a vow of celibacy.

> prophets and for his most outstanding and incomparable creatures. . . . It is for this reason, we believe, that the pure and immaculate embodiment of the Mother of God, the Virgin Mary, the Temple of the Holy Spirit, that is to say, her saintly body, was carried up to Heaven by the angels.[229]

Within Anglicanism, many of the "high-church" or "Anglo-Catholic" faction believe in a Mariology not unlike that of the Catholic Church, both doctrinally and devotionally.

[229] From Thurian, *Mary: Mother of All Christians*, 197-198; written in 1568, *De Origine Erroris*, 16.

Chapter Ten

The Papacy and Infallibility

"Keys of the kingdom"

The ecumenical First Vatican Council, in 1870, defined once and for all the dogma of papal infallibility as follows:

> We teach and define that it is a dogma divinely revealed: that the Roman Pontiff, when he speaks *ex cathedra*, that is, when, in discharge of the office of pastor and teacher of all Christians, by virtue of his supreme Apostolic authority, he defines a doctrine regarding faith or morals to be held by the universal Church, is, by the divine assistance promised to him in Blessed Peter, possessed of that infallibility with which the divine Redeemer willed that His Church should be endowed in defining doctrine regarding faith or morals; and that, therefore, such definitions of the Roman Pontiff are of themselves, and not from the consent of the Church, irreformable.[230]

[230] In *Dogmatic Canons and Decrees* (Rockford, Illinois: TAN Books, 1977), 256. (Documents of Councils of Trent and Vatican I, plus Decree on the Immaculate Conception and the *Syllabus of Errors* of Pope Pius IX). See also CCC, pars. 891, 2035; Hardon, CC, 224-233; Hardon *PCD*, 194-195. For conciliar infallibility, see CCC, pars. 891-892, 2035.

The charge is often made that the Catholic Church "invents" dogmas late in the game, which were not present in earlier centuries. The papacy, and papal infallibility, have indeed been in existence from the very earliest days of the Church, starting with the apostle Peter, and what he and other Christians believed about his leadership and jurisdiction.[231] As is to be expected, however, both the office of the Pope and the notion of papal infallibility did undergo much development through the centuries.

To illustrate how the definition of 1870 drew on centuries of reflection and practice, we will cite St. Francis de Sales's teaching from around 1596:

> When he teaches the whole Church as shepherd, in general matters of faith and morals, then there is nothing but doctrine and truth. And in fact everything a king says is not a law or an edict, but that only which a king says as king and as a legislator. So everything the Pope says is not canon law or of legal obligation; he must mean to define and to lay down the law for the sheep, and he must keep the due order and form.
>
> We must not think that in everything and everywhere his judgment is infallible, but then only when he gives judgment on a matter of Faith in questions necessary to the whole Church; for in particular cases which depend on human fact he can err, there is no doubt, although it is not for us to control him in these cases, save with all reverence, submission, and discretion. Theologians have said, in a word, that he can err in questions of fact, not in questions of right; that he can err *extra cathedram*, outside the chair of Peter; that is, as a private individual, by writings and bad example.

[231] CCC, pars. 552-553, 765, 862, 880-882, 936-937, 1444.

> But he cannot err when he is *in cathedra*, that is, when he intends to make an instruction and decree for the guidance of the whole Church, when he means to confirm his brethren as supreme pastor, and to conduct them into the pastures of the Faith. For then it is not so much man who determines, resolves, and defines as it is the Blessed Holy Spirit by man, which Spirit, according to the promise made by our Lord to the Apostles, teaches all truth to the Church.[232]

Robert Hugh Benson (1871-1914), a convert to Catholicism whose father, Edward W. Benson (1829-1896), had been the Archbishop of Canterbury, the highest office in Anglicanism, wrote concerning the development of the papacy:

> It was not, then, until the head had been fully established as supreme over the body that men had eyes to see how it had been so ordained and indicated from the beginning. After it had come to pass, it was seen to have been inevitable. All this is paralleled, of course, by the ordinary course of affairs. Laws of nature, as well as laws of grace, act quite apart from man's perception or appreciation of them; and it is not until the law is recognized that its significance and inevitability, its illustrations and effects, are intelligibly recognized either.[233]

Likewise, Cardinal Newman, in his masterpiece *Essay on the Development of Christian Doctrine*, offers similar analysis:

> Whether communion with the Pope was necessary for Catholicity would not and could not be debated till a suspension

[232] St. Francis de Sales, *CON*, 306-307.

[233] Robert Hugh Benson, *The Religion of the Plain Man* (Long Prairie, Minnesota: Neumann Press, 1906), 109.

> of that communion had actually occurred. It is not a greater difficulty that St. Ignatius does not write to the Asian Greeks about Popes, than that St. Paul does not write to the Corinthians about Bishops. And it is less a difficulty that the Papal supremacy was not formally acknowledged in the second century, than that there was no formal acknowledgment on the part of the Church of the doctrine of the Holy Trinity till the fourth. No doctrine is defined till it is violated. . . .
>
> Moreover, an international bond and a common authority could not be consolidated . . . while persecutions lasted. If the Imperial Power checked the development of Councils, it availed also for keeping back the power of the Papacy. The Creed, the Canon, in like manner, both remained undefined. . . . All began to form, as soon as the Empire relaxed its tyrannous oppression of the Church. . . .
>
> Supposing there be otherwise good reason for saying that the Papal Supremacy is part of Christianity, there is nothing in the early history of the Church to contradict it. . . .
>
> Doctrine cannot but develop as time proceeds and need arises, and . . . therefore it is lawful, or rather necessary, to interpret the words and deeds of the earlier Church by the determinate teaching of the later.[234]

Cardinal Gibbons eloquently defended papal infallibility against the common objections of Protestants and other non-Catholics:

> You will tell me that infallibility is too great a prerogative to be conferred on man. I answer: Has not God, in former times, clothed His Apostles with powers far more exalted? They were endowed with the gifts of working miracles, of

[234] John Henry Newman, *An Essay on the Development of Christian Doctrine*, Pt. 1, ch. 4, sect. 3, nos. 4-5, 7-8. Newman was received into the Catholic Church the year this book of his was completed.

> prophecy and inspiration; they were the mouthpiece communicating God's revelation, of which the Popes are merely the custodians. If God could make man the organ of His revealed Word, is it impossible for Him to make man its infallible guardian and interpreter? For, surely, greater is the Apostle who gives us the inspired Word than the Pope who preserves it from error. . . .
>
> Let us see, sir, whether an infallible Bible is sufficient for you. Either you are infallibly certain that your interpretation of the Bible is correct or you are not.
>
> If you are infallibly certain, then you assert for yourself, and of course for every reader of the Scripture, a personal infallibility which you deny to the Pope, and which we claim only for him. You make every man his own Pope.
>
> If you are not infallibly certain that you understand the true meaning of the whole Bible . . . then, I ask, of what use to you is the objective infallibility of the Bible without an infallible interpreter?[235]

Although the Pope is supreme Head of the Church and preeminent in authority, nevertheless, he acts in concert with both the college of bishops (especially when meeting in an ecumenical council, such as Trent or Vatican II),[236] and the "sense of the faithful" (or *sensus fidelium*).[237] It is this united jurisdiction of bishops and Pope (distantly analogous to the U.S. Congress and President, with the Supreme Court similar to Catholic Canon Law) which is the distinctive mark of Catholic ecclesiology,[238] as opposed to Eastern Orthodoxy, which accepts bishops but acknowledges no Pope, and Protestantism, which does not formally recognize the

[235] Gibbons, *The Faith of Our Fathers*, 108-109.

[236] CCC, pars. 877, 879, 887.

[237] CCC, par. 889.

[238] CCC, pars. 765, 816, 880-881, 883-885, 895, 1444, 2034.

papacy, and many denominations of which (perhaps the majority) lack bishops. Catholics claim that this arrangement is mirrored in the biblical relationship of St. Peter and the other original disciples, and that it is required by the demands of apostolic succession (see Appendix Two), which is itself suggested in the Bible.[239]

Bishop Vincent Gasser, in his famous defense of papal infallibility (the *Relatio*) at the First Vatican Council, discussed the aspects of collegiality and community:

> We do defend the infallibility of the person of the Roman Pontiff, not as an individual person, but as the person of the Roman Pontiff or a public person, that is, as head of the Church in his relation to the Church Universal. . . .
>
> We do not exclude the cooperation of the Church because the infallibility of the Roman Pontiff does not come to him in the manner of inspiration or of revelation, but through a divine assistance. Therefore, the Pope, by reason of his office and the gravity of the matter, is held to use the means suitable for properly discerning and aptly enunciating the truth. These means are councils, or the advice of the bishops, cardinals, theologians, etc. Indeed the means are diverse according to the diversity of situations, and we should piously believe that, in the divine assistance promised to Peter and his successors by Christ, there is simultaneously contained a promise about the means which are necessary and suitable to make an infallible pontifical judgment.
>
> Finally we do not separate the Pope, even minimally, from the consent of the Church, as long as that consent is not laid down as a condition which is either antecedent or consequent. We are not able to separate the Pope from the consent of the Church because this consent is never able to

[239]CCC, pars. 77, 551, 833, 860-862, 869, 875, 886, 888, 890, 892, 894-896, 935, 938.

> be lacking to him. Indeed, since we believe that the Pope is infallible through the divine assistance, by that very fact we also believe that the assent of the Church will not be lacking to his definitions, since it is not able to happen that the body of bishops be separated from its head, and since the Church universal is not able to fail.[240]

Nevertheless, the Pope is ultimately supreme, even over ecumenical councils, which he ratifies in all particulars (a power that might be compared in part to the veto of the American President). The famous English convert and apologist Ronald Knox (1888-1957) explains:

> [It is a] quite unworkable idea that the authority of the Pope depends on the authority of the Council. There is no way of deciding which councils were ecumenical councils except by saying that those councils were ecumenical which had their decisions ratified by the Pope. Now, either that ratification is infallible of itself, or else you will immediately have to summon a fresh ecumenical council to find out whether the Pope's ratification was infallible or not, and so on *ad infinitum*. You can't keep on going round and round in a vicious circle; in the long run, the last word of decision must lie with one man, and that man is obviously the Pope. In the last resort the Pope must be the umpire, must have the casting vote. If, therefore, there is to be any infallibility in the Church, that infallibility must reside in the Pope, even when he speaks in his own name, without summoning a council to fortify his decision.[241]

[240] In Vincent Gasser, *The Gift of Infallibility*, James T. O'Connor, trans. (Boston: Daughters of St. Paul, 1986), 41-44.

[241] Ronald Knox, *In Soft Garments* (Garden City, New York: Doubleday Image, 1941), 130.

Contrary to common assumptions, the doctrine of the papacy is well grounded in Scripture, and the institution is present in increasingly developing stages throughout the history of the Church. Moreover, the constant, remarkable primacy of Rome in the history of Christianity is equally undeniable. Because the very existence of this historical institution (in the early Church) is so often denied (for example, many arbitrarily maintain that Pope Leo the Great in the fifth century was the first Pope, and others claim the same for Gregory the Great in the sixth), more attention than usual will be paid to the actual history of the papacy and the theological justifications historically put forth in defense of it.

Scriptural evidence for the papacy and the apostolic primacy of St. Peter

St. Peter as the Rock (Matthew 16:18)

> **Matthew 16:18:** "And I tell you, you are Peter, and on this rock I will build my church, and the powers of death shall not prevail against it."

Catholics contend that the "rock" is Peter himself, not his faith, or Jesus (although arguably his faith is assumed by Christ in naming Peter "rock" in the first place). This interpretation is found in the Church Fathers at least as early as Tertullian (d. c. 230). The next verse (16:19) is in the singular, which supports this view, which is in fact the consensus of the majority of biblical commentators today, according to the article on Peter in the *Encyclopaedia Britannica* (1985 edition).[242]

It has often been argued to the contrary that Jesus called Peter *petros* (literally, "stone"), not *petra* (the word for "rock" in the

[242] *Micropedia*, 330-333. D. W. O'Connor, the author of the article, is himself Protestant and author of *Peter in Rome: The Literary, Liturgical, and Archaeological Evidence* (1969).

passage), so that the "rock" wasn't Peter; but this is simply explained by the necessity for a proper male name in Greek to be in the masculine gender. But in Aramaic, the language Jesus spoke, the name *kepha* would have been used for both "rock" and "Peter." Matthew could just as easily have used another Greek word for "stone" — *lithos* — in contrast to "rock," but this would have distorted the unmistakable word-play of the passage, which is the whole point!

Many prominent Protestant scholars and exegetes have agreed that Peter is the "rock" in Matthew 16:18; these include Alford, Broadus, Keil, Kittel, Cullmann,[243] Albright,[244] Robert McAfee Brown,[245] and more recently, respected Evangelical commentators R. T. France[246] and D. A. Carson.[247] Also, popular one-volume Protestant Bible commentaries such as *Peake's Commentary*,[248] *New Bible Commentary* (NBC), and numerous others concur.[249]

[243] Oscar Cullmann, *Peter: Disciple, Apostle, Martyr* (second revised edition, 1962).

[244] Anchor Bible (Garden City, New York: Doubleday, 1971), Vol. 26, 195, 197-198.

[245] In Peter J. McCord, ed., *A Pope For All Christians?* (New York: Paulist Press, 1976), 7. This book is an ecumenical project, offering views on the papacy from many perspectives. Brown is a Presbyterian and a prominent ecumenist.

[246] Leon Morris, gen. ed., *Tyndale New Testament Commentaries* (Leicester, England: Inter-Varsity Press/Grand Rapids, Michigan: Eerdmans Pub. Co., 1985), Vol. 1: *Matthew*, R. T. France, 254, 256.

[247] Frank E. Gaebelein, gen. ed., *Expositor's Bible Commentary* (Grand Rapids, Michigan: Zondervan, 1984), Vol. 8: *Matthew, Mark, Luke* (Matthew: D. A. Carson), 368.

[248] Second revised edition (London: Nelson, 1962), 787.

[249] According to Raymond E. Brown, Karl P. Donfried, and John Reumann, eds., *Peter in the New Testament* (Minneapolis: Augsburg Publishing House/New York: Paulist Press, 1973), 92-93, which also takes the same view. This is probably the most important ecumenical work on Peter and is thus cited

Both Carson and France surprisingly assert that only Protestant overreaction to Catholic Petrine and papal claims have brought about the denial that Peter himself is the "rock."

The great Protestant Greek scholar Marvin Vincent was one who took the traditional view, in his standard reference work *Word Studies in the New Testament*, originally published in 1887:

> The word refers neither to *Christ* as a *rock*, distinguished from *Simon*, a *stone*, nor to *Peter's confession*, but to *Peter himself*. . . . The reference of *petra* to Christ is forced and unnatural. The obvious reference of the word is to Peter. The emphatic *this* naturally refers to the nearest antecedent; and besides, the metaphor is thus weakened, since Christ appears here, not as the *foundation*, but as the *architect*: "On *this rock* will I build." Again, Christ is the great foundation, the *chief cornerstone*, but the New Testament writers recognize no impropriety in applying to the members of Christ's church certain terms which are applied to him. For instance, Peter himself (1 Pet. 2:4) calls Christ a *living stone* and . . . addresses the church as *living stones* (1 Pet. 2:5). . . .
>
> Equally untenable is the explanation which refers *petra* to Simon's confession. Both the play upon the words and the natural reading of the passage are against it, and besides, it does not conform to the fact, since the church is built, not on *confessions*, but on *confessors* — living men. . . .
>
> The reference to Simon himself is confirmed by the actual relation of Peter to the early church. . . . See Acts 1:15; 2:14, 37; 3:2; 4:8; 5:15, 29; 9:34, 40; 10:25-6; Galatians 1:18.[250]

first in a long bibliography in the *Encyclopaedia Britannica*. It is a common statement by a panel of eleven Catholic and Lutheran scholars.

[250] Marvin R. Vincent, *Word Studies in the New Testament* (Grand Rapids, Michigan: Eerdmans, 1946), Vol. 1, 91-92; emphasis in original.

St. Francis de Sales, a leader of the Catholic Reformation, draws out the implications of this passage for the papacy:

> Our Lord, then, who is comparing his Church to a building, when he says that he will build it on St. Peter, shows that St. Peter will be its foundation-stone. . . . When he makes St. Peter its foundation, he makes him head and superior of this family. By these words, our Lord shows the perpetuity and immovableness of this foundation. The stone on which one raises the building is the first; the others rest on it. Other stones may be removed without overthrowing the edifice, but he who takes away the foundation knocks down the house. If, then, the gates of Hell can in no wise prevail against the Church, they can in no wise prevail against its foundation and head, which they cannot take away and overturn without entirely overturning the whole edifice. . . .
>
> The supreme charge which St. Peter had . . . as chief and governor, is not *beside* the authority of his Master, but is only a participation in this, so that he is not the foundation of this hierarchy *besides* our Lord, but rather in our Lord: as we call him most holy Father in our Lord, outside whom he would be nothing. . . .
>
> St. Peter is foundation, not founder, of the whole Church; foundation but founded on another foundation, which is our Lord . . . in fine, administrator and not lord, and in no way the foundation of our faith, hope, and charity, nor of the efficacy of the Sacraments. . . . So, although [Christ] is the Good Shepherd, he gives us shepherds (Eph. 4:11) under himself, between whom and his Majesty there is so great a difference that he declares himself to be the only shepherd (John 10:11; Ezek. 34:23).[251]

[251] St. Francis de Sales, *CON*, 242-243, 245-247.

Chesterton made a marvelously insightful comment concerning Christ's selection of Peter as the "rock":

> When Christ at a symbolic moment was establishing His great society, he chose for its cornerstone neither the brilliant Paul nor the mystic John, but a shuffler, a snob, a coward — in a word, a man. And upon this rock he has built His Church, and the gates of Hell have not prevailed against it. All the empires and the kingdoms have failed, because of this inherent and continual weakness, that they were founded by strong men and upon strong men. But this one thing, the historic Christian Church, was founded on a weak man, and for that reason it is indestructible. For no chain is stronger than its weakest link.[252]

The keys of the kingdom (Matthew 16:19)

Matthew 16:19: "I will give you the keys of the kingdom of Heaven."

Isaiah 22:20-22: "In that day I will call my servant Eliakim, the son of Hilkiah . . . and he shall be a father to the inhabitants of Jerusalem and to the house of Judah. And I will place on his shoulder the key of the house of David; he shall open, and none shall shut; and he shall shut, and none shall open."

Revelation 3:7 [Christ describing Himself]: ". . . the holy one, the true one, who has the key of David, who opens and no one shall shut, who shuts and no one opens."

[252] G. K. Chesterton, *Heretics* (London: The Bodley Head, 1950), 60-61. Chesterton was not yet formally Catholic at the time of this quote (1905). He would be received into the Catholic Church seventeen years later, in 1922.

The power of the "keys," in the Hebrew mind, had to do with administrative authority and ecclesiastical discipline and, in a broad sense, might be thought to encompass the use of excommunication, penitential decrees, a barring from the sacraments and lesser censures, and legislative and executive functions. Like the name "rock," this privilege was bestowed only upon St. Peter and no other disciple or apostle. He was to become God's "vice-regent," so to speak.[253]

In the Old Testament, a steward was a man *over a house* (Gen. 43:19, 44:4; 1 Kings 4:6, 16:9, 18:3; 2 Kings 10:5, 15:5, 18:18; Isa. 22:15). The steward was also called a "governor" in the Old Testament and has been described by commentators as a type of prime minister.

In the New Testament, the two words often translated as "steward" are *oikonomos* (Luke 16:2-3; 1 Cor. 4:1-2; Titus 1:7; 1 Pet. 4:10) and *epitropos* (Matt. 20:8; Gal. 4:2).

Several Protestant commentaries and dictionaries take the position that Christ is clearly hearkening back to Isaiah 22:15-22 when he makes this pronouncement, and that it has something to do with delegated authority in the Church that he is establishing (in the same context).[254] He applies the same language to himself in Revelation 3:7 (cf. Job 12:14), so that his commission to Peter may be interpreted as an assignment of powers to the recipient in his stead, as a sort of authoritative representative or ambassador.

[253] J. D. Douglas, ed., *The New Bible Dictionary (NBD)* (Grand Rapids, Michigan: Eerdmans, 1962), 1018.

[254] Ibid., 1018, 1216; Guthrie, *NBC*, 603, 837; France, *Tyndale New Testament Commentaries*, 256; Cullmann, *Peter: Disciple, Apostle, Martyr*, 183-184 (in 1952 French edition). Cullmann describes Peter as Jesus' "superintendent." The ecumenical work *Peter in the New Testament* (Brown, ed.) also espouses the same view (96-97).

The "opening" and "shutting" (Isa. 22:2) appear to refer to a jurisdictional power that no one but the king (in the ancient kingdom of Judah) could override. Literally, it refers to the prime minister's prerogative to deny or allow entry to the palace and access to the king. In Isaiah's time, this office was over three hundred years old and is thought to have been derived by Solomon from the Egyptian model of palace functionary, or the Pharaoh's "vizier," who was second in command after the Pharaoh. This was exactly the office granted to Joseph in Egypt (Gen. 41:40-44, 45:8).[255]

The symbol of keys always represented authority in the Middle East. This standpoint comes down to us in our own culture when we observe mayors giving an honored visitor the "key to the city."

The Commentary on the Whole Bible expounds Isaiah 22:15, 22 as follows:

> [The steward is] the *king's friend*, or *principal officer of the court* (1 Kings 4:5; 18:3; 1 Chron. 27:33), the *king's counselor)*. . . .
>
> Keys are carried sometimes in the East hanging from the kerchief on the shoulder. But the phrase is rather figurative for *sustaining the government on one's shoulders*. Eliakim, as his name implies, is here plainly a type of the God-man Christ, the son of "David," of whom Isaiah (9:6) uses the same language as the former clause of this verse *[and the government will be upon his shoulder]*.[256]

One can confidently conclude, therefore, that when Old Testament usage and the culture of the hearers is closely examined, the phrase "keys of the kingdom of Heaven" must have great

[255] See Stanley Jaki, *The Keys of the Kingdom* (Chicago: Franciscan Herald Press, 1986), 27-28.

[256] *Commentary on the Whole Bible*, 536.

significance (for Peter and for the papacy) indeed, all the more so since Christ granted this honor only to St. Peter.

The power to bind and loose

> **Matthew 16:19:** "Whatever you bind on earth shall be bound in Heaven, and whatever you loose on earth shall be loosed in Heaven."

Binding and *loosing* were technical rabbinical terms meaning, respectively, "to forbid" and "to permit," with regard to interpretations of Jewish Law. In secondary usage, they could mean "to condemn" and "to acquit." This power is also given to the Apostles in Matthew 18:17-18, where it apparently refers particularly to discipline and excommunication in local jurisdictions (whereas Peter's commission seems to apply to the universal Church).

In John 20:23, it is also granted to the Apostles (in a different terminology, which suggests the power to impose penance and grant indulgences and absolution). Generally speaking, *binding* and *loosing* usually meant the prerogative to formulate Christian doctrine and to require allegiance to it, as well as to condemn heresies that were opposed to the true doctrine (Jude 3).[257]

Marvin Vincent writes:

> No other terms were in more constant use in Rabbinic canon-law than those of *binding* and *loosing*. They represented the *legislative* and *judicial* powers of the Rabbinic office. These powers Christ now transferred . . . in their reality, to his Apostles; the first, here, to Peter, as their representative, the second, after his Resurrection, to the Church (John 20:23). . . .[258]

[257] See, e.g., Allen C. Myers, ed., *Eerdmans Bible Dictionary* (Grand Rapids, Michigan: Eerdmans, 1987), 158; Guthrie, NBC, 837; France, *Tyndale New Testament Commentaries*, 256.

[258] Vincent, *Word Studies in the New Testament*, Vol. 1, 96.

St. Peter commanded to "feed my sheep"

John 21:15-17: "Jesus said to Simon Peter, 'Simon, son of John, do you love me more than these?' He said to him, 'Yes, Lord; you know that I love you.' He said to him, 'Feed my lambs.' A second time he said to him, 'Simon, son of John, do you love me?' He said to him, 'Yes, Lord; you know that I love you.' He said to him, 'Tend my sheep.' He said to him the third time, 'Simon, son of John, do you love me?' Peter was grieved because he said to him the third time, 'Do you love me?' And he said to him, 'Lord, you know everything; you know that I love you.' Jesus said to him, 'Feed my sheep.' "

Revelation 7:17: "For the Lamb in the midst of the throne will be their shepherd, and he will guide them to springs of living water."

The Greek word for "tend" in 21:16 is *poimaino*, which is applied to Jesus Christ in Revelation 7:17 above, and also in Matthew 2:6 and Revelation 2:27, 12:5, and 19:15. It is used of bishops in Acts 20:28 and 1 Peter 5:2 (which seems to be a passage perhaps reminiscent in St. Peter's mind of the Lord's charge to him). Clearly, an awesome amount of spiritual authority is being given to Peter, which includes, according to the Protestant Greek scholar W. E. Vine, "discipline, authority, restoration, material assistance of individuals."[259]

The commission of Christ to Peter, then, to "tend my sheep," while not exclusive to Peter in the sense that no one else (besides Christ) exercises this function (St. Peter himself says as much in 1 Peter 5:2), nevertheless is supremely unique and important insofar

[259] Vine, *An Expository Dictionary of New Testament Words*, Vol. 2, 88.

as no other *individual* disciple is likewise instructed by our Lord — and in such momentous terms (considering all of the biblical data).

Peter's ministry to the Church is always universal; his jurisdiction knows no bounds, and the language that Christ himself applies to him is strikingly sublime and profound. For to no one else was it granted the keys of the kingdom of Heaven. No one else was renamed "Rock," and proclaimed by Jesus to be the foundation upon which he would build his Church.

And although the power to bind and loose was given to the disciples as a whole in Matthew 18:18, nevertheless, Peter is the only *individual* to be given this power by Christ. In other words, St. Peter has extraordinary privileges unique to himself, and in cases where they are not exclusive, they are obviously applied to him in a pre-eminent sense.

We find then, that the scriptural relation between Christ, Peter, and the disciples (by extension, bishops and priests), is precisely that found in the teaching and practice of the Catholic Church, where the Pope, more than just the "foremost among equals," as the Orthodox and some Lutherans and Anglicans hold, is the supreme shepherd and leader of the Church, yet not in such a fashion as to exclude Christ as the Head or the cardinals and bishops (and even laymen) as fellow members of the Body in Christ acting in organic harmony.

Always, it is the Pope and the cardinals, the Pope and the council, the Pope acting with due consideration of the faithful lay members of the Church, but the Pope is supreme. It is simply not necessary to dichotomize the relationship between the Pope and lesser clergy. With regard to the papacy, only Catholicism does justice to both the scriptural data and the course of the early Church in the formative years of her development.

One need not fall into the trap of denying the Pope's existence (and thereby doing violence to the Petrine texts as well), nor of caricaturing the Catholic Church's doctrine of the papacy as strictly a "top-down," "autocratic," "monarchical" conception of Church government. In any event, the abundant Petrine evidence in the Bible must be dealt with in an open and consistent manner, whatever position one holds.

St. Peter charged to strengthen his brethren

> **Luke 22:31-32:** "Simon, Simon, behold, Satan demanded to have you, that he might sift you like wheat, but I have prayed for you that your faith may not fail; and when you have turned again, strengthen your brethren."

The Jesuit apologist Nicholas Russo and St. Francis de Sales explain how this charge to St. Peter suggests the need for an ongoing, infallible papacy:

> In this passage there is question of infallibility. For infallibility is nothing else but a supernatural gift by which the recipient is shielded from all error against faith. But — a) this is clearly expressed in the words, "that thy faith fail not"; b) it is implied in the command to confirm his brethren; c) it is supposed in the very failure of Satan's attempts to destroy the Church, which is personified in the Apostles, and which depends essentially upon faith. . . .
>
> The temptation is common, but the prayer was offered for Peter alone; not because our Lord was less solicitous for the rest of the Apostles, says Bossuet, but because by strengthening the head, He wished to prevent the rest from staggering. Now, this duty of confirming his brethren was to last as long as the Church; and Peter, accordingly, abides always in his successors. . . . Strange, indeed, would it be to suppose that the doctrinal infallibility of the Head of the Church should cease just when the need becomes greater and more

urgent. Christ would, in this supposition, have rendered His first vicar infallible . . . and denied this divine assistance to all the rest of His vicars on earth, when in their times the dangers were to be greater. . . . If this consequence be absurd, our position is unassailable.[260]

He prays for St. Peter as for the confirmer and support of the others; and what is this but to declare him head of the others? Truly one could not give St. Peter the command to confirm the Apostles without charging him to have care of them. . . . Is this not to again call him foundation of the Church? If he supports, secures, strengthens the very foundation-stones, how shall he not confirm all the rest? If he has the charge of supporting the columns of the Church, how shall he not support all the rest of the building? If he has the charge of feeding the pastors, must he not be sovereign pastor himself? . . . Our Lord . . . having planted this holy assembly of the disciples, prayed for the head and the root, in order that the water of faith might not fail to him who was therewith to supply all the rest, and in order that, through the head, the Faith might always be preserved in the Church.[261]

St. Paul's rebuke of St. Peter

Galatians 2:9, 11-14: "And when they perceived the grace that was given to me, James and Cephas [Peter] and John, who were reputed to be pillars, gave to me and Barnabas the right hand of fellowship. . . . But when Cephas came to Antioch, I opposed him to his face, because he stood condemned. For before certain men came from James, he ate with the Gentiles;

[260] Russo, *The True Religion*, 124-126.

[261] St. Francis de Sales, *CON*, 258-259.

> but when they came he drew back and separated himself, fearing the circumcision party. And with him the rest of the Jews acted insincerely, so that even Barnabas was carried away by their insincerity. But when I saw that they were not straightforward about the truth of the gospel, I said to Cephas before them all, 'If you, though a Jew, live like a Gentile and not like a Jew, how can you compel the Gentiles to live like Jews?' "

Bertrand Conway puts this incident in the proper perspective for us:

> St. Paul's rebuke of St. Peter, instead of implying a *denial* of his supremacy, implies just the *opposite*. He tells us that the example of St. Peter *compelled* the Gentiles to live as the Jews. St. Paul's example had not the same compelling power.
>
> The duty of fraternal correction (Matt. 18:15) may often require an inferior to rebuke a superior in defense of justice and truth. St. Bernard, St. Thomas of Canterbury, and St. Catherine of Siena have rebuked Popes, while fully acknowledging their supreme authority. . . .
>
> The rebuke, however, did not refer to the *doctrine*, but to the *conduct* of St. Peter. . . . St. Peter had not changed the views he had himself set forth at the Council of Jerusalem (Acts 15:10). But at Antioch he withdrew from the table of the Gentiles, because he feared giving offense to the Jewish converts. They at once mistook his kindliness for an approval of the false teaching of certain Judaizers, who wished to make the Mosaic Law obligatory upon all Christians. His action was most *imprudent*, and calculated to do harm because of his great influence and authority. St. Paul, therefore, had a perfect right to uphold the Gospel

liberty by a direct appeal to St. Peter's own example and teaching.[262]

Leslie Rumble and Charles Carty, who co-wrote the three-volume *Radio Replies*, a popular and bestselling defense of Catholicism, agree:

> No doctrinal error was involved in this particular case. . . . To cease from doing a lawful thing for fear lest others be scandalized is not a matter of doctrine. It is a question of prudence or imprudence. St. Paul did not act as if he were St. Peter's superior. Nor did he boast. To show the urgency of the matter, he practically said, "I had to resist even Peter — to whom chief authority belongs." And his words derive their full significance only from the fact that St. Peter was head of the Apostles.[263]

If St. Peter were guilty in this instance of hypocrisy (which appears to be the case), this is no disproof whatsoever of the Catholic dogma of papal infallibility, since that teaching does not extend to behavior and applies only to decrees on Faith and morals, which are intended to bind all the faithful to a certain doctrinal standpoint. Granted, hypocrisy and bad example are not conducive to the successful propagation of a viewpoint, yet one must critique an idea according to its actual content. Thus, the attempt to undermine papal infallibility by means of this scriptural passage fails, due to misunderstanding of the Catholic claims for the Pope's divinely appointed charism (in other words, it is a "straw man" argument). The *New Bible Dictionary*, an authoritative Evangelical reference work, states that the disagreement here had nothing to

[262] Conway, *The Question Box*, 152-153 (emphasis added).

[263] Leslie Rumble, and Charles M. Carty, *Radio Replies* (St. Paul, Minnesota: Radio Replies Press, 1940), Vol. 1, 82-83, question 357.

do with any theological dispute between Paul and Peter, but rather, with the unfortunate inconsistency of belief and behavior on Peter's part, and denies the "old theory" that there was some sort of "rivalry" between these two pillars of the early Church.[264]

St. Peter at the Jerusalem Council (Acts 15)

The apostolic supremacy of St. Peter is also often disputed by the counter-assertion that he did not preside over the Council of Jerusalem, the first record we have of a corporate Christian assembly, convened to settle doctrinal and practical matters. Conway and Rumble and Carty show how this, too, is an untenable position:

> St. Peter, not St. James, presided at the Council of Jerusalem. The question at issue was whether the Gentiles were bound to obey the Mosaic Law. Paul, Barnabas, James, and the rest were present as teachers and judges . . . but Peter was their head, and the supreme arbiter of the controversy. . . .
>
> St. Peter spoke first and decided the matter unhesitatingly [Acts 15:7-11], declaring that the Gentile converts were not bound by the Mosaic Law. He claimed to exercise authority in the name of his special election by God to receive the Gentiles (Acts 15:7), and he severely rebuked those who held the opposite view (Acts 15:10). After he had spoken, "all the multitude held their peace" (Acts 15:12) [immediately before Peter spoke, there had been much debate — 15:7]. Those who spoke after him merely confirmed his decision. . . . James gave no special decision on the question. . . . Moreover the decree is attributed to the Council of Apostles and Presbyters . . . (Acts 16:4), and not to James personally.[265]

[264] Douglas, *NBD*, 973.

[265] Conway, *The Question Box*, 152.

St. James, as local Bishop of Jerusalem, would naturally have a prominent position at the meeting, since it took place in Jerusalem. But there can be no doubt about his deference to the ecumenical position of St. Peter as chief of the Apostles [for example, he starts by saying, "Symeon [Peter] has related . . ."].[265]

Petrine panoply: fifty New Testament proofs for the pre-eminence of St. Peter

The papacy is biblically based and is derived from the evident primacy of St. Peter among the Apostles. Like all Christian doctrines, it has undergone development through the centuries, but it hasn't departed from the essential components already existing in the leadership and prerogatives of St. Peter.

These were given to him by our Lord Jesus Christ, acknowledged by his contemporaries, and accepted by the early Church. The biblical Petrine data is quite strong and is inescapably compelling by virtue of its cumulative weight. This is especially made clear with the assistance of biblical commentaries. The evidence of Holy Scripture follows:

1. Peter alone is the Rock upon which Jesus builds his Church (Matt. 16:18). Christ appears here, not as the foundation, but as the architect who "builds." Moreover, *Rock* embodies a metaphor applied to him by Christ in a sense analogous to the suffering and despised Messiah (1 Pet. 2:4-8; cf. Matt. 21:42). Without a solid foundation, a house falls. The Good Shepherd (John 10:11) gives us other shepherds (pastors) as well (Eph. 4:11).

2. Peter alone is given the keys of the kingdom of Heaven (Matt. 16:19).

3. Peter is individually given the power to bind and loose (Matt. 16:19).

[266] Rumble and Carty, *Radio Replies*, Vol. 2, 91, question 344.

4. Peter's name occurs first in all lists of Apostles (Matt. 10:2; Mark 3:16; Luke 6:14; Acts 1:13). Matthew even calls him the "first" (10:2). (Judas Iscariot is invariably mentioned last.)

5. Peter is almost always named first whenever he appears with anyone else. In one (only?) example to the contrary, Galatians 2:9, where he (Cephas) is listed after James and before John, he is clearly pre-eminent in the entire context (e.g., 1:18-19, 2:7-8).

6. Peter alone among the Apostles receives a new name, Rock, solemnly conferred (John 1:42; Matt. 16:18).

7. Likewise, Peter is regarded by Jesus as the Chief Shepherd after himself (John 21:15-17), singularly by name, and over the universal Church, even though others have a similar but subordinate role (Acts 20:28; 1 Pet. 5:2).

8. Peter alone among the Apostles is mentioned by name as having been prayed for by Jesus Christ in order that his faith may not fail (Luke 22:32).

9. Peter alone among the Apostles is exhorted by Jesus to "strengthen your brethren" (Luke 22:32).

10. Peter is the first to confess Christ's Messiahship and divinity (Matt. 16:16).

11. Peter alone is told that he has received divine knowledge by a special revelation (Matt. 16:17).

12. Peter is regarded by the Jews (Acts 4:1-13) as the leader and spokesman of Christianity.

13. Peter is regarded by the common people in the same way (Acts 2:37-41; 5:15).

14. Jesus Christ uniquely associates himself and Peter in the miracle of the tribute-money (Matt. 17:24-27).

15. Christ teaches from Peter's boat, and the miraculous catch of fish follows (Luke 5:1-11): perhaps a metaphor for the Pope as a "fisher of men" (cf. Matt. 4:19).

16. Peter was the first apostle to set out for and enter the empty tomb (Luke 24:12; John 20:6).

17. Peter is specified by an angel as the leader and representative of the Apostles (Mark 16:7).

18. Peter leads the Apostles in fishing (John 21:2-3, 11). The "bark" (boat) of Peter has been regarded by Catholics as a figure of the Church, with Peter at the helm.

19. Peter alone casts himself into the sea to come to Jesus (John 21:7).

20. Peter's words are the first recorded and most important in the upper room before Pentecost (Acts 1:15-22).

21. Peter takes the lead in calling for a replacement for Judas (Acts 1:22).

22. Peter is the first person to speak (and the only one recorded) after Pentecost, so he was the first Christian to "preach the gospel" in the Church era (Acts 2:14-36).

23. Peter works the first miracle of the Church Age, healing a lame man (Acts 3:6-12).

24. Peter utters the first anathema (on Ananias and Sapphira), which is emphatically affirmed by God (Acts 5:2-11).

25. Peter's shadow works miracles (Acts 5:15).

26. Peter is the first after Christ to raise the dead (Acts 9:40).

27. Cornelius is told by an angel to seek out Peter for instruction in Christianity (Acts 10:1-6).

28. Peter is the first to receive the Gentiles, after a revelation from God (Acts 10:9-48).

29. Peter instructs the other Apostles on the catholicity (universality) of the Church (Acts 11:5-17).

30. Peter is the object of the first divine interposition on behalf of an individual in the Church Age (an angel delivers him from prison: Acts 12:1-17).

31. The whole Church (strongly implied) offers earnest prayer for Peter when he is imprisoned (Acts 12:5).

32. Peter opens and presides over the first council of Christianity and lays down principles afterward accepted by it (Acts 15:7-11).

33. Paul distinguishes the Lord's post-Resurrection appearances to Peter from those to other apostles (1 Cor. 15:4-8). The two disciples on the road to Emmaus make the same distinction (Luke 24:34), in this instance mentioning only Peter (Simon), even though they themselves had just seen the risen Jesus within the previous hour (Luke 24:33).

34. Peter is often spoken of as distinct among Apostles (Mark 1:36; Luke 9:28, 32; Acts 2:37, 5:29; 1 Cor. 9:5).

35. Peter is often spokesman for the other Apostles, especially at climactic moments (Mark 8:29; Matt. 18:21; Luke 9:5, 12:41; John 6:67 ff.).

36. Peter's name is always the first listed of the "inner circle" of the disciples (Peter, James, and John — Matt. 17:1, 26:37, 40; Mark 5:37, 14:37).

37. Peter is often the central figure relating to Jesus in dramatic Gospel scenes, such as walking on the water (Matt. 14:28-32; Luke 5:1 ff.; Mark 10:28; Matt. 17:24 ff.).

38. Peter is the first to recognize and refute heresy, in Simon Magus (Acts 8:14-24).

39. Peter's name is mentioned more often than all the other disciples put together: 191 times (162 as Peter or Simon Peter, twenty-three as Simon, and six as Cephas). John is next in frequency, with only forty-eight appearances, and Peter is present fifty percent of the time we find John in the Bible.[267] Fulton Sheen reckoned that all the other disciples combined were mentioned 130 times.[268] If

[267] This number includes thirteen generally accepted instances of St. John's humble referral to himself as "the disciple," or, "the disciple whom Jesus loved" in John 18-21. We know this from John 21:24, John's style, and deductive logic. Also included are five occurrences in Revelation, assuming the same John is its author (which is questioned by many biblical scholars).

[268] Fulton J. Sheen, *Life of Christ* (Garden City, New York: Doubleday Image, 1958), 106. Sheen's figures for Peter and

this is correct, Peter is named a remarkable sixty percent of the time any disciple is referred to.

40. Peter's proclamation at Pentecost (Acts 2:14-41) contains a fully authoritative interpretation of Scripture, a doctrinal decision, and a disciplinary decree concerning members of the House of Israel (2:36) — an example of binding and loosing.

41. Peter was the first "charismatic," having judged authoritatively the first instance of the gift of tongues as genuine (Acts 2:14-21).

42. Peter is the first to preach Christian repentance and Baptism (Acts 2:38).

43. Peter (presumably) leads the first recorded mass Baptism (Acts 2:41).

44. Peter commanded the first Gentile Christians to be baptized (Acts 10:44-48).

45. Peter was the first traveling missionary and first exercised what would now be called "visitation of the churches" (Acts 9:32-38, 43). Paul preached at Damascus immediately after his conversion (Acts 9:20), but hadn't traveled there for that purpose. (God changed his plans!) His missionary journeys begin in Acts 13:2.

46. Paul went to Jerusalem specifically to see Peter for fifteen days in the beginning of his ministry (Gal. 1:18) and was commissioned by Peter, James, and John (Gal. 2:9) to preach to the Gentiles.

47. Peter acts, by strong implication, as the chief bishop/shepherd of the Church (1 Pet. 5:1), since he exhorts all the other bishops, or elders.

48. Peter interprets prophecy (2 Pet. 1:16-21).

49. Peter corrects those who misuse Paul's writings (2 Pet. 3:15-16).

John were 195 and twenty-nine. I used my own tallies from *Strong's Concordance*.

50. Peter wrote his first epistle from Rome, according to most scholars, as its bishop, and as the universal bishop (or Pope) of the early Church. "Babylon" (1 Pet. 5:13) is regarded by many commentators as a code name for Rome.

In conclusion, it strains credulity to hold that God would present St. Peter with such prominence in the Bible, without some meaning and import for later Church government. The papacy is the most plausible interpretation and actual institutional fulfillment of this biblical evidence. For why would God foreordain such a leadership function, only to cease after Peter's death? Clearly, the *office* of the papacy is paramount, not individual popes, and this was to be perpetual (apostolic succession), just as are the offices of bishop, deacon, teacher, and evangelist.

Appendix One

The "Perspicuity" of Scripture

Most conservative, classical, Evangelical, "Reformation" Protestants hold to the view that — when all is said and done — the Bible is basically *perspicuous* (able to be clearly understood) in and of itself, without the absolute necessity for theological teaching, scholarly interpretation, and the authority of the Church (however defined).

This is not to say that Protestants are consciously taught to ignore Christian historical precedent altogether and shun theological instruction (although, sadly, the tendency of ahistoricism and anti-intellectualism is strong in many circles). Rather, perspicuity is said to apply to doctrines "essential" for salvation. Accordingly, it follows that whatever is necessary for salvation can be found in the Bible by any literate individual without the requisite assistance of an ecclesiastical body. This is presupposed in, for example, the widespread practice of passing out Bibles to the newly evangelized, oftentimes with no provision made for further guidance and supervision.

Many Protestant evangelists, it should be happily acknowledged (notably, Billy Graham), do urge church involvement and membership, but not to the extent that this would undermine the premise of perspicuity itself. Given the denial of some sort of binding, compulsory Christian Tradition, this state of affairs is pretty much inevitable, as a result of the Protestant axiom of the primacy of the individual and his conscience.

But what could possibly be imagined as more fatal to this abstract view than the tragic multiplicity of Protestant denominations? The Bible is indeed more often than not quite clear when approached open-mindedly and with a moral willingness to accept its teachings. But in actual fact many Christians (and also heretics or "cultists") distort and misunderstand the Bible, or at the very least, arrive at contradictory, sincerely held convictions. This is the whole point from the Catholic perspective. Error is necessarily present wherever contradictions exist — clearly not a desirable situation, as all falsehood is harmful (e.g., John 8:44, 16:13; 2 Thess. 2:10-12; 1 John 4:6). Perspicuity might theoretically be a good thing in principle, and on paper, but in practice it is unworkable and untenable. History has proven this beyond all doubt.

Yet Protestant freedom of conscience is valued more than unity and the certainty of doctrinal truth in all matters (not just the core issues alone). The inquirer with newfound zeal for Christ is in trouble if he expects easily to attain any comprehensive certainty within Protestantism. All he can do is take a "head count" of scholars and pastors and evangelists and Bible Dictionaries and see who lines up where on the various sides of the numerous disagreements. Or else he can uncritically accept the word of whatever denomination with which he is associated.

In effect, then, he is no better off than a beginning philosophy student who prefers Kierkegaard to Kant — the whole procedure (however well-intentioned, and I readily grant that it is) is arbitrary and destined to produce further confusion.

The usual Protestant reply to this critique is that denominations differ mostly over secondary issues, not fundamental or central doctrines. This is often and casually stated, but when scrutinized, it collapses under its own weight. From the beginning, the fault lines of Protestantism appeared when Zwingli and Oecolampadius (two lesser Reformers) differed with Luther on the Real Presence, and the Anabaptists dissented on the Eucharist, infant Baptism, Ordination, and the function of civil authority. Martin Luther regarded these fellow Protestants as "damned" and "out of the Church" for these reasons. He didn't care much at all for doctrinal disunity among Christians, either.

Reformers John Calvin and Martin Bucer held to a third position on the Eucharist (broadly speaking), intermediate between Luther's Real Presence (consubstantiation) and Zwingli's purely symbolic belief. By 1577, the book *200 Interpretations of the Words, "This is My Body"* was published at Ingolstadt, Germany. This is the fruit of perspicuity, and it was quick to appear.

Protestants will often maintain that the Eucharist and Baptism, for instance, are neither primary nor essential doctrines. This is curious, since these are the two sacraments that the majority of Protestants accept. Jesus said: "Unless you eat the flesh of the Son of man and drink his blood, you have no life in you" (John 6:53).

This certainly sounds essential, even to the extent that a man's salvation might be in jeopardy. St. Paul, too, regards Communion with equally great seriousness and of the utmost importance to one's spiritual well-being and relationship with Jesus Christ (1 Cor. 10:14-22; 11:23-30). Thus, we are already in the realm of salvation — a primary doctrine. Lutherans and many Anglicans (for example, the Oxford Tractarians and C. S. Lewis), believe in the Real Presence, whereas most Evangelicals do not, yet this is not considered cause for alarm or even discomfort.

Protestants differ on other soteriological issues as well: most Methodists, Anglicans, Lutherans, pentecostals, some Baptists, and many nondenominationalists and other groups are Arminian and accept free will and the possibility of falling away from salvation (apostasy), while Presbyterians, Reformed, and a few Baptist denominations and other groups are Calvinist and deny free will and the possibility of apostasy for the elect.

In contrast to the former denominations, the latter groups have a stronger view of the nature of Original Sin, deny that the Atonement is universal, and believe that God predestines the reprobate sinners to Hell before the foundation of the world, with no free will exercised by these damned sinners as to their eternal destiny.

Traditional, orthodox Methodists and many "high church" Anglicans have had views of sanctification (that is, the relationship of faith and works, and of God's enabling and preceding grace and man's cooperation) akin to that of Catholicism. These are questions of how one repents and is saved (justification) and of what is required afterward either to manifest or to maintain this salvation (sanctification and perseverance). Thus, they are primary doctrines, even by standard Protestant criteria.

The same state of affairs is true concerning Baptism, where Protestants are split into infant and adult camps. Furthermore, the infant camp contains those who accept baptismal regeneration (Lutherans, Anglicans, and to some extent, Methodists), as does the adult camp (Churches of Christ and Disciples of Christ). Regeneration absolutely has a bearing on salvation, and therefore is a primary doctrine. The Salvation Army and the Quakers do not baptize at all (the latter does not even celebrate the Eucharist). Thus, there are five distinct competing belief-systems among Protestants with regard to Baptism.

Scripture seems to refer clearly to baptismal regeneration in Acts 2:38 (forgiveness of sins), 22:16 (wash away your sins); Romans 6:3-4; 1 Corinthians 6:11; Titus 3:5 (he saved us . . . by the washing of regeneration), and other passages.

For this reason, many prominent Protestant individuals and denominations have held to the position of baptismal regeneration, which is anathema to the Baptist/Presbyterian/Reformed branch of Protestantism — the predominant evangelical outlook at present (judging by scholarly influence, at any rate).

We need look no further than Martin Luther himself, from whom all Protestants inherit their understanding of both *sola Scriptura* and *sola fide* as the prerequisites for salvation and justification. Luther largely agrees with the Catholic position on sacramental and regenerative infant Baptism:

> Little children . . . are free in every way, secure and saved solely through the glory of their baptism. . . . Through the prayer of the believing church which presents it . . . the infant is changed, cleansed, and renewed by inpoured faith. Nor should I doubt that even a godless adult could be changed, in any of the sacraments, if the same church prayed for and presented him, as we read of the paralytic in the Gospel, who was healed through the faith of others (Mark 2:3-12). I should be ready to admit that in this sense the sacraments of the New Law are efficacious in conferring grace, not only to those who do not, but even to those who do most obstinately present an obstacle.[269]

Likewise, in his *Large Catechism* (1529), Luther writes:

> Expressed in the simplest form, the power, the effect, the benefit, the fruit, and the purpose of Baptism is to save. No one is baptized that he may become a prince, but, as the words declare [of Mark 16:16], "that he may be saved." But to be saved, we know very well, is to be delivered from sin, death, and Satan, and to enter Christ's kingdom and live forever with him. . . . Through the Word, baptism receives the power to become the washing of regeneration, as St.

[269] *The Babylonian Captivity of the Church*, 1520, from the translation of A. T. W. Steinhauser (Philadelphia: Fortress Press, 1970), 197.

> Paul calls it in Titus 3:5. . . . Faith clings to the water and believes it to be baptism which effects pure salvation and life. . . .
>
> When sin and conscience oppress us . . . you may say: It is a fact that I am baptized, but, being baptized, I have the promise that I shall be saved and obtain eternal life for both soul and body. . . . Hence, no greater jewel can adorn our body or soul than baptism; for through it perfect holiness and salvation become accessible to us. . . .[270]

Anglicanism concurs with Luther on this matter. In its authoritative *Thirty-Nine Articles* (1563, language revised 1801), Article 27, "Of Baptism," reads as follows:

> Baptism is not only a sign of profession, and mark of difference, whereby Christian men are discerned from others that be not christened, but it is also a sign of Regeneration or New-Birth, whereby, as by an instrument, they that receive Baptism rightly are grafted into the Church; the promises of the forgiveness of sin, and of our adoption to be the sons of God by the Holy Ghost, are visibly signed and sealed; Faith is confirmed, and Grace increased by virtue of prayer unto God.
>
> The Baptism of young children is in any wise to be retained in the Church, as most agreeable with the institution of Christ.[271]

John Wesley, who is widely admired by Protestants and Catholics alike, agreed, too, that children are regenerated (and justified initially) by means of infant Baptism. From this position he never

[270] Martin Luther, *Large Catechism* (Minneapolis: Augsburg Publishing House, 1935), sects. 223-224, 230, 162, 165.

[271] From *The Book of Common Prayer* (New York: The Seabury Press, 1979), 873.

wavered. In his *Articles of Religion* (1784), which is a revised version of the Anglican *Articles*, he retains an abridged form of the clause on Baptism (no. 17), stating that it is "a sign of regeneration, or the new birth."

The doctrine of Baptism in particular, as well as other doctrinal disputes mentioned above, illustrate the irresolvable Protestant dilemma with regard to its fallacious notion of perspicuity. Again, the Bible is obviously not perspicuous enough to eliminate these differences, unless one arrogantly maintains that sin always blinds those in opposing camps from seeing obvious truths, which even a "plowboy" (Luther's famous phrase) ought to be able to grasp. Obviously, an authoritative (and even infallible) interpreter is needed whether or not the Bible is perspicuous enough to be theoretically understood without help. Nothing could be clearer than that. "Paper infallibility" is no substitute for papal infallibility.

The conclusion is inescapable: either biblical perspicuity is a falsehood, or one or more of the doctrines of regeneration, justification, sanctification, salvation, election, free will, predestination, perseverance, eternal security, the Atonement, Original Sin, the Eucharist, and Baptism, all "five points" of Calvinism (TULIP[272]), and the very gospel itself are not central. Protestants can't have it both ways.

Of course, people like Martin Luther, John Wesley, C. S. Lewis, and denominations such as Methodists, Anglicans, Lutherans, Churches of Christ, and the Salvation Army can be read out of the Christian Faith due to their unorthodoxy, as defined by the self-proclaimed "mainstream" Evangelicals such as Baptists, Presbyterians, and "Reformed" (even the last two groups baptize infants, although they vehemently deny that this causes regeneration).

[272] TULIP is an acronym for the basic ideas of Calvinism: total depravity, unconditional election, limited atonement, irresistible grace, and perseverance of the saints

Since most Protestants are unwilling to anathematize other Protestants, perspicuity dissolves into a boiling cauldron of incomprehensible contradictions, and as such, must be discarded or seriously reformulated in order to harmonize with the Bible and logic.

The Catholic Church at least courageously takes a stand on any given doctrine and refuses to leave whole areas of theology and practice perpetually up for grabs and — too often — mere individualistic whim, fancy, or subjective preference, divorced from considerations of Christian history and consensus. For this so-called "dogmatism" and lack of "flexibility," the Catholic Church is often reviled and despised. But for those of us who are seeking to be faithful to Christ within her fold, this is regarded, to the contrary, as her unique glory and majesty.

Orthodox Catholics believe that Christians can place full confidence in the firmly established Tradition that is found, not only in holy Scripture, but also in the received doctrines of the Catholic Church, appointed by our Lord Jesus Christ as the guardian and custodian of "the Faith that was once for all delivered to the saints" (Jude 3).

Appendix Two

The Visible, Hierarchical, Apostolic Church

In the Nicene Creed, which is accepted by most Christians, the Christian Church is described as being "one, holy, catholic, and apostolic." These are known as the four marks of the Church. The notions of *holiness* and *catholicity* are not much in dispute. The mark of holiness may be defined as the possession and dissemination of the sublime, holy, Christ-centered moral code of Christianity (as best exemplified by saints or otherwise great, godly figures). All parties — while disagreeing on many particulars — concur that this is a central function of the Church. *Catholicity* simply means "universal." Here Protestants and Catholics disagree only on the nature of that Church which is to be considered universal and all-encompassing.

This brings us to the *oneness* and *apostolicity* of the Church, where the disagreements are great indeed. Most Protestants (especially evangelicals) see unity and oneness subsisting primarily or solely in the inner, invisible, spiritual unity of those who are in fact in Christ by virtue of being justified, or "born again," or regenerated (with or without Baptism, depending on denomination). For them, the church consists of the Spirit-filled, predestined elect, who will persevere and are saved, now and in eternity.

The Catholic Church has always proclaimed this unifying characteristic also, under the broad and rich concept of the Mystical

Church (under which it acknowledges Protestantism), yet it does not pit the Mystical Church against the institutional, or visible Church, as most Evangelicals do. For Catholics, then, the issue of oneness is substantially related to organizational and practical aspects of ecclesiology. Catholics believe that the Church is both organism and organization, not merely the former. The Mystical and visible "Churches" are like two circles that largely intersect, but which are not synonymous. They exist together — somewhat paradoxically and with tension — until the "end of the age." But what kind of organization is this Church, which includes within itself these two aspects (as well as many others)?

At this point in the discussion, Catholics appeal to the hierarchical, or episcopal (that is, under the jurisdiction of bishops), nature of Church government. Furthermore, Catholics maintain that this form is divinely instituted and biblical, therefore not optional or of secondary theological importance.

Finally, Catholics believe that bishops are — by the intention of Jesus Christ — the successors of the Apostles (the concept of apostolic succession). This is the methodology whereby the Catholic Church traces herself back historically in an unbroken succession to the Apostles and the early Church. Catholicism thus greatly emphasizes historical and doctrinal continuity, whereas Evangelical Protestants are more concerned with maintaining the passion and intense commitment and zeal of the Apostles and early Christians, and are less interested in governmental forms or doctrines that are now regarded as Catholic "distinctives." They tend to see clearly in the Bible and early Church those doctrines with which they agree, but they overlook those which are more in accordance with Catholicism, such as the episcopacy, Purgatory, and apostolicity.

We shall examine the marks of the Church with which Protestants (notwithstanding many individual exceptions) largely disagree: her visibility, the hierarchy of bishops, apostolic succession, and related issues, such as Ordination, the duties of priests, and sectarianism. Most of these questions are concerned ultimately with authority per se. Protestants emphasize biblical authority, and Catholics ecclesiastical and episcopal leadership, and Tradition. But if the Bible points to and encourages submission to the latter, then the two types of authority cannot (biblically) be opposed.

One of the undeniable aspects of unity and oneness in the Bible is the constant warning (especially in the writings of St. Paul) against (and prohibition of) divisions, schism, and sectarianism, either by command, or by counterexample (Matt. 12:25, 16:18; John 10:16, 17:20-23; Acts 4:32; Rom. 13:13, 16:17; 1 Cor. 1:10-13, 3:3-4, 10:17, 11:18-19, 12:12-27, 14:33; 2 Cor. 12:2; Gal. 5:19-21; Eph. 4:3-6; Phil. 1:27, 2:2-3; 1 Tim. 6:3-5; Titus 3:9-10; James 3:16; 2 Pet. 2:1). This is clearly no trifling matter. Our Lord even makes unity a means by which the world might believe that the Father sent the Son (John 17:21, 23) and prays that it will be as profound as the unity of the Trinity itself (John 17:21-22). St. Paul makes stirring up division a grounds for virtual exclusion from the Christian community (Rom. 16:17) and says that divisions (in effect) divide Christ (1 Cor. 1:13). This has always been one of the strengths of the Catholic position over Protestantism, and Protestants are themselves increasingly alarmed over what they consider to be a scandalous concurrence between denominationalism and sectarianism, which all agree is condemned in Scripture.

One of the sincere and seemingly reasonable grounds for forming a new sect is the desire to separate from sinners and sin, which may be infecting the group left. Yet the Bible clearly teaches that the Church (especially in its institutional sense) comprises saints and sinners, good and bad. We see this most indisputably in several parables of Jesus about the kingdom of Heaven (that is, the Church), such as the wheat and the weeds (or tares), where Jesus says that they will grow together until the final Judgment, or harvest time (Matt. 13:24-30; cf. Matt. 3:12). He compares the Church to a fishnet, which draws good and bad fish, ultimately separated (Matt. 13:47-50), and to a marriage banquet, from which one guest was cast out into the outer darkness (Matt. 22:1-14). This parable ends with the famous phrase, "Many are called, but few are chosen," which may be interpreted as the distinction between lukewarm, or dead, or nominal Christians and the actual elect, who will be saved in the end. Both are present in the Church, according to Jesus. A similar state of affairs is seen in the parables of the ten virgins (Matt. 25:1-13) and the talents (Matt. 25:14-30). And Jesus' description of Christians and the Church as a city set on a hill (Matt. 5:14; cf. 5:15-16), is an obvious reference to the visibility of the Church. In no way can this city be regarded as invisible.

Jesus chose Judas as his disciple, even though he knew the future, and he was truly an apostle (Matt. 10:1, 4; Mark 3:14; John 6:70-71; Acts 1:17). Likewise, St. Paul, in addressing elders (Acts 20:17), states that the Holy Spirit himself has made them bishops (RSV, *guardians*; Greek, *episkopos* — Acts 20:28), yet from among these very same men, heretics and schismatics would arise (Acts 20:30). He echoes this thought in the parable-like verse 2 Timothy 2:20 (see also 2:15-19).

Protestants often cite Jesus' analogy of sheep and shepherd (John 10:1-16; cf. 2 Tim. 2:19; 1 John 2:19), who *know* each other (John 10:14), as evidence that the Church consists of the elect only. Yet the analogy breaks down when we find that Scripture also applies the term *sheep* to the unsaved reprobate (Ps. 74:1), the straying (Ps. 119:176), Israel as a nation (Ezek. 34:2-3, 13, 23, 30), and, indeed, all men (Isa. 53:6).

Other passages that presuppose a visible, identifiable, "concrete" Church include Matthew 18:15-17, in which believers are exhorted by our Lord to take errant and obstinate brothers to the Church, which will then determine the appropriate verdict. It would be contrary to the tenor of the New Testament if this were a reference to a local church alone — even apart from the utterly impractical consequences of such a scenario (where the sinner would simply attend another denomination and move on with his life, as is tragically all too often the case today).

And St. Paul, in 1 Timothy 3:15, describes the church of the living God as "the pillar and bulwark of the truth." This statement is similarly almost nonsensical in the context of competing and often contradictory denominations. Where would a sincere, uninformed, unsophisticated religious seeker go to find this certain truth? Only within the sphere of a serious attempt at actual visible oneness of doctrine can this verse attain any pragmatic possibility.

It is also incorrect to regard St. Paul as some kind of spiritual "lone ranger," on his own, with no particular ecclesiastical allegiance, since he was commissioned by Jesus himself as an apostle. In his very conversion experience, Jesus informed Paul that he would be told what to do (Acts 9:6; cf. 9:17). He went to see St. Peter in Jerusalem for fifteen days in order to be confirmed in his calling (Gal. 1:18) and fourteen years later was commissioned by Peter, James, and John (Gal. 2:1-2, 9). He was also sent out by the Church at Antioch (Acts 13:1-4), which was in contact with the Church at Jerusalem (Acts 11:19-27). Later on, Paul reported back to Antioch (Acts 14:26-28).

The New Testament refers basically to three types of permanent offices in the Church (apostles and prophets were to cease): bishops *(episkopos)*, elders *(presbyteros*, from which are derived *Presbyterian* and *priest)*, and deacons *(diakonos)*. Bishops are mentioned in Acts 1:20, 20:28; Philippians 1:1; 1 Timothy 3:1-2; Titus 1:7; and 1 Peter 2:25. *Presbyteros* (usually *elder)* appears in passages such as Acts 15:2-6, 21:18; Hebrews 11:2; 1 Peter 5:1; and 1 Timothy 5:17. Protestants view these leaders as analogous to current-day pastors, while Catholics regard them as priests. Deacons (often *ministers* in English translations) are mentioned in the same fashion as Christian elders with similar frequency (e.g., 1 Cor. 3:5; Phil. 1:1; 1 Thess. 3:2; and 1 Tim. 3:8-13).

As is often the case in theology and practice among the earliest Christians, there is some fluidity and overlapping of these three vocations (for example, compare Acts 20:17 with 20:28; 1 Timothy 3:1-7 with Titus 1:5-9). But this does not prove that three offices of ministry did not exist. For instance, St. Paul often referred to himself as a deacon or minister (1 Cor. 3:5, 4:1; 2 Cor. 3:6, 6:4, 11:23; Eph. 3:7; Col.1:23-25), yet no one would assert that he was merely a deacon, and nothing else. Likewise, St. Peter calls himself a fellow elder (1 Pet. 5:1), whereas Jesus calls him the rock upon which he would build his Church, and gave him alone the keys of the kingdom of Heaven (Matt. 16:18-19). These examples are usually indicative of a healthy humility, according to Christ's injunctions of servanthood (Matt. 23:11-12; Mark 10:43-44).

Upon closer observation, clear distinctions of office appear, and the hierarchical nature of Church government in the New Testament emerges. Bishops are always referred to in the singular, while elders are usually mentioned plurally. The primary controversy among Christians has to do with the nature and functions of bishops and elders (deacons have largely the same duties among both Protestants and Catholics).

Catholics contend that the elders/presbyters in Scripture carry out all the functions of the Catholic priest:

- *Sent and commissioned by Jesus* (the notion of being called): Mark 6:7; John 15:5, 20:21; Romans 10:15; 2 Corinthians 5:20.

- *Representatives of Jesus:* Luke 10:16; John 13:20.

- *Authority to "bind" and "loose"* (Penance and absolution): Matthew 18:18 (cf. Matthew 16:19).

- *Power to forgive sins in Jesus' name:* Luke 24:47; John 20:21-23; 2 Corinthians 2:5-11; James 5:15.

- *Authority to administer penance:* Acts 5:2-11; 1 Corinthians 5:3-13; 2 Corinthians 5:18; 1 Timothy 1:18-20; Titus 3:10.

- *Power to conduct the Eucharist:* Luke 22:19; Acts 2:42 (cf. Luke 24:35; Acts 2:46, 20:7; 1 Corinthians 10:16).

- *Power to dispense sacraments:* 1 Corinthians 4:1; James 5:13-15.

- *Power to baptize:* Matthew 28:19; Acts 2:38, 41.

- *Ordained:* Acts 14:23; 1 Timothy 4:14, 5:23.

- *Pastors (shepherds):* Acts 20:17, 28; Ephesians 4:11; 1 Peter 5:1-4.

- *Authority to preach and teach:* 1 Timothy 3:1-2; 5:17.

- *Authority to evangelize:* Matthew 16:15, 28:19-20; Mark 3:14; Luke 9:2, 6, 24:47; Acts 1:8.

- *Power to heal:* Matthew 10:1; Luke 9:1-2, 6.

- *Power to cast out demons:* Matthew 10:1; Mark 3:15; Luke 9:1.

- *Authority to hear confessions:* Acts 19:18 (cf. Matthew 3:6; Mark 1:5; James 5:16; 1 John 1:8-9; presupposed in John 20:23).

- *Celibacy for those called to it:* Matthew 19:12; 1 Corinthians 7:7-9, 20, 25-38 (especially 7:35).

- *Enjoy Christ's perpetual presence and assistance in a special way:* Matthew 28:20.

Protestants — following Luther — cite 1 Peter 2:5, 9 (see also Revelation 1:6) to prove that *all* Christians are priests. But this does not exclude a specially ordained, sacramental priesthood, since St. Peter was reflecting the language of Exodus 19:6, where the Jews were described in this fashion. Since the Jews had a separate Levitical priesthood, by analogy 1 Peter 2:9 cannot logically exclude a New Testament ordained priesthood. These texts are concerned with priestly *holiness*, as opposed to priestly *function*. The universal sense, for instance, never refers to the Eucharist or to the sacraments. Every Christian is a priest in terms of offering the sacrifices of prayer (Heb. 13:15), almsgiving (Heb. 13:16), and faith in Jesus (Phil. 2:17).

Bishops *(episkopos)* possess all the powers, duties, and jurisdiction of priests, with these important additional responsibilities:

- *Jurisdiction over priests and local churches, and the power to ordain priests:* Acts 14:22; 1 Timothy 5:22; 2 Timothy 1:6; Titus 1:5.

- *Special responsibility to defend the Faith:* Acts 20:28-31; 2 Timothy 4:1-5; Titus 1:9-10; 2 Peter 3:15-16.

- *Power to rebuke false doctrine and to excommunicate:* Acts 8:14-24; 1 Corinthians 16:22; 1 Timothy 5:20; 2 Timothy 4:2; Titus 1:10-11.

- *Power to bestow Confirmation* (the receiving of the indwelling Holy Spirit): Acts 8:14-17; 19:5-6.

- *Management of Church finances:* 1 Timothy 3:3-4; 1 Peter 5:2.

In the Septuagint, *episkopos* is used for "overseer" in various senses, for example: officers (Judg. 9:28; Isa. 60:17), supervisors of funds (2 Chron. 34:12, 17), overseers of priests and Levites (Neh. 11:9; 2 Kings 11:18), and of temple and tabernacle functions (Num. 4:16). God is called *episkopos* in Job 20:29, referring to his role as Judge, and Christ is an *episkopos* in 1 Peter 2:25 (RSV: "Shepherd and Guardian of your souls").

The Council of Jerusalem (Acts 15:1-29) bears witness to a definite hierarchical, episcopal structure of government in the early Church. St. Peter, the chief elder (the office of Pope) of the entire Church (1 Peter 5:1; cf. John 21:15-17), presided and issued the authoritative pronouncement (15:7-11). Then James, Bishop of Jerusalem (rather like the host-mayor of a conference) gives a concurring (Acts 15:14) concluding statement (15:13-29). That James was the sole, "monarchical" bishop of Jerusalem is fairly apparent from Scripture (Acts 12:17, 15:13, 19, 21:18; Gal. 1:19, 2:12). This fact is also attested by the first Christian historian, Eusebius (*History of the Church*, 7:19).

Much historical and patristic evidence also exists for the bishopric of St. Peter at Rome. No one disputes the fact that St. Clement (d. c. 101) was the sole Bishop of Rome a little later, or that St. Ignatius (d. c. 110) was the Bishop of Antioch, starting around 69 A.D. Thus, the "monarchical" bishop is both a biblical concept and an unarguable fact of the early Church. By the time we get to the mid-second century, virtually all historians hold that single bishops led each Christian community. This was to be the case in all Christendom, East and West, until Luther transferred this power to the secular princes in the sixteenth century, and the Anabaptist tradition eschewed ecclesiastical office either altogether or in large part. Today many denominations have no bishops at all.

One may concede all the foregoing as true, yet deny apostolic succession, whereby these offices are passed down, or handed down, through the generations and centuries, much like sacred Tradition. But this belief of the Catholic Church (along with Eastern Orthodoxy and Anglicanism) is also grounded in Scripture.

St. Paul teaches us (Eph. 2:20) that the Church is built on the foundation of the Apostles, whom Christ himself chose (John 6:70; Acts 1:2, 13; cf. Matt. 16:18). In Mark 6:30, the twelve original disciples of Jesus are called Apostles, and Matthew 10:1-5 and Revelation 21:14 speak of the twelve Apostles. After Judas defected, the remaining eleven Apostles appointed his successor, Matthias (Acts 1:20-26). Since Judas is called a bishop (*episkopos*) in this passage (1:20), then, by logical extension, all the Apostles can be considered bishops (albeit of an extraordinary sort).

If the Apostles are bishops, and one of them was replaced by another, after the death, Resurrection, and Ascension of Christ, then we have an explicit example of apostolic succession in the Bible, taking place before 35 A.D. In like fashion, St. Paul appears to pass on his office to Timothy (2 Tim. 4:1-6), shortly before his death, around 65 A.D. This succession shows an authoritative equivalency between Apostles and bishops, who are the successors of the Apostles. As a corollary, we are also informed in Scripture that the Church herself is perpetual, infallible, and indefectible (Matt. 16:18; John 14:26, 16:18). Why should the early Church be set up in one form and the later Church in another?

All of this biblical data is harmonious with the ecclesiological views of the Catholic Church. There has been some development over the centuries, but in all essentials, the biblical Church and clergy and the Catholic Church and clergy are one and the same.

The historical evidence of the earliest Christians after the Apostles and the Church Fathers is quite compelling as well: there exists virtually unanimous consent as to the episcopal, hierarchical, visible nature of the Church, which proceeds authoritatively down through history by virtue of apostolic succession.

St. Clement, Bishop of Rome, teaches apostolic succession around 80 A.D. (*Epistle to Corinthians*, 42:4-5, 44:1-3), and St. Irenaeus is a very strong witness to and advocate of this tradition in the last two decades of the second century (*Against Heresies*, 3:3:1, 4; 4:26:2; 5:20:1; 33:8). Eusebius, the first historian of the Church, in his *History of the Church* (c. 325), begins by saying that one of the "chief matters" to be dealt with in his work is "the lines of succession from the holy Apostles."[273]

With regard to the threefold ministry of bishop, priest (elder; *presbyteros*), and deacon, St. Ignatius, Bishop of Antioch, offers

[273] Eusebius, *History of the Church*, G. A. Williamson, trans. (Baltimore: Penguin Books, 1965), 31.

remarkable testimony, around 110: *Letter to the Magnesians*, 2, 6:1, 13:1-2; *Letter to the Trallians*, 2:1-3, 3:1-2, 7:2; *Letter to the Philadelphians*, 7:1-2; *Letter to the Smyrnaeans*, 8:1-2 — the last also being the first reference to the "Catholic Church." St. Clement of Rome refers to the "high priest" and "priests" of Christians around 96 (*1 Clement*, 40). Other prominent early witnesses include St. Hippolytus (*Apostolic Tradition*, 9) and St. Clement of Alexandria (*Stromateis*, 6:13:107:2), both in the early third century.

John Calvin himself, contrary to many of his later followers, taught that the Church was visible and a "Mother" (*Institutes of the Christian Religion*, IV, 1, 1; IV, 1, 4; IV, 1, 13-14), the wrongness of sectarianism and schism (IV, 1, 5; IV, 1, 10-15), and that the Church includes sinners and "hypocrites" (IV, 1, 7; IV, 1, 13-15 — he cites Matthew 13:24-30, 47-58).

Appendix Three

The Historical Case for the "Apocrypha"

The Old Testament in Catholic Bibles contains seven more books than are found in Protestant Bibles (forty-six and thirty-nine, respectively). Protestants call these books the Apocrypha, and Catholics know them as the deuterocanonical books: Tobit, Judith, 1 and 2 Maccabees, Wisdom of Solomon, Ecclesiasticus (or Sirach), and Baruch. Also, Catholic Bibles contain an additional six chapters (107 verses) in the book of Esther and an additional three (174 verses) in the book of Daniel. These books and chapters were found in Bible manuscripts in Greek only and were not part of the Hebrew Canon of the Old Testament, as determined by the Jews.

All of these were dogmatically acknowledged as Scripture at the Council of Trent in 1548 (which means that Catholics were henceforth not allowed to question their canonicity), although the tradition of their inclusion was ancient. At the same time, the council rejected 1 and 2 Esdras and the Prayer of Manasses as part of Sacred Scripture (these are often included in collections of the "Apocrypha" as a separate unit).

The Catholic perspective on this issue is widely misunderstood (insofar as it can be said to be known at all). Protestants accuse Catholics of "adding" books to the Bible, while Catholics retort that Protestants have "booted out" part of Scripture. Catholics are able to offer very solid and reasonable arguments in defense of the scriptural status of the deuterocanonical books. These can be summarized as follows:

• They were included in the Septuagint, which was the "Bible" of the Apostles. They usually quoted the Old Testament Scriptures (in the text of the New Testament) from the Septuagint.

• Almost all of the Church Fathers regarded the Septuagint as the standard form of the Old Testament. The deuterocanonical books were in no way differentiated from the other books in the Septuagint, and were generally regarded as canonical. St. Augustine thought the Septuagint was apostolically sanctioned and inspired, and this was the consensus in the early Church.

• Many Church Fathers (such as St. Irenaeus, St. Cyprian, and Tertullian) cite these books as Scripture without distinction. Others, mostly from the East (for example, St. Athanasius, St. Cyril of Jerusalem, and St. Gregory Nazianzen) recognized some distinction, but nevertheless still customarily cited the deuterocanonical books as Scripture. St. Jerome, who translated the Hebrew Bible into Latin (the Vulgate, early fifth century), was an exception to the rule (the Church has never held that individual Fathers are infallible).

• The Church councils at Hippo (393) and Carthage (397, 419), influenced heavily by St. Augustine, listed the deuterocanonical books as Scripture, which was simply an endorsement of what had become the general consensus of the Church in the West and most of the East. Thus, the Council of Trent merely reiterated in stronger terms what had already been decided eleven and a half centuries earlier, and which had never been seriously challenged until the onset of Protestantism.

• Since these councils also finalized the sixty-six canonical books that all Christians accept, it is quite arbitrary for Protestants selectively to delete seven books from this authoritative Canon.

This is all the more curious when the complicated, controversial history of the New Testament Canon is understood.

• Pope Innocent I concurred with and sanctioned the canonical ruling of the above councils *(Letter to Exsuperius, Bishop of Toulouse)* in 405.

• The earliest Greek manuscripts of the Old Testament, such as *Codex Sinaiticus* (fourth century) and *Codex Alexandrinus* (c. 450) include all of the deuterocanonical books mixed in with the others and not separated.

• The practice of collecting the deuterocanonical books into a separate unit dates back no further than 1520 (in other words, it was a novel innovation of Protestantism). This is admitted by, for example, the Protestant New English Bible in its "Introduction to the Apocrypha."[274]

• Protestants, following Martin Luther, removed the deuterocanonical books from their Bibles, due to their clear teaching of doctrines that had been recently repudiated by Protestants, such as prayers for the dead (Tob. 12:12; 2 Mac. 12:39-45; cf. 1 Cor. 15:29), the intercession of dead saints (2 Mac. 15:14; cf. Rev. 6:9-10), and the intermediary intercession of angels (Tob. 12:12, 15; cf. Rev. 5:8, 8:3-4). We know this from plain statements of Luther and other Reformers.

• Luther was not content even to let the matter rest there, and proceeded to cast doubt on many other books of the Bible that are accepted as canonical by all Protestants. He considered Job and Jonah mere fables, and Ecclesiastes incoherent and incomplete. He wished that Esther (along with 2 Maccabees) "did not exist," and wanted to "toss it into the Elbe" River.

[274] New English Bible (Oxford: Oxford University Press, 1976), iii.

• The New Testament fared scarcely better under Luther's gaze. He rejected from the New Testament Canon ("chief books") Hebrews, James ("epistle of straw"), Jude, and Revelation, and he placed them at the end of his translation, as a New Testament Apocrypha. He regarded them as nonapostolic. Of the book of Revelation he said, "Christ is not taught or known in it." These opinions are found in Luther's Prefaces to biblical books, in his German translation of 1522.

• Although the New Testament does not quote any of these books directly, it does closely reflect the thought of the deuterocanonical books in many passages. For example, Revelation 1:4 and 8:3-4 appear to make reference to Tobit 12:15:

> **Revelation 1:4:** "Grace to you . . . from the seven spirits who are before his throne" (see also 3:1; 4:5; 5:6).
>
> **Revelation 8:3-4:** "And another angel came and stood at the altar with a golden censer; and he was given much incense to mingle with the prayers of all the saints upon the golden altar before the throne; and the smoke of the incense rose with the prayers of the saints from the hand of the angel before God" (see also 5:8).
>
> **Tobit 12:15:** "I am Raphael, one of the seven holy angels who present the prayers of the saints and enter into the presence of the glory of the Holy One."

St. Paul, in 1 Corinthians 15:29, seems to have 2 Maccabees 12:44 in mind. This saying is one of the most difficult in the New Testament for Protestants to interpret, given their theology:

> **1 Corinthians 15:29:** "Otherwise, what do people mean by being baptized on behalf of the dead? If the

> dead are not raised at all, why are people baptized on their behalf?"
>
> **2 Maccabees 12:44:** "For if he were not expecting that those who had fallen would rise again, it would have been superfluous and foolish to pray for the dead."

This passage of St. Paul shows that it was the custom of the early Church to watch, pray, and fast for the souls of the deceased. In Scripture, to be baptized is often a metaphor for affliction or (in the Catholic understanding) penance (e.g., Matt. 3:11; Mark 10:38-39; Luke 3:16, 12:50). Since those in Heaven have no need of prayer, and those in Hell can't benefit from it, these practices, sanctioned by St. Paul, must be directed toward those in Purgatory. Otherwise, prayers and penances for the dead make no sense, and this seems to be largely what Paul is trying to bring out. The "penance interpretation" is contextually supported by the next three verses, where St. Paul speaks of "Why am I in peril every hour? . . . I die every day," and so forth.

As a third example, Hebrews 11:35 mirrors the thought of 2 Maccabees 7:29:

> **Hebrews 11:35:** "Women received their dead by resurrection. Some were tortured, refusing to accept release, that they might rise again to a better life."
>
> **2 Maccabees 7:29:** "Do not fear this butcher, but prove worthy of your brothers. Accept death, so that in God's mercy I may get you back again with your brothers (a mother speaking to her son: see 7:25-26)."

• Ironically, in some of the same verses in which the New Testament is virtually quoting the "Apocrypha," doctrines are taught that are rejected by Protestants, and which were a major reason why the deuterocanonical books were "demoted" by them. Therefore, it was not as easy to eliminate these disputed doctrines from the Bible as it was (and is) supposed, and Protestants still must grapple with much New Testament data that do not comport with their beliefs.

- Despite this lowering of the status of the deuterocanonical books by Protestantism, the books were still widely retained separately in Protestant Bibles for a long period (unlike the prevailing practice today). John Wycliffe, considered a forerunner of Protestantism, included them in his English translation. Luther himself kept them separately in his Bible, describing them generally as (although subscriptural) "useful and good to read." Zwingli and the Swiss Protestants, and the Anglicans maintained them in this secondary sense also. The English Geneva Bible (1560) and Bishop's Bible (1568) both included them as a unit. Even the Authorized, or King James, Version of 1611 contained the "Apocrypha" as a matter of course. And up to the present, many Protestant Bibles continue this practice. The revision of the King James Bible (completed in 1895) included these books, as did the Revised Standard Version (1957), the New English Bible (1970), and the Goodspeed Bible (1939), among others.

- The deuterocanonical books are read regularly in public worship in Anglicanism, and also among the Eastern Orthodox, and most Protestants and Jews fully accept their value as historical and religious documents, useful for teaching, even though they deny the books full canonical status.

It is apparent, then, that the Catholic "case" for these books carries a great deal of weight, certainly at the very least equal to the Protestant view.

Appendix Four

The Biblical Basis for Clerical Celibacy

With regard to clerical, or priestly, celibacy, Protestants (and today, many Catholics) often mirror Luther's viewpoint that chastity is well-nigh impossible. Orthodox Catholics contend that such a view is not biblical. Our Lord Jesus and St. Paul were of a different opinion. Jesus said:

> For there are eunuchs who have been so from birth, and there are eunuchs who have been made eunuchs by men, and there are eunuchs who have made themselves eunuchs for the sake of the kingdom of Heaven. He who is able to receive this, let him receive it" (Matt. 19:12).

Other modern translations use the phrase "others have renounced marriage." One might argue that Jesus was merely describing this state of affairs, not sanctioning it, but this is made implausible by his concluding comment, "He who is able to receive this, let him receive it."

But if it is to be denied that Jesus taught the desirability of celibacy for those called to it, there can be little doubt about St. Paul's position, expressed in great detail in 1 Corinthians 7:7-9, 20, 27-28, 32-35, 38:

> I wish that all were as I myself am. But each has his own special gift from God, one of one kind and one of another. To

> the unmarried and the widows I say that it is well for them to remain single as I do. But if they cannot exercise self-control, they should marry. For it is better to marry than to be aflame with passion. . . . Every one should remain in the state in which he was called. . . .
>
> Are you bound to a wife? Do not seek to be free. Are you free from a wife? Do not seek marriage. But if you marry, you do not sin. . . . Yet those who marry will have worldly troubles, and I would spare you that. . . .
>
> I want you to be free from anxieties. The unmarried man is anxious about the affairs of the Lord, how to please the Lord; but the married man is anxious about worldly affairs, how to please his wife, and his interests are divided. And the unmarried woman or girl is anxious about the affairs of the Lord, how to be holy in body and spirit; but the married woman is anxious about worldly affairs, how to please her husband.
>
> I say this for your own benefit, not to lay any restraint upon you, but to promote good order and to secure your undivided devotion to the Lord. . . . So that he who marries his betrothed does well; and he who refrains from marriage will do better.

These verses are the scriptural rationale for the much-maligned Catholic requirement of celibacy for priests, monks, and nuns. St. Paul's argument is clear enough, for anyone able to receive it. The celibate priest can single-heartedly devote himself both to God and to his flock. The practical advantages of having more time and not being burdened by multiple loyalties are obvious.

Why, then, is there so much uproar today (as there was in Luther's era) over this disciplinary requirement? (It is neither a dogma nor irreversible, although it is firmly established in Catholic Tradition.) I submit that it is a lack of belief in the power of

God to assist one in such a difficult life-choice, especially given the present sexually crazed atmosphere. Opponents of celibacy often simply assume, like Luther, that a life without sex is utterly impossible, whereas our Lord Jesus and St. Paul undeniably teach the contrary, and the desirability — even preferability — of celibacy for those so called. One must make a choice for or against the biblical teaching. If sexual abstinence is impossible and "unnatural," men and women are reduced to the level of mere beasts, devoid of God's image and strengthening power, utterly unable to control their appetites and passions. This is not the Christian view!

It needs to be stressed at this point that no one is *forced* to be celibate. It is a matter of personal choice and, on a deeper level, an acceptance of one's calling, as given by God. Paul acknowledges both the divine impetus (1 Cor. 7:7, 20) and the free-will initiative of human beings (1 Cor. 7:35, 38). These two are not contradictory, but rather, complementary. In other words, if a man is called to celibacy (and further, to the priesthood in the Latin, Western Rites), he will be given both the desire and the ability to carry out this lifestyle successfully (see Phil. 2:13). If one is not called, like most of us, to celibacy or the priesthood, or both, then he or she ought to get married (1 Cor. 7:7, 9, 20, 28, 38).

The issue is not a matter of either-or, with one option being good and the other bad. Both are good, but one has a certain practical superiority and a somewhat heroic aspect. To renounce personally something is not equivalent to regarding the state or thing renounced as evil. I may give up eating potatoes, reading fiction, ice-skating, or swimming, for various reasons, but this does not make any of them evil in and of themselves.

Likewise, the Catholic Church is not in any sense whatsoever against marriage or sexuality (1 Cor. 7:38), as long as these are within the proper biblical and moral guidelines. Marriage and Ordination are both sacraments in Catholicism; both are positive and wonderful means of God's grace. The Catholic view of holy

Matrimony, which considers a valid, sacramental marriage between two baptized Catholics absolutely indissoluble, provides women in particular with the greatest degree of security and dignity known to history (we are already reaping the bitter fruit of today's "easy divorcism"). The Church wants only to see everyone fulfill the estate in life to which they are called (1 Cor. 7:20).

Every Roman Catholic priest takes vows of chastity and obedience. No one is compelled to become a Catholic priest, and the complaining and moaning of those who have ill-advisedly taken on such a commitment, or, who (through loss of the supernatural virtue of faith) no longer believe it to be possible, is unjustified. Anyone who is not called to celibacy is free to become a married priest in the Orthodox or Anglican Churches (or even in the Eastern Rites of the Catholic Church, where married men can be ordained).

When Catholic priests today forsake their vows of Ordination (usually taking on wives), this is no disproof whatsoever of the Catholic doctrine of the desirability of celibacy, but rather, an indication that (oftentimes) something was seriously awry in the intellectual honesty of these men or in the perception of God's calling in their lives. Again, no one forced any of these men to take the vows they did, and it is improper for them to complain about it after the fact. This is as foolish and silly as a man's whining that he cannot join the army because he cannot stand constantly being with thirty other men!

Numerous other analogies could be given. Every institution has the inherent right to create whatever rules and regulations it deems necessary for its purposes. In this case, the Catholic Church is simply trying to follow the clear recommendations of its Lord and one of the premier apostles, St. Paul, and to go against the grain of today's decadent culture, where unrestrained sex has often replaced the quest for God and righteousness and has become an idol.

Furthermore, today there seems to be a lack of understanding (or downright denigration) of the validity and seriousness of vows and oaths, from the biblical and Christian perspective. We see how lightly the marital vows are taken by many in our time; "for better or worse" and "till death do us part" are almost forgotten by thousands, it seems. The Law of Moses made vows and oaths sacredly and solemnly binding (Exod. 20:7; Lev. 19:12; Deut. 5:11, 23:21-23). Ezekiel says that perjury is punishable by death (Ezek. 17:16-18). Jesus taught that oaths were binding (Matt. 5:33). St. Paul once had his hair cut off as the result of a vow of some sort (Acts 18:18). Even God bound Himself by an oath (Heb. 6:13-18). The notion of covenant is closely related to oath-taking. A deceptive vow is an affront to God and brings about His curse (Mal. 1:14; Eccles. 5:4-5). Vowing is completely voluntary and optional in biblical thought, but once made, the vow must be performed and is a very serious matter indeed.

Sadly, many "former" priests, rather than face honestly their own inadequacies, choose instead to cast doubt on the Church's teaching on celibacy in general, which causes them ultimately to deny the affirmations of both Jesus and St. Paul on this subject. No amount of admitted difficulty (no one maintains the easiness of abstention) or self-serving rationalization can undo the plain teaching of holy Scripture in this regard. There is an old proverb to the effect that "all heresy begins below the belt." This is certainly not the reason for all priestly defections, but it is undoubtedly true far more often than is admitted. Priests, even "good" ones, are fallen and fallible human beings — like all of us — subject to temptations and moral lapses, and are special targets of Satan due to their lofty office. They need our prayers continually.

Appendix Five

A Dialogue on Infant Baptism

Zeke the "Jesus Freak": Hey, Cathy, why do Catholics baptize babies? It's pointless since babies don't know what's going on and can't *repent*, according to Acts 2:38 and Mark 6:16.

Cathy the Catholic: But where in the Bible does it specifically *prohibit* the Baptism of babies?

Zeke: Well . . . I guess it never says *that*. But . . .

Cathy: But don't you only follow what's plainly taught in the pages of Scripture?

Zeke: It's a conclusion that follows from *ideas* that are clearly in Scripture. It's still a *biblical doctrine*.

Cathy: Ah! That's a big difference. Now we're both in the same boat, since the Bible doesn't *explicitly* teach about Baptism of infants. We must make inferences. Catholics maintain that there are many strong *indications* of our view.

Zeke: Where? I've never seen any in seventeen years of being saved.

Cathy: In Acts 16:15, 33, 18:8 [cf. 11:14], and 1 Corinthians 1:16, it is stated that an individual and his whole household were baptized. It would be hard to say this involved no small children. Paul in Colossians 2:11-13 makes a connection between Baptism and circumcision. Israel was the church before Christ [Acts 7:38; Rom. 9:4]. Circumcision, given to eight-day-old boys, was the seal of the covenant God made with Abraham, which applies to us also [Gal. 3:14, 29]. It was a sign of repentance and future faith [Rom. 4:11]. Infants were just as much a part of the covenant as adults were [Gen. 17:7; Deut. 29:10-12; cf. Matt. 19:14]. Likewise, Baptism is the seal of the New Covenant in Christ. It signifies cleansing from sin, just as circumcision did [Deut. 10:16, 30:6; Jer. 4:4, 9:25; Rom. 2:28-29; Phil. 3:3]. Infants are wholly saved by God's grace, just as adults are, only apart from their rational and willful consent. Their parents act in their behalf.

Zeke: That's not possible. You have to repent and be born again in order to receive salvation, as John 3:5 says.

Cathy: It doesn't exactly say that. It says that one "must be born of water and the Spirit." Catholics, along with the Church Fathers such as St. Augustine and many Protestants (for example, Lutherans and Anglicans), interpret this as a reference to Baptism, and a proof of the necessity of infant Baptism.

Zeke: That doesn't make sense. *Water* here refers to the amniotic sac when a baby is born. Babies can't be born again. Jesus is contrasting natural with spiritual birth.

Cathy: Are you saying then that a baby can't be *saved* and will go to Hell if he dies before the "age of reason"?

Zeke: No, no. I would never say that. God is too merciful to let that happen to an innocent little baby.

Cathy: But you believe in Original Sin [1 Cor. 15:22], inherited by all people from the Fall of Adam and Eve, right?

Zeke: Well, yeah. What are you getting at?

Cathy: Once you say that a baby can be saved, then clearly there is a justification for baptizing infants, since there are factors other than their own consent that enter into the question of their salvation. Thus, you have arrived at a more communal, covenantal view of salvation — see, for example, 1 Corinthians 7:14, 12:13 — rather than the individualistic notion that many Evangelicals have. The reality of Original Sin makes Baptism desirable as soon as possible, since it removes the punishment and guilt due to sin and infuses sanctifying grace. This is why most Protestants through history, including Lutherans, Anglicans, Methodists, Reformed, and Presbyterians, have baptized infants.

Zeke: Now, wait a minute. Surely you don't believe that Baptism actually *does* anything, do you? It's only a symbol.

Cathy: You Evangelicals always seem to deny that matter can be a conveyor of grace and too often frown on the idea of sacraments, which are physical, visible means whereby grace is conferred.

Zeke: We don't believe in those things because they're not biblical. The Bible talks about the Spirit giving grace [John 6:63; Rom. 8:1-10], not matter. Catholics are always getting weird about *things*, such as statues, relics, rosary beads, the wafer of Communion, and holy water. This usually degenerates into idolatry.

Cathy: I disagree. God himself took on flesh in Christ. Paul's handkerchiefs healed the sick [Acts 19:12], as did Peter's shadow [Acts 5:15]! Likewise, Baptism is said to regenerate sinners. Acts 2:38 speaks of being baptized for the forgiveness of your sins. 1 Peter 3:21 says, "Baptism . . . now saves you" [cf. Mark 16:16; Rom. 6:3-4]. Paul recalls how Ananias told him to "be baptized, and wash away your sins" [Acts 22:16]. In 1 Corinthians 6:11, Paul sure seems to imply an organic connection between Baptism (washed), sanctification, and justification, whereas Evangelicals separate all three. Titus 3:5 says that "he saved us . . . by the washing of regeneration." What more biblical proof is needed? Is this all to be explained as "symbolic"?

Zeke: I gotta run. I have some questions for my pastor. . . .

Appendix Six

A Dialogue on Liturgy and "Vain Worship"

Nona the nondenominational Protestant: I don't understand, Peter, why Catholics keep putting up with the same old empty form prayers and rituals every Sunday at Mass. Don't you ever have the desire to grow in the Lord and feel God's presence and praise him exuberantly?

Peter the "Papist": How do you know that all Catholics don't "feel" anything, or desire to grow? That seems pretty judgmental to me. Sure, many Catholics are nominal and spiritually cold, but we don't have a monopoly on that characteristic — not by a long shot!

Nona: I can say that because the Mass is simply vain repetition, which Jesus condemned in Matthew 6:7. Since it isn't spontaneous, it can't be from the Holy Spirit, but merely a dead tradition of men. It's not alive and spiritual, like our service. We're on fire.

Peter: I think that you make a lot of unwarranted conclusions. First of all, repetition in and of itself isn't always a bad thing. You overlook the fact that Jesus says *vain* repetition. *Vain* means having excessive pride or conceit. So the Lord is condemning prayers uttered without the proper reverence or respect for God. As usual, he is concerned with the inner dispositions of the worshiper — see, for example, Isaiah 1:11-15 and Matthew 7:20-23, 15:9 — not with outward appearance, as you seem to emphasize. God sees the heart. Besides, if repetition itself is wrong, Protestants are as guilty of it as we are. Lutherans, Anglicans, and Methodists are just as liturgical as Catholics, with Presbyterians not far behind. All have form prayers and creeds, such as the Nicene Creed, which are repeated every Sunday. Even the Baptists have a set routine they stick to.

Nona: Don't lump me in with *them*. I'm a nondenominational Christian. I'm not a Protestant. That's just a label and tradition of men. I go by the Bible alone.

Peter: Evangelical Protestants are always saying that they're merely following the Bible's clear teaching, but that's another subject. Anyway, pentecostal, charismatic, "Spirit-filled" services are just as repetitious as more liturgical, ordered churches. Your position amounts to a plain old prejudice against written, traditional prayer. This proves too much, since the Lord's Prayer, and many of the Psalms would become vain repetition as well; for example, in Psalm 136, the same exact phrase is repeated for twenty-six straight verses! Since Scripture is "God-breathed," if you're correct, this would mean that God himself indulged in the very practice he condemns elsewhere.

Nona: Well, I guess you've got a point there, but I still say that our services are more on fire since they're led by the spontaneous leading of the Spirit.

Peter: Having participated in both types of worship, I can tell you that your services — edifying as they may be — have just as much form and repetition, conscious or not, as anyone's. The music and prayer portions always seem to last the same amount of time, and then comes prophecy, the collection, a forty-five-minute sermon, and so on. The praises almost invariably are "Praise you, Jesus," "Hallelujah," "Glory to you, Lord," over and over. The prophecies vary little. I heard a "prophecy" on two occasions at my church where a person blurted out, "I am the *alfalfa* and the

Omega [laughs]."[275] If Catholic worship is supposedly so "dead," I could say that informal worship can be excessively emotional and sometimes downright silly — not always "spiritual." No Christian group is above criticism or unable to benefit from others in many ways.

Nona: You know, I've never thought about all this in the way you have. But I've been on both sides, too. When I was Catholic, I used to get so bored at Mass. I wasn't convicted or challenged. It was so dry and meaningless, and the homilies left much to be desired. I never heard the gospel until I got saved twelve years ago.

Peter: I don't know how you could never get challenged or not hear the gospel. At every Sunday Mass, there are four Bible readings from the Old Testament, the Psalms, the Gospels, and the Epistles — far more than at Protestant services. Sure, the homilies aren't always as interesting and "meaty" (in a certain sense) as Protestant ones. I admit that you guys win hands down today when it comes to fiery, stirring oratory, but as an adult, you can easily read all the theology and sermons you want. The potential for learning is unlimited. For example, if you want great preaching and food for thought from Catholics, I suggest you read the sermons of St. Augustine, or St. John Chrysostom, or John Henry Newman. Evangelicals love to read Scripture; they could benefit by reading the works of great Christians of the past also. There is a long, fabulous Christian heritage just waiting to be discovered by each Christian.

Nona: Perhaps you're right about that, but isn't the purpose of going to church to be fed and to gear up for the week, with all its problems and stress? I need to be exhorted and encouraged.

Peter: Those aspects are valid, but I would say with all due respect, that being "fed" is for spiritual babies [1 Cor. 3:1-2; Heb.

[275] See Rev. 1:8, 11. Actual experience of the author, formerly a "nondenominational," charismatic Evangelical Protestant.

5:12-14]. The rest of us can feed ourselves. The Mass requires some work and active participation, as Vatican II stresses. The word *liturgy* means "work of the people." The informed, committed Catholic doesn't go to church primarily to "feel good," to "get fed," or to "get moral support," but to engage in the work of worshiping God with his whole being, including his mind [Luke 10:27], and to receive him in Communion. Even if one doesn't feel anything, it is worthwhile to be obedient to God and worship him simply for who he is.

Nona: I . . . um . . . maybe I've been too harsh on Catholics, and judgmental. I suppose Mass wasn't all bad all the time. Perhaps I was uninformed and lax and didn't make enough effort to learn its true meaning.

Peter: You know, Nona, there are charismatic Masses, which combine both traditional and contemporary worship — in a sense, the best of both worlds. They're usually a little more spontaneous and have more lively worship-singing. (I admit, Catholics generally sing terribly or not at all!) Yet, the structure of the Mass and the Liturgy is respected and not violated. You might like the homilies a little better, too.

Nona: I have to admit you've really challenged me to examine some of my positions. I'll have to think about this some more. Thanks, and let's discuss this again.

Recommended Apologetic and Historical Works

See my extensive web page: *Catholic Books, Authors, and Cultural Heritage:* http://ic.net/~erasmus/BOOKREV.HTM. Also, see links to used theological books online, on my web page: *Christian Online Books and Search:* http://ic.net/~erasmus/RAZ17.HTM.

Catholic Doctrine and Beliefs

Adam, Karl, *The Spirit of Catholicism*, Justin McCann, trans. (Garden City, New York: Doubleday Image, 1954).

Denzinger, Henry, *Enchiridion Symbolorum*, Roy J. Deferrari, trans. (St. Louis: B. Herder Books, 1957).

Fournier, Keith A., *Evangelical Catholics* (Nashville: Thomas Nelson, 1990).

Gibbons, James Cardinal, *The Faith of Our Fathers* (New York: P. J. Kenedy and Sons, 1917).

Guardini, Romano, *The Faith and Modern Man*, Charlotte E. Forsyth, trans. (New York: Pantheon Books, 1952).

Howard, Thomas, *Splendor in the Ordinary* (Manchester, New Hampshire: Sophia Institute Press, 2000).

Howard, Thomas, *On Being Catholic* (San Francisco: Ignatius Press, 1997).

Keating, Karl, *Catholicism and Fundamentalism* (San Francisco: Ignatius Press, 1988).

Knox, Ronald, *The Belief of Catholics* (Garden City, New York: Doubleday Image, 1927).

Kreeft, Peter, *Fundamentals of the Faith* (San Francisco: Ignatius Press, 1988).

Kreeft, Peter, *Everything You Ever Wanted to Know About Heaven* (San Francisco: Ignatius Press, 1990).

Kreeft, Peter, *Angels (and Demons)* (San Francisco: Ignatius Press, 1995).

O'Brien, John A., *The Faith of Millions* (Huntington, Indiana: Our Sunday Visitor).

Ott, Ludwig, *Fundamentals of Catholic Dogma*, Patrick Lynch, trans. (Rockford, Illinois: TAN Books).

Premm, Matthias, *Dogmatic Theology for the Laity*, David Heimann, trans. (Rockford, Illinois: TAN Books and Pub., 1977).

Ryan, Kenneth and J. D. Conway, eds., *What Would You Like to Know About the Catholic Church?* (St. Paul: Carillon Books, 1976).

Ryan, Kenneth, *What More Would You Like to Know About the Church?* (St. Paul: Carillon Books).

Schreck, Alan, *Catholic and Christian* (Ann Arbor, Michigan: Servant Books, 1984).

Scott, Martin J., *Things Catholics Are Asked About* (New York: P. J. Kenedy and Sons, 1927).

Sheed, Frank J., *Theology for Beginners* (New York: Sheed and Ward, 1957).

Stravinskas, Peter M. J., ed., *Catholic Encyclopedia* (Huntington, Indiana: Our Sunday Visitor, 1991).

Trese, Leo J., *The Faith Explained* (Chicago: Fides Pub. Assoc., 1959).

Catholic Catechisms

Catechism of the Catholic Church (Liguori, Missouri: Liguori Publications, 1994).

Catechism of the Council of Trent, John A. McHugh and Charles J. Callan, trans. (New York: Joseph F. Wagner, 1936).

German Bishops Conference, *The Church's Confession of Faith: A Catholic Catechism for Adults*, Stephen Wentworth Arndt, trans., Mark Jordan, ed. (San Francisco: Ignatius Press, 1987).

Hardon, John A., *The Catholic Catechism* (Garden City, New York: Doubleday, 1975).

Hardon, John A., *Pocket Catholic Catechism* (New York: Doubleday Image, 1989).

Hardon, John A., *Pocket Catholic Dictionary* (New York: Doubleday Image, 1980).

Hardon, John A., *The Question and Answer Catechism* (New York: Doubleday Image, 1981).

Lawler, Ronald, Donald W. Wuerl, Thomas C. Lawler, eds., *The Teaching of Christ: A Catholic Catechism for Adults* (Huntington, Indiana: Our Sunday Visitor, 1976).

Schreck, Alan, *Basics of the Faith: A Catholic Catechism* (Ann Arbor, Michigan: Servant Books, 1987).

Catholic Apologetics

Chesterton, G. K., *Orthodoxy* (Garden City, New York: Doubleday Image, 1959).

Chesterton, G. K., *The Everlasting Man* (Garden City, New York: Doubleday Image, 1955).

Conway, Bertrand L., *The Question Box* (New York: Paulist Press, 1929).

St. Francis de Sales, *The Catholic Controversy*, Henry B. Mackey, trans. (Rockford, Illinois: TAN Books, 1989).

Gibbons, James Cardinal, *Our Christian Heritage* (Baltimore: John Murphy Co., 1889).

Graham, Henry G., *Where We Got the Bible* (St. Louis: B. Herder, 1924).

Keating, Karl, *What Catholics Really Believe* (San Francisco: Ignatius Press, 1992).

Kreeft, Peter and Ronald K. Tacelli, *Handbook of Christian Apologetics* (Downers Grove, Illinois: InterVarsity Press, 1994).

Madrid, Patrick, *Any Friend of God's Is a Friend of Mine* (San Diego: Basilica Press, 1996).

Mirus, Jeffrey A., ed., *Reasons for Hope* (Front Royal, Virginia: Christendom Press, 1982).

Most, William G., *Catholic Apologetics Today* (Rockford, Illinois: TAN Books, 1986).

Novak, Michael, *Confession of a Catholic* (San Francisco: Harper and Row, 1983).

Ray, Steve, *Crossing the Tiber* (San Francisco: Ignatius Press, 1997).

Shea, Mark P., *By What Authority?: An Evangelical Discovers Catholic Tradition* (Huntington, Indiana: Our Sunday Visitor, 1996).

Sheed, Frank J., *Theology and Sanity* (New York: Sheed and Ward, 1946).

Sheed, Frank J. and Maisie Ward, *Catholic Evidence Training Outlines* (Ann Arbor, Michigan: Catholic Evidence Guild, 1992).

Stravinskas, Peter M. J., *The Bible and the Mass* (Ann Arbor, Michigan: Servant Books, 1989).

Stravinskas, Peter M. J., *The Catholic Answer Book* (Huntington, Indiana: Our Sunday Visitor, 1990).

Stravinskas, Peter M. J., *The Catholic Answer Book 2* (Huntington, Indiana: Our Sunday Visitor, 1994).

Sungenis, Robert A., *Not by Faith Alone: The Biblical Evidence for the Catholic Doctrine of Justification* (Santa Barbara, California: Queenship Publishing, 1997).

Sungenis, Robert A., ed., *Not by Scripture Alone: A Catholic Critique of the Protestant Doctrine of* Sola Scriptura (Santa Barbara, California: Queenship Publishing, 1997).

Recommended Apologetic and Historical Works

Books by or about Catholic Converts

St. Augustine, *Confessions*, R. S. Pine-Coffin trans. (New York: Penguin, 1961).

Baram, Robert, ed., *Spiritual Journeys* (Boston: St. Paul Books and Media, 1988): twenty-seven conversion stories.

Bouyer, Louis, *Newman: His Life and Spirituality*, J. Lewis May trans. (New York: Meridian, 1958).

Chervin, Ronda, ed., *Bread From Heaven: Stories of Jews Who Found the Messiah* (New Hope, Kentucky: Remnant of Israel, 1994).

Chesterton, G. K., *The Catholic Church and Conversion* (New York: Macmillan, 1926).

Currie, David B., *Born Fundamentalist, Born Again Catholic* (San Francisco: Ignatius Press, 1995).

Dulles, Avery, *A Testimonial to Grace* (New York: Sheed and Ward, 1946).

Ffinch, Michael, *G. K. Chesterton: A Biography* (San Francisco: Harper and Row, 1986).

Grodi, Marcus, ed., *Journeys Home* (Santa Barbara, California: Queenship Publishing, 1997).

Hahn, Scott and Kimberly, *Rome Sweet Home* (San Francisco: Ignatius Press, 1993).

Howard, Thomas, *Evangelical Is Not Enough* (Nashville: Nelson, 1984).

Howard, Thomas, *Lead, Kindly Light* (Steubenville, Ohio: Franciscan University Press, 1994).

Ker, Ian, *John Henry Newman: A Biography* (Oxford: Oxford University Press, 1988).

Knox, Ronald, *A Spiritual Aeneid* (New York: Sheed and Ward, 1950).

Knox, Ronald, *The Quotable Knox*, George J. Marlin, Richard P. Rabatin, and John L. Swan, ed. (San Francisco: Ignatius Press, 1996).

Madrid, Patrick, ed., *Surprised by Truth* (San Diego: Basilica Press, 1994): eleven conversion stories, including that of Dave Armstrong.

Madrid, Patrick, ed., *Surprised by Truth 2* (Manchester, New Hampshire: Sophia Institute Press, 2000).

Madrid, Patrick, ed., *Surprised by Truth* 3 (Manchester, New Hampshire: Sophia Institute Press, 2002).

Muggeridge, Malcolm, *Confessions of a Twentieth-Century Pilgrim* (San Francisco: Harper and Row, 1988).

Newman, John Henry, *Apologia Pro Vita Sua* (Garden City, New York: Doubleday Image, 1956).

Nordhagen, Lynn, ed., *When Only One Converts* (Huntington, Indiana: Our Sunday Visitor, 2001).

O'Brien, John A., ed., *Giants of the Faith* (Garden City, New York: Doubleday Image, 1957).

O'Brien, John A., ed., *The Road to Damascus* (Garden City, New York: Doubleday Image, 1949): fifteen conversion stories.

O'Neill, Dan, ed., *The New Catholics* (New York: Crossroad, 1989): seventeen conversion stories.

Pearce, Joseph, *Wisdom and Innocence: A Biography of* G. K. *Chesterton* (San Francisco: Ignatius Press, 1997).

Stoddard, John L., *Rebuilding a Lost Faith* (New York: P. J. Kenedy and Sons, 1922).

Talbot, John Michael, *Changes: A Spiritual Journal* (New York: Crossroad, 1984).

Vanauken, Sheldon, *Under the Mercy* (Nashville: Thomas Nelson Publications, 1985).

Catholic Historical Documents and Writings

St. Thomas Aquinas, *Summa Theologica*.

St. Augustine, *The City of God*, Gerald G. Walsh et al., trans. abridged edition (Garden City, New York: Doubleday Image, 1958).

Bettenson, Henry, ed., *Documents of the Christian Church* (London: Oxford University Press, 1947).

Dogmatic Canons and Decrees (Rockford, Illinois: TAN Books, 1977): documents of Councils of Trent and Vatican I, plus *Decree on the Immaculate Conception* and the *Syllabus of Errors* of Pope Pius IX.

Flannery, Austin, ed., *Vatican Council II: The Conciliar and Post-Conciliar Documents* (Northport, New York: Costello, 1988).

Fremantle, Anne, ed., *A Treasury of Early Christianity* (New York: Mentor, 1953).

Fremantle, Anne, ed., *The Papal Encyclicals* (New York: Mentor, 1956).

Jurgens, William A., ed. and trans., *The Faith of the Early Fathers*, 3 vols. (Collegeville, Minnesota: Liturgical Press, 1970, 1979).

Lightfoot, Joseph B. and J. R. Harmer, trans., *The Apostolic Fathers*, Michael W. Holmes, ed. (Grand Rapids, Michigan: Baker Book House, 1989).

Neuner, Josef and Jacques Dupuis, eds., *The Christian Faith in the Doctrinal Documents of the Catholic Church* (New York: Alba House, 1990).

Quasten, Johannes, *Patrology*, 4 vols. (Allen, Texas: Christian Classics, 1977).

Staniforth, Maxwell, trans., *Early Christian Writings: The Apostolic Fathers* (New York: Penguin, 1968).

History of the Catholic Church: Overviews

Belloc, Hilaire, *Europe and the Faith* (Rockford, Illinois: TAN Books, 1992).

Belloc, Hilaire, *The Catholic Church and History* (New York: Macmillan, 1927).

Chapman, John, *Bishop Gore and the Catholic Claims* (London: Longmans, Green, and Co., 1905).

Civardi, Luigi, *How Christ Changed the World*, Sylvester Andriano, trans. (Rockford, Illinois: TAN Books, 1991).

Farrow, John, *Pageant of the Popes* (New York: Sheed and Ward, 1950).

Grandi, Domenico and Antonio Galli, *The Story of the Church*, John Chapin, trans. (Garden City, New York: Doubleday Image, 1960).

Hughes, Philip, *A Popular History of the Catholic Church* (Garden City, New York: Doubleday Image, 1949).

Hughes, Philip, *The Church in Crisis: History of the General Councils, 325-1870* (Garden City, New York: Doubleday Image, 1961).

Laux, John, *Church History* (New York: Benziger Bros., 1930).

Lortz, Joseph, *History of the Church*, Edwin G. Kaiser, trans. (Milwaukee: Bruce Pub. Co., 1939).

Luce, Clare Boothe, ed., *Saints for Now* (New York: Sheed and Ward, 1952).

Newman, John Henry Cardinal, *An Essay on the Development of Christian Doctrine* (Notre Dame, Indiana: University of Notre Dame Press, 1989).

Schreck, Alan, *The Compact History of the Catholic Church* (Ann Arbor, Michigan: Servant Books, 1987).

Sheed, Frank J., ed., *Saints Are Not Sad* (New York: Sheed and Ward, 1949).

Early Church History

Adam, Karl, *The Son of God*, Philip Hereford, trans. (Garden City, New York: Doubleday Image, 1934).

Barbet, Pierre, *A Doctor at Calvary*, Earl of Wicklow, trans. (Garden City, New York: Doubleday Image, 1950).

Recommended Apologetic and Historical Works

Bruce, F. F., *The Canon of Scripture* (Downers Grove, Illinois: InterVarsity Press, 1988; Protestant).

Carroll, Warren H., *The Founding of Christendom: A History of Christendom*, Vol. 1 (Front Royal, Virginia: Christendom Press, 1985).

Carroll, Warren H., *The Building of Christendom: A History of Christendom*, Vol. 2 (Front Royal, Virginia: Christendom Press, 1987).

Daniel-Rops, Henri, *Jesus and His Times*, Ruby Millar trans. (New York: E. P. Dutton and Co., 1954).

Eusebius, *Ecclesiastical History*, G. A. Williamson, trans. (Baltimore: Penguin, 1965).

Guardini, Romano, *The Lord*, Elinor C. Briefs, trans. (Chicago: Henry Regnery Co., 1954).

Pelikan, Jaroslav, *The Christian Tradition: A History of the Development of Doctrine:* Vol. 1 of 5: The Emergence of the Catholic Tradition (Chicago: University of Chicago Press, 1971; Lutheran).

Pope, Hugh, *St. Augustine of Hippo* (Garden City, New York: Doubleday Image, 1937).

Prat, Fernand, *The Theology of St. Paul*, 2 vols., John L. Stoddard, trans. (Westminster, Maryland: The Newman Bookshop, 1926).

Ricciotti, Giuseppe, *Paul the Apostle*, Alba I. Zizzamia, trans. (Milwaukee: Bruce Pub. Co., 1946).

Sheen, Fulton, *Life of Christ* (Garden City, New York: Doubleday Image, 1958).

Walsh, William Thomas, *Saints in Action* (Garden City, New York: Doubleday Image, 1961).

Ward, Maisie, *Saints Who Made History* (New York: Sheed and Ward, 1959).

Wilson, Ian, *The Shroud of Turin* (Garden City, New York: Doubleday Image, 1979).

Church History in the Middle Ages

Carroll, Warren H., *The Glory of Christendom: A History of Christendom*, Vol. 3 (Front Royal, Virginia: Christendom Press, 1993).

Chesterton, G. K., *St. Francis of Assisi* (Garden City, New York: Doubleday Image, 1924).

Chesterton, G. K., *Saint Thomas Aquinas: "The Dumb Ox"* (Garden City, New York: Doubleday Image, 1933).

Daniel-Rops, Henri, *Cathedral and Crusade*, Vol. 1, John Warrington, trans. (Garden City, New York: Doubleday Image, 1956).

Dawson, Christopher, *Religion and the Rise of Western Culture* (Garden City, New York: Doubleday Image, 1950).

Dawson, Christopher, *The Historic Reality of Christian Culture* (New York: Harper and Row, 1960).

DeWulf, Maurice, *Philosophy and Civilization in the Middle Ages* (New York: Dover, 1922).

Duggan, Alfred, *The Story of the Crusades* (Garden City, New York: Doubleday Image, 1963).

Jorgensen, Johannes, *St. Francis of Assisi*, T. O'Conor Sloane, trans. (Garden City, New York: Doubleday Image, 1907).

Leclercq, Jean, *The Love of Learning and the Desire for God*, Catharine Misrahi, trans. (New York: Mentor Omega, 1961).

Peters, Edward, *Inquisition* (Berkeley: University of California Press, 1989).

Rand, Edward K., *Founders of the Middle Ages* (New York: Dover, 1928).

Walsh, William Thomas, *Isabella of Spain* (New York: Robert M. McBride and Co., 1930).

Walsh, William Thomas, *Characters of the Inquisition* (Rockford, Illinois: TAN Books, 1987).

Church History: 1600 to the Present

Ball, Ann, *Modern Saints* (Rockford, Illinois: TAN Book, 1983).

Belloc, Hilaire, *Survivals and New Arrivals* (New York: Sheed and Ward, 1929).

Brodrick, James, *Galileo* (New York: Harper and Row, 1964).

Daniel-Rops, Henri, *The Church in an Age of Revolution (1789-1879)*, John Warrington, trans. (New York: E. P. Dutton and Co., 1960).

Janelle, Pierre, *The Catholic Reformation* (Milwaukee: Bruce Pub. Co., 1963).

Pope John XXIII, *Journal of a Soul*, Dorothy White, trans. (New York: McGraw-Hill Book Co., 1965).

Hitchcock, James, *The Decline and Fall of Radical Catholicism* (Garden City, New York: Doubleday Image, 1971).

Kelly, George A., *The Crisis of Authority* (Chicago: Regnery Gateway, 1982).

Kelly, George A., *Inside My Father's House* (New York: Doubleday Image, 1989).

Kelly, George A., *Keeping the Church Catholic with John Paul II* (San Francisco: Ignatius Press, 1993).

Lapide, Pinchas, *Three Popes and the Jews* (New York: Hawthorn Books, 1967; Jewish).

Martin, Ralph, *A Crisis of Truth* (Ann Arbor, Michigan: Servant Books, 1982).

Martin, Ralph, *The Catholic Church at the End of an Age* (San Francisco: Ignatius Press, 1994).

Maynard, Theodore, *The Story of American Catholicism*, 2 vols. (Garden City, New York: Doubleday Image, 1941).

Muggeridge, Malcolm, *Something Beautiful for God* [Mother Teresa] (New York: Harper and Row, 1971).

Neuhaus, Richard John, *The Catholic Moment* (San Francisco: Harper and Row, 1987).

Protestantism and the Reformation

Adam, Karl, *The Roots of the Reformation*, Cecily Hastings, trans. (New York: Sheed and Ward, 1951; portion of One and Holy, 1948).

Belloc, Hilaire, *Characters of the Reformation* (Garden City, New York: Doubleday Image, 1958).

Belloc, Hilaire, *How the Reformation Happened* (New York: Robert M. McBride and Co., 1928).

Bouyer, Louis, *The Spirit and Forms of Protestantism*, A. V. Littledale, trans. (London: Harvill Press, 1956).

Daniel-Rops, Henri, *The Protestant Reformation*, Vol. 2, Audrey Butler, trans. (Garden City, New York: Doubleday Image, 1961).

Dawson, Christopher, *The Dividing of Christendom* (New York: Sheed and Ward, 1965).

Grisar, Hartmann, *Luther*, E. M. Lamond, trans., Luigi Cappadelta, ed., 6 vols. (London: Kegan Paul, Trench, Trubner and Co., 1917).

Grisar, Hartmann, *Martin Luther: His Life and Work*, Frank J. Eble, trans. (Westminster, Maryland: The Newman Press, 1950).

Hughes, Philip, *A Popular History of the Reformation* (Garden City, New York: Doubleday Image, 1957).

Hughes, Philip, *The Reformation in England* (New York: Macmillan, 1951).

Janssen, Johannes, *History of the German People from the Close of the Middle Ages*, A. M. Christie, trans. 16 vols. (St. Louis: B. Herder, 1910).

Knox, Ronald, *Enthusiasm* (Oxford: Oxford University Press, 1950).

Lortz, Joseph, *How the Reformation Came* (New York: Herder and Herder, 1964).

Tavard, Georges, *Understanding Protestantism*, Rachel Attwater, trans. (Glen Rock, New Jersey: Deus/Century Books, 1963).

Eastern Orthodoxy

Attwater, Donald, *The Christian Churches of the East*, Vol. 2 (Milwaukee: Bruce Pub. Co., 1962).

Congar, Yves, *After Nine Hundred Years* (New York: Fordham University Press, 1959).

Daniel-Rops, Henri, *The Protestant Reformation*, Vol. 1, Audrey Butler, trans. (Garden City, New York: Doubleday Image, 1963), Pt. 2: "A Crisis of Unity: Christendom Disintegrates and Loses the East," 80-150.

Dvornik, Francis, *The Photian Schism* (Cambridge: Cambridge University Press, 1938).

Englert, Clement C., *Catholics and Orthodox: Can They Unite?* (New York: Paulist Press, 1961).

Fortescue, Adrian, *The Orthodox Eastern Church* (London: Catholic Truth Society, 1911).

Hardon, John A., *Religions of the World*, Vol. 2 (Garden City, New York: Doubleday Image, 1968), ch.15: "Eastern Orthodoxy," 112-159.

Le Guillou, M. J., *The Spirit of Eastern Orthodoxy*, Donald Attwater, trans. (Glen Rock, New Jersey: Paulist Press, 1964).

Soloviev, Vladimir, *Russia and the Universal Church* (London: Geoffrey Bles, 1948).

The Blessed Virgin Mary

Bouyer, Louis, *The Seat of Wisdom*, A. V. Littledale, trans. (Chicago: Henry Regnery Co., 1965).

Daniel-Rops, Henri, *The Book of Mary*, Alastair Guinan, trans. (Garden City, New York: Doubleday Image, 1960).

Delaney, John J., ed., *A Woman Clothed with the Sun* (Garden City, New York: Doubleday Image, 1961).

Gambero, Luigi, *Mary and the Fathers of the Church*, Thomas Buffer, trans. (San Francisco: Ignatius Press, 1999).

Graef, Hilda, *Mary: A History of Doctrine and Devotion*, Vol. 1 [to the Reformation] (New York: Sheed and Ward, 1963).

Howell, Kenneth, *Mary of Nazareth* (Santa Barbara, California: Queenship Publishing, 1998).

Miravelle, Mark I., ed., *Mary: Coredemptrix, Mediatrix, Advocate: Theological Foundations* (Santa Barbara, California: Queenship Publishing, 1995).

Most, William G., *Mary in Our Life* (Garden City, New York: Doubleday Image, 1963).

Sheen, Fulton J., *The World's First Love* (Garden City, New York: Doubleday Image, 1956).

Stravinskas, Peter M. J., ed., *The Catholic Answer Book of Mary* (Huntington, Indiana: Our Sunday Visitor, 2000); includes a chapter by Dave Armstrong: "The Imitation of Mary."

Thurian, Max, *Mary: Mother of All Christians*, Neville B. Cryer, trans. (New York: Herder and Herder, 1963).

Walsh, William Thomas, *Our Lady of Fatima* (Garden City, New York: Doubleday Image, 1947).

The Papacy

von Balthasar, Hans Urs, *The Office of Peter and the Structure of the Church*, Andree Emery, trans. (San Francisco: Ignatius Press, 1986).

Butler, B. C., *The Church and Infallibility* (New York: Sheed and Ward, 1954).

Butler, Scott, Norman Dahlgren, and David Hess, Jesus, *Peter and the Keys* (Santa Barbara, California: Queenship Publishing Co., 1996).

Chapman, John, *Studies on the Early Papacy* (London: Sheed and Ward, 1928).

D'Ormesson, Wladimir, *The Papacy, Michael Derrick*, trans. (New York: Hawthorn Books, 1959).

Jaki, Stanley, *And on This Rock* (Manassas, Virginia: Trinity Communications, 1987).

Jaki, Stanley, *The Keys of the Kingdom* (Chicago: Franciscan Herald Press, 1986).

Madrid, Patrick, *Pope Fiction* (San Diego: Basilica Press, 1999).

Ray, Stephen K., *Upon This Rock* (San Francisco: Ignatius Press, 1999).

Ripley, Francis J., *The Pope: Vicar of Jesus Christ* (Dublin: Catholic Truth Society, 1965).

Rivington, Luke, *The Primitive Church and the See of Peter* (London: Longmans, Green and Co., 1894).

Walsh, John Evangelist, *The Bones of St. Peter* (Garden City, New York: Doubleday Image, 1985).

Marriage, Gender, and the Family

Bouyer, Louis, *Women in the Church*, Marilyn Teichert, trans. (San Francisco: Ignatius Press, 1979).

Boyle, John F., ed., *Creative Love: The Ethics of Human Reproduction* (Front Royal, Virginia: Christendom Press, 1989).

Chervin, Ronda, *Feminine, Free, and Faithful* (San Francisco: Ignatius Press, 1986).

Ford, John C., Germain Grisez, Joseph Boyle, John Finnis, and William E. May, *The Teaching of Humanae Vitae: A Defense* (San Francisco: Ignatius, 1988).

von Hildebrand, Dietrich, *Man and Woman* (Manchester, New Hampshire: Sophia Institute Press, 1992).

von Hildebrand, Dietrich, *Marriage* (Manchester, New Hampshire: Sophia Institute Press, 1984).

Pope John Paul II, *Familiaris Consortio* (On the Family), Apostolic Exhortation (Washington: United States Catholic Conference, December 15, 1981).

Pope John Paul II, *Mulieris Dignitatem* (On the Dignity and Vocation of Women), Apostolic Letter (Boston: St. Paul Books and Media, 1988).

Kippley, John F. and Sheila K., *The Art of Natural Family Planning* (Cincinnati: Couple to Couple League, 1987).

Catholic Philosophy and Moral Theology

Copleston, Frederick C., *Aquinas* (Baltimore: Penguin Books, 1955).

Copleston, Frederick C., *Medieval Philosophy* (New York: Harper and Bros., 1952).

Fremantle, Anne, ed., *The Social Teachings of the Church* (New York: Mentor-Omega, 1963).

Gilson, Etienne, *Reason and Revelation in the Middle Ages* (New York: Charles Scribner's Sons, 1938).

Gilson, Etienne, *Elements of Christian Philosophy* (New York: Mentor-Omega, 1960).

Gilson, Etienne, *The Spirit of Thomism* (New York: Harper and Row, 1964).

Howard, Thomas, *Chance or the Dance?* (San Francisco: Ignatius Press, 1969).

Johnson, Paul, *Intellectuals* (New York: Harper and Row, 1988).

Kreeft, Peter, *Back to Virtue* (San Francisco: Ignatius Press, 1995).

Kreeft, Peter, *Christianity for Modern Pagans* [commentary on Pascal's *Pensées*] (San Francisco: Ignatius Press, 1993).

Kreeft, Peter, *Ecumenical Jihad* (San Francisco: Ignatius Press, 1996).

Kreeft, Peter, *Making Sense Out of Suffering* (Ann Arbor, Michigan: Servant Books, 1986).

Laux, John, *Catholic Morality* (Rockford, Illinois: TAN Books and Pub., 1990).

Pope Leo XIII, *The Church Speaks to the Modern World*, Etienne Gilson, ed. (Garden City, New York: Doubleday Image, 1954).

Maritain, Jacques, *The Range of Reason* (New York: Charles Scribner's Sons, 1942).

Maritain, Jacques, *Moral Philosophy* (New York: Charles Scribner's Sons, 1960).

Newman, John Henry, *An Essay in Aid of a Grammar of Assent* (Garden City, New York: Doubleday Image, 1955).

Rutler, George William, *Beyond Modernity* (San Francisco: Ignatius Press, 1987).

Sheen, Fulton, *God and Intelligence in Modern Philosophy* (Garden City, New York: Doubleday Image).

Biographical Note

Dave Armstrong

Dave Armstrong is a Catholic writer, apologist, and evangelist, who has been actively proclaiming and defending Christianity for more than twenty years. Formerly a campus missionary, as a Protestant, Armstrong was received into the Catholic Church in 1991 by the late, well-known catechist and theologian Fr. John A. Hardon, S.J.

Armstrong's conversion story appeared in the bestselling book *Surprised by Truth* and his articles have been published in a number of Catholic periodicals, including *The Catholic Answer, This Rock, Envoy, Hands On Apologetics, The Coming Home Journal*, and *The Latin Mass*. His apologetic and writing apostolate was the subject of a feature article in the May 2002 issue of *Envoy*. Armstrong is the author of the book *More Biblical Evidence for Catholicism* and of forty-four apologetics articles in *The Catholic Answer Bible*.

His website (www.biblicalcatholic.com), *Biblical Evidence for Catholicism*, online since March 1997, received the 1998 Catholic Website of the Year award from *Envoy*, which also nominated Armstrong himself for Best New Evangelist.

Armstrong and his wife, Judy, and their four children live near Detroit, Michigan.

Sophia Institute Press®

Sophia Institute® is a nonprofit institution that seeks to restore man's knowledge of eternal truth, including man's knowledge of his own nature, his relation to other persons, and his relation to God. Sophia Institute Press® serves this end in numerous ways: it publishes translations of foreign works to make them accessible to English-speaking readers; it brings out-of-print books back into print; and it publishes important new books that fulfill the ideals of Sophia Institute®. These books afford readers a rich source of the enduring wisdom of mankind. Sophia Institute Press® makes these high-quality books available to the public by using advanced technology and by soliciting donations to subsidize its publishing costs. Your generosity can help Sophia Institute Press® to provide the public with editions of works containing the enduring wisdom of the ages. Please send your tax-deductible contribution to the address below. We welcome your questions, comments, and suggestions.

For your free catalog, call:
Toll-free: 1-800-888-9344

Sophia Institute Press® • Box 5284 • Manchester, NH 03108
www.sophiainstitute.com

Sophia Institute® is a tax-exempt institution as defined by the Internal Revenue Code, Section 501(c)(3). Tax I.D. 22-2548708.